Since his retirement as Israel's controversial longtime Prime Minister, Yitzhak Shamir has set down the story of his life, from the years of conspiracy and deep cover in the underground that fought for Jewish independence in the Palestine of the 1940s to the decade he spent in the shadows of the Mossad, the Israeli intelligence service, and to his emergence into national and international prominence as the helmsman of Israel's complex, often painful, always precarious foreign and domestic involvements.

Yitzhak Shamir not only discloses his own view of the intricacies of the peace process and present-day US–Israeli relations but also provides insights into such personalities as Menachem Begin, Anwar Sadat, Ronald Reagan, George Bush and John Major and into Israel's right wing, its origins, its philosophies and its political heroes.

Finally Shamir analyses the rewards, hazards and price of public service in one of the world's most read-about and talked-about countries and gives his unconventional personal view of the Norway Accord with the PLO. For the first time, this is the story of one of the most important figures in the Middle East – in his own words.

SUMMING UP

Summing Up

An Autobiography

Yitzhak Shamir

Little, Brown and Company

Boston   New York   Toronto   London

First American Edition

Library of Congress Cataloging-in-Publication Data
Shamir, Itzhak.
    Summing up : an autobiography / Yitzhak Shamir.
        p.   cm.
    Includes index.
    ISBN 0-316-96825-0
    1. Shamir, Itzhak, 1915-   . 2. Prime ministers — Israel —
Biography. 3. Revisionist Zionists — Biography. 4. Israel —
Biography.   I. Title.
DS126.6.S365A3   1994
956.9405'4'092 — dc20
    [B]   94-17365

10 9 8 7 6 5 4 3 2 1

HAD

Published simultaneously in Canada by Little, Brown & Company
(Canada) Limited

Printed in the United States of America

CONTENTS

ILLUSTRATIONS

Unless otherwise stated, the photographs come from Yitzhak Shamir's private collection. GPO refers to the Israel Government Press Office.

Between pages 84 and 85

My father, Shlomo Yezernitsky, opening a summer camp for poor children, Rujenoy, 1930s.

My sister Miriam with her husband, Mottel Skalevich, 1930s.

My sister Rivka Pitkovsky in the late 1920s.

On my graduation day at the age of sixteen, Rujenoy, 1932.

Shulamit on her graduation day in Sofia, Bulgaria, 1940.

With a group of friends on a Tel Aviv roof-top, 1938.

Underground fighter, 1940s (*Beit Yair*).

British police 'wanted poster' (*Jabotinsky Institute*).

'Yair' – Abraham Stern (*Beit Yair*).

Exiled in Djibouti, 1947.

Shulamit with Yair in 1948, when I was in exile.

Back home, 1948.

Lehi leaders after emerging from the underground, 1949.

With Shulamit, Tel Aviv, 1950s.

At the Western Wall after the Six Day War, 1967.

Menachem Begin, Anwar Sadat and myself, as Speaker of the Knesset, during Sadat's historic visit to Jerusalem, 1977 (*GPO*).

Newly appointed Foreign Minister with Prime Minister Begin, 1980 (*Rahamim Israeli*).

With President Sadat in 1983 (*Sygma*).

With President Hosni Mubarak after Sadat's funeral, Cairo, 1981 (*GPO*).

My first Government, October 1983 (*GPO*).

My first day in the Prime Minister's Office, October 1983.

To Shulamit

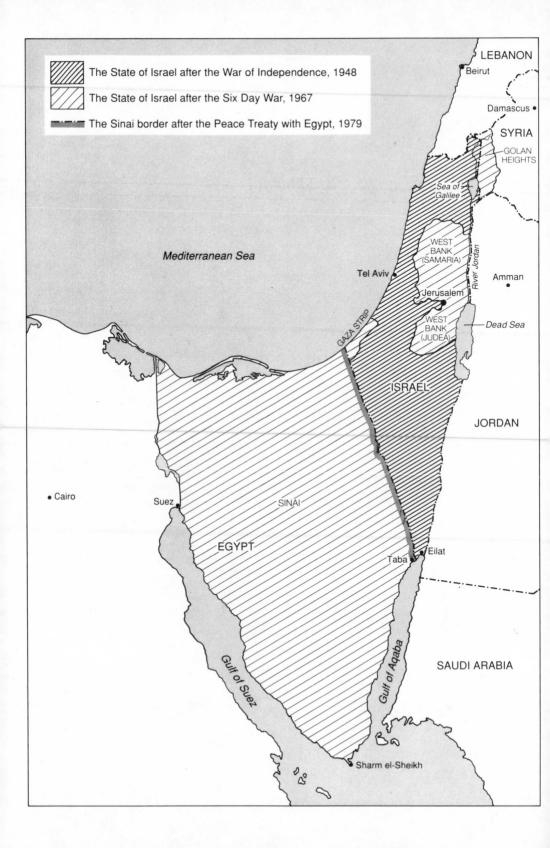

The State of Israel after the War of Independence, 1948

The State of Israel after the Six Day War, 1967

The Sinai border after the Peace Treaty with Egypt, 1979

LEBANON

Beirut

Damascus •

SYRIA

GOLAN
HEIGHTS

Sea of
Galilee

River Jordan

WEST
BANK
(SAMARIA)

Amman
•

Mediterranean Sea

Tel Aviv •

Jerusalem •

WEST
BANK
(JUDEA)

Dead Sea

GAZA STRIP

ISRAEL

JORDAN

• Cairo

Suez •

SINAI

EGYPT

Taba

Eilat

Gulf of Suez

Gulf of Aqaba

SAUDI ARABIA

Sharm el-Sheikh •

SUMMING UP

1

EARLY DAYS

VERY LITTLE THAT I have experienced or that has really mattered to me could have been foreseen when I was growing up in the very small town in Poland where I was born in 1915. Rujenoy was one of those Eastern European towns that changed hands often, first being part of Poland, then of Russia, then of Poland and then of Russia again; it was so small that no train stopped there – nor even, for part of my childhood, did the bus. If we had to travel anywhere, it was by cart. And, of course, in those days, no one in town owned a car. Of the population of 5,000, some 3,500 were Jews. They earned their living in various ways but none could be called prosperous. My father – his name was Shlomo Yezernitzky – had a little leather factory and, by Rujenoy's very modest standards, we were considered fairly well-to-do. We were three children: my two older sisters, Miriam and Rivka, and me, reared in a warm, constantly crowded home. In my memory there were always people in the house: the men who came to my father for advice and a glass of tea, even for arbitration in especially sharp local quarrels; my sisters' friends; the women gently forced by my mother to perform good deeds such as baking a Sabbath *challah* for the poor or helping to organize a summer 'camp' in the woods for underprivileged children. My mother, Perla, was not only kind; she was bright, aware of what was happening around her and for ever busy performing some sort of useful action. Now and then, she would ask me to sit down with her for a few minutes and read some article from the Yiddish press to her. It was a way of keeping in touch with the world outside – and with me, I think.

But the liveliness I recall was not just because of the stream of guests or charitable activities. My parents were also very involved with major matters, with Zionism and Jewish education. In their youth, they had both been politically active, if only for a short time, through the Bund, the fiercely secular anti-Zionist Jewish Socialist

Party, founded in Russia at the turn of the century, which had a significant following among the Jews of Eastern Europe, including the three million Jews of Poland. For most of their adult lives, however, my mother and father were dedicated followers of the Zionist cause, believers in the right of the Jews to a national home in the Land of Israel, and my father's insistence on the cardinal importance of a Hebrew education for me (though we naturally spoke Yiddish at home) was part of this commitment. So was the town's Hebrew school for which he always helped to find the funds.

I can't imagine what shape my life would have taken if I hadn't been educated exclusively in Hebrew, if in the Polish diaspora I had not – each day of my childhood and until I went to university – attended a Hebrew school; not afternoon or extra-curricular or synagogue-related classes, but a bona-fide school in which the language of instruction was Hebrew. It was part of that dynamic, irretrievably lost network of nearly 200 Hebrew schools maintained, mainly in Poland, by Tarbut (Hebrew for 'culture'), an organization that ran elementary and high schools, kindergartens and teachers' seminaries – all strongly Zionist in orientation, but essentially secular and up-to-date in method. I took this special schooling entirely for granted. It wasn't that I felt I lived in a ghetto. Not at all. Nor did I feel superior or inferior to the outer environment. I was just not connected to it. Poland, the Polish language and Polish history were secondary for me to the Land of Israel; my imagination, curiosity and energy were perpetually stimulated and nourished by a language, a history and the landscapes of a distant country that bore no resemblance to, and were actually almost unknown in, the non-Jewish world that surrounded me, and of which I increasingly felt myself to be only a temporary resident, a transient en route to another place.

The school was, of course, private, supported by contributions. Still the tuition was high, very high for my parents as I well knew. But I also knew their principles and why my father was so adamant about my going there though he paid for this schooling with great difficulty in hard-won zlotys. Everything about my growing up had to do with *Eretz Israel*, with what was happening there and with my certainty – I can find no other word for it – that there would, one day, be a Jewish state and that I personally must work towards this. Not all my schoolmates felt this way. Some were indifferent; some turned to Communism, later to suffer for their beliefs, to be arrested, tortured and exiled. There were even once whispers in the community that I too looked towards Moscow. 'See who his friends are,' some people said, but although the seemingly endless political conversations may well have radicalized me, it was towards a radical Zionism that I turned.

In general, whatever happened in Palestine found some echo in Rujenoy. I remember, for instance, the opening of the Hebrew University in Jerusalem in the spring of 1925 almost as vividly as if I had been there. It was a real holiday for the Jews of Rujenoy, a celebration: children were let out of school; there was a public assembly at which a speaker (who had come all the way from Lodz for the occasion) addressed the crowd, and flag-bearers, waving the blue-and-white Zionist colours, made their way through town. Everyone talked that day, and for days afterwards, about the great figures who had attended the historic ceremony on Jerusalem's Mount Scopus: Lord Balfour, General Allenby, Dr Chaim Weizmann and the Hebrew poet, Chaim Nachman Bialik, many of whose long poems I had learned by heart and can still recite. Perhaps our greatest excitement, ironically enough, was over Sir Herbert Samuel, the British Jew who became the first High Commissioner to Palestine and who then signified for us, for Jews everywhere, the glorious reality of a Jewish national home. Little did we know that his administration would seek, unsuccessfully, to pacify the Arabs by forbidding Jewish settlement in Trans-Jordan and subjecting Jewish immigration to Palestine to the grotesque criterion of 'absorptive capacity'.

It would be hard to overstate my involvement, in those long-gone days, with the heroes of the Old Testament – Moses, David, Saul, Jonathan and many others – who peopled my daydreams and were the subjects of my games. I knew how they looked and sounded and felt; and I had favourites among them and was wonderfully free to share their adventures and struggles and triumphs. They lived in my mind as models and companions. But in real life, without doubt, the strongest influence on me was my father. He was a born leader; this was his role in Rujenoy and he would probably have been such in a much larger place too. Two characteristics made him outstanding: his unfailing tolerance (matched by my mother's) and his total lack of any prejudice. He was always ready to listen, to discuss, to suggest if necessary – whether he was talking to a Polish farmer, to rabbis (whose internal disputes were frequently more vehement than any Knesset debate has been), or to me. He was a man who fought with profound conviction for what he believed – whether it was against the Tsar, or for Zionism, or for the equality of Jews in Poland. He never imposed his will on anyone, but his tall, quiet presence was impressive and, in the end, his judgments were usually accepted. Inevitably, in time he became head of Rujenoy's Jewish community, but by then I had left. To me, he gave the priceless gift of feeling free, all my life, to think as I please, a gift I hope I have, in turn, passed on to my own children. Nothing, I believe, is as important as independence of thought, which among other things leads to the ability to respect, if not to agree with, the opinions and ideas of others. I have not always, I know, met the standards my father set so many years ago, but nor have I ever lost sight of them.

He was steeped in Jewishness, something best described in Yiddish as *Yiddishkeit*. A lover of Jewish tradition, he attended synagogue each Saturday, always taking me with him. Religion for him – as it was, perhaps inevitably, to become for me – was primarily that complex code of thought and behaviour that strengthens the bond between Jews and enriches their shared legacy. It had nothing to do with that religious zealousness that frequently seeks to divide and control and is politicized – and which he abhorred. Even now I can summon up the special quality of those weekly walks to synagogue, the nods of greeting en route to friends and neighbours, the brief chats with people who needed something from him, and my pride in him and my sense of kinship with the community; all of us were dressed in our *Shabbos* best, doing the same thing, knowing that it had always been so, sure that it would be so in all the years ahead, and feeling secure in the unchanging routines of Jewish life.

As for the non-Jews, we lived, mainly peaceably, alongside them, my father accepted both as a friend and as a spokesman for the Jews. To use a word that has since entered common usage, it was a form of co-existence, sometimes uneasy. In theory, since 1919 Polish Jews had equal rights with non-Jews, but Poland's depressed economy, the post-World War I prominence of Jews in city life and in the free professions, and the ease with which Poles have always taken to anti-Semitism, made simpler the Jews' role as scapegoats. Job discrimination, special taxation and anti-Jewish riots were standard in the world outside Rujenoy. But within Rujenoy things were different, or at least, when I think back to my childhood (which I rarely do), those early years present themselves to me as orderly and pleasant, filled with Jewish content – though there had once been two cases of blood libel, and I went to school with a boy whose father was one of six Jews killed on their way home from synagogue by deserters from the Polish army.

My father had been born in a tiny village, not far from Rujenoy, where his family had lived for decades, the only Jews in the vicinity. My grandfather, who owned some land, had founded a large family: I had twelve uncles in what I thought of as 'the country', Rujenoy being in my mind a metropolis. The summer months I spent at my grandparents were filled with joy: riding through fields on horseback, swimming in creeks, helping to take care of farm animals. My parents came to see me often during those holidays. My father especially liked going back for a day or two to what had been his home and to his village friends, all Christians of course. They also came often to Rujenoy and were among the most jovial of our many guests, so we looked forward to their visits and enjoyed them.

Was it really so idyllic in sheltered Rujenoy? I think so and yet the small flames were already lit when the Nazis came to fan them into the fires of the Holocaust that consumed a third of the Jewish people. There were, as I shall tell, a few true prophets of doom, but other than these, who could have believed that the worst that man has ever inflicted on man, in all human history, would happen – against those ordinary backgrounds to the ordinary people I loved – and be observed, at best with indifference, by other ordinary people whom I had known so well and for so long?

Although I know that it was so, it is hard to believe that on 2 November 1942 the Jews of Rujenoy were taken away, in carts, to Volkovysk and from there to Treblinka, where my mother and my sister Rivka perished at the hands of the Nazis and their helpers. Miriam's husband, Mottel, so I was told much later in Israel by a woman I met once and never saw again, tried hard to save his family. Somehow he had understood that terrible things were in the making and he prepared a hiding-place, a hut in the forest, with the aid of a woodsman who had worked for him for many years. One day they moved to the forest. As promised, the woodsman was there, waiting, when my brother-in-law brought Miriam and the children to the shelter – and, as they approached, he shot and killed them, one by one. I expect he did it so that the hut could be his. My father, having been separated from the rest of the family, turned to old friends from 'his' village for help, to men on whose backs I used to climb in childhood and whose big, smiling faces I still see; they too betrayed his trust – and murdered him.

That was long after I had settled in Palestine. But within months of my arrival there, I began to press my parents to join me, appeals that became more emphatic as time passed. This, though I knew how difficult it would be for them to raise the £1,000 sterling which the British demanded as a guarantee against each certificate of entry given to Jewish immigrants who, as would have been true of my mother and father, belonged to the category which the Palestine Administration vaguely labelled 'capitalist'. It had been hard enough to borrow the money for me to come to Palestine though I had been able to repay it fairly soon.

'I promise that one day we will come but now it is impossible. We are very busy with our summer camps. The children can't just be abandoned. If we leave, who will care for them?' My father wrote to me late in 1938. 'And the money? Where will we find it?' But the summer camps and the needy children weren't the main reason for not coming; it was the money. It was almost impossible at that stage to sell property to the Poles, many of whom were already waiting to get it very cheaply – as, indeed, Syrian Jews are now having a hard time finding purchasers for property which will surely become available later for less money. For my family, very soon it was too late; the price had been set too high.

Earlier, in the late 1920s, before the catastrophe, the family moved to Volkovysk, a nearby town numbering some 10,000 to 15,000 souls where trains did stop and where I finished two years of Hebrew high school. After that I was sent, at God knows what expense, to the Hebrew high school in Bialystok, a city known among Jews for three things: for the savagery of the pogroms that had broken out there in 1905, leaving seventy Jewish dead (a toll unprecedented in those relatively innocent days); for the brightness and depth of its Jewish cultural activities; and for the vigour of its Zionist movement.

I lived in a rented room with another boy from Volkovysk, David Niv, with whom, as a university student, I was also to share quarters in Warsaw. Years later, when I was Speaker of the Knesset, he edited the Israeli equivalent of Hansard, the British Parliamentary proceedings. Although the books I read and knew best were in Hebrew and Yiddish, I was stirred by the long Polish struggle for national independence and learned by heart great stretches of Adam Mickiewicz's epic poem *Konrad Walenrod*, written to keep alive Polish faith in ultimate freedom. It happened that my class sat for state matriculation exams the very first time that the Polish Government permitted the Hebrew high schools to participate in them. We felt it our grave responsibility to do especially well, even though the Government sent its toughest examiners to us, directing them to bear down on classical Polish literature as though, through this, also testing our allegiance to Poland. It was my good fortune to be questioned on Mickiewicz's works, so I passed the exam with high marks, *élan* and much satisfaction!

Today I have neither the opportunity nor the desire to speak Polish, though there was one notable exception. As Israel's Foreign Minister, I was received in the Vatican by the Polish-born Pope, and it pleased me to express to him in Polish my admiration for the then-popular Polish workers' freedom movement, Solidarnosc (Solidarity), with which he sympathized. I think he was impressed by the fluency with which I still spoke the language and was pleased by the substance of my few words, though not sufficiently so to utter more than a non-committal sentence or two about Israel (which the Vatican has yet to recognize). He did, however, speak with sorrow of friends who had been murdered in Poland.

I leave to others the closer investigation of Polish behaviour during the Nazi occupation, questions concerning the adequacy of the recognition given by Jews to Poles who risked their lives to save Jews, the still unfulfilled demand for public Polish atonement, all of the subsequent intricate painful areas that remain to be researched and documented. I tried hard, first as Israel's Foreign Minister and then as Prime Minister, to further diplomatic and commercial ties between the State of Israel and Poland, which I consider necessary and proper. But for me, personally, there remains only the knowledge that there, in Poland, in that country in which Jews lived for close to 1,000 years, among the millions who were abandoned, tormented and slaughtered was my entire family. I cannot forget and will not forgive.

Revolution was much in the air in that period between the wars when I attended university. Warsaw, one of the great cities of Europe, was the capital of the 'new' Polish state (established only in 1919), the first cosmopolitan place I had known. It was exciting and full of ferment, though for Jews, by 1932, there was already cause for alarm. Many Jewish students walked around equipped with some means of defence against gangs of anti-Semitic hooligans whose attacks were becoming increasingly frequent. Later in life I got used to being armed, though I never developed either a liking for or any interest in weapons, but in those first weeks in Warsaw, it was jarring for me to have to remember to slip a knife in my pocket – as more experienced Jewish students told me to do – before I set out to study.

The endless conversations of students outside lecture halls were what opened up new worlds for me, far more than did any formal education. The talk was largely political. I listened, I read, I questioned and, when I was alone, I thought hard and long about the issues being discussed so emotionally and so seriously. Here, too, some of my friends were Communists, hoping to save me from myself and from what they saw as the 'suffocating' narrowness of Zionism; they heaped their standard (and illegal) literature on me and almost talked me to death. Over many small cups of cheap chicory coffee and glasses of bad brandy, I learned a lot about Communism, its dialectic, its methodologies and its gods. I was fascinated by the lives of Lenin, Trotsky and their predecessors, starting with the men and women of Tsarist Russia's Narodnya Volya (The Peoples' Freedom) and their terrorist activities, on through to the Social Revolutionaries (SRs) and including the personalities who founded or led the various contemporary Communist Parties. Fascinated I was, but I felt no more connected with these than with the martyrs of the Irish uprisings about which I also read whatever I could lay my hands on. Oddly enough, it was to the heroes of the Irish revolution that I was to pay tribute years afterwards by choosing 'Michael' as my underground alias when I joined Lehi (acronym of the Hebrew for 'Fighters for the Freedom of Israel', best-known outside Israel as the Stern Group). I was stirred in some special manner by what I had read about Michael Collins, the Irish leader, director of intelligence for the IRA and later among the heads of the new Ireland and its army, who, in 1922, was ambushed and shot to death by his opponents. The spirit and circumstances of his struggle against the British came to life for me in faraway Poland and remained with me, though not consciously, for years. The name 'Shamir', on the other hand, belongs to my underground years. It was the name on the forged ID certificate which was on me when the British arrested and exiled me in 1946. So I kept it, partly because I rather liked it, but mostly for what might be considered sentimental reasons.

What became my *raison d'être*, what moved me and was to rivet my attention, undiminished, for the rest of my life, had to do with the return of the Jews to the Land of Israel – a drive so intense, an idea so powerful, that all other options before me in Warsaw could in no way compete. Zionism had come to me as part of my upbringing, but there was also a moment when I decided to join a Zionist youth group and 'officially' enter the ranks. It came in 1929, when I was fourteen and in high school in Volkovysk, and was sparked off by the Arab riots that broke out in Palestine that year.

News and commentary arrived very slowly in those days. There was, of course, no television and no radio at home; the printed word was all. We waited in a state of suspended animation for the newspapers to arrive; the most important, published in Warsaw (it appeared daily until September 1939), being the Yiddish *Haynt* ('Today') that provided extensive daily coverage on what was happening. But it was the less frequent bundle of Hebrew papers (to which my father determinedly subscribed) from the Land itself which gave us the sense of immediacy that nothing else could capture. The unfolding story of the riots shocked and enraged me: the savage Arab assaults on the isolated Jewish quarter in Jerusalem, the murder and mutilation of Jews – men, women and children – in Hebron, Safed and Motza as directed by the Mufti of Jerusalem (who had also been responsible for the riots of 1920 in that city), the destruction and looting of Jewish farming settlements. The Palestine Administration eventually restored peace in a manner that assured the aggressors, especially the Mufti, that Britain was not going to exert itself either to protect the Jews or to punish the Arabs. On the contrary, since the Jewish national home so upset the Arabs, they had to be placated by curbing Jewish immigration into the Land so festively promised us only a dozen years earlier.

That year I joined Betar (its name derived from the Hebrew '*Brit Trumpeldor*', or 'Trumpeldor's Covenant'), the Zionist youth movement created in 1923 and headed by Vladimir (Zeev) Jabotinsky. Significantly, Betar was also the name of the last stronghold of Jewish resistance against the Romans during the three-year revolt led by Shimon Bar Kochba, which ended in 135 AD with a great killing and the expulsion of the surviving Jews from Judea.

Without doubt, Jabotinsky was the most dynamic and controversial of the many gifted men who left their mark on the Zionist movement and, subsequently, on the State of Israel. No one who met him, who heard him speak in public, or who read his brilliantly lucid articles regarding the situation and aims of the Zionist revolution remained disaffected. For ever the target of strong feelings, he was at once hated, worshipped, feared and admired; accepted as a supreme leader by some, he was rejected by others as a dangerous extremist whose concepts and supporters, if allowed to prevail, would degrade and destroy the essence of the Zionist cause. Though he never achieved leadership of the official Zionist establishment, knowing only the dubious joys of heading a perpetual minority, and although he died in 1940, before the birth of Israel, his contributions to it and his impact upon it are, in my view, no less than fundamental to its existence.

Today Jabotinsky's name and spirit are kept alive mostly through the Likud Party, which, to a significant degree, represents and articulates his basic philosophy and is, so to speak, executor of his political testament. It is, by the way, no coincidence that of all the Zionist leaders, only Jabotinsky, I think, succeeded in leaving behind him so well-defined a political entity, so identifiable a school of thought and so clear-cut an ideology.

None the less, while the Likud does much to keep his memory green and there is hardly a town in Israel without its Jabotinsky

Street, I am reasonably sure that most young Israelis (those born within the past thirty years or so), and certainly most young Diaspora Jews, know little, if anything, about him. I want therefore to relate something, however briefly, of his life, views, achievements – and disappointments. I did not know him personally, nor did I always agree with his opinions, approve of his actions or follow his edicts, but the vistas he opened up for me and their effect on my life were such that, in the final analysis, I see them as having helped to shape it.

A Russian Jew, born in the Black Sea port city of Odessa in 1880, blessed by striking literary and linguistic talent (he wrote several novels and was fluent in seven languages) and a magnetic public speaker, Jabotinsky was well on his way, even as a student, to a notable career in journalism when, in 1903, the Jewish problem forced itself on his attention. As had happened earlier to Theodor Herzl, founder of the Zionist movement, and also a journalist from a largely secular background, Jabotinsky was lastingly affected by the outbreak of vicious anti-Semitism. He became interested in Zionism, intrigued by the boldness of the plan for the restoration of a Jewish state and by Herzl himself, and threw himself into the cause, concentrating on political work and what is now known as public relations.

World War I found Jabotinsky in Egypt, a correspondent for a leading Russian daily. Believing that Turkey would lose the war, and its Ottoman empire, to the Allies, convinced that the Jews might then indeed make an effective bid for independence in Palestine – a much neglected province of that empire but one in which some 40,000 Jews already lived – Jabotinsky set about creating the one instrument he was convinced would make such a bid feasible, even attractive: the participation of Jews as Jews in the Allied victory he anticipated. Fortune, or fate, brought him together with a man who was perhaps ideally suited for this project. Joseph Trumpeldor, formerly a Russian army officer, had settled in Palestine and then, along with other Palestinian Jews, been exiled to Egypt in 1914 by the Turks. In Egypt, he and Jabotinsky headed a group of exiles who resolved 'to form a Jewish Legion and propose to England to make use of it in Palestine'.

It took effort and patience, but, in 1915, the Zion Mule (transport) Corps was created by the British and sent to the Gallipoli front. Trumpeldor was triumphant, but Jabotinsky was not satisfied. Almost alone, he went on trying to create a Jewish Legion that would fight on the Palestine front as part of the British combat force. In 1917, a

Jewish battalion was finally formed, and Jabotinsky led the first company across the River Jordan. In 1918, two other battalions were added; by 1919, the Legion numbered more than 5,000 men in active service (mostly Russian immigrants), including volunteers from Palestine, the United States, Great Britain and Canada.

What is most telling, I think, about the story of the Legion (other than proving once more the accuracy of Herzl's motto: 'If you will it, it is no legend') is the discouragement that Jabotinsky faced from the Zionist leadership – with one or two exceptions. That the outcome might be the first real step towards realization of the Zionist dream was less pressing a consideration for most Zionists than the possibility that the Legion might not be a success, or that Turkey might not be defeated after all, or that the Zionist endeavour in Palestine might be harmed. The habits of settling for immediate, if deceptive, calm, of taking the easier path, of doing what the Zionists thought was expected of them rather than holding out for what they believed in, of pragmatism at the expense of faith – and patience – were already entrenched and indicated a kind of pessimism inappropriate to the daring concepts that were both Herzl's and Jabotinsky's. Nor has the passage of time or statehood erased or much blurred these differences of concept and approach, but of that more later.

Essentially, Jabotinsky's vision of Zionism achieved can be compressed into one sentence: a Jewish majority in a Jewish state in the whole of the biblical Land of Israel. This, he believed, would be gained through courage, action, imagination, what he termed 'iron' – meaning when necessary fighting back – and no deviation from, or compromise with, the central aims. His advocacy of free enterprise in that Jewish state of whose future existence he was always sure, his deeply rooted liberalism (diametrically opposed to the 'fascism' of which he and his adherents were ceaselessly accused), his strong objection to 'acts of an extra-legal nature' – all these were obscured by the intense hatred directed against him, initially by the Zionist Socialists of the Diaspora and then by their successors in Israel, by the jealousies he aroused and by the threat he posed to the official Zionist power structure and its vested interests.

Whatever Jabotinsky had to say on substantive matters relevant to Zionism was either distorted or ignored – even when it concerned human lives. This was as true of the reception accorded his prophetic anxiety regarding the real state of affairs in Europe (it led him, long before World War II, to seek alliances with governments that might help bring a million and a half Eastern European Jews to Palestine within a few years) as it was of his early advocacy of the 'illegal' immigration of Jews to Palestine – if all other channels were closed. Both urgent campaigns were opposed by many as 'fanatical' and 'extremist'; ironically, my father – who so encouraged and advocated *aliyah* (the Hebrew for settling in Israel) – greatly disapproved of Jabotinsky's so-called 'evacuation' plan for European Jewry on the grounds that, as he wrote to me, 'How can Jabotinsky demand that Jews be evacuated from Poland when we have contributed so much to its history?'

In truth, Jabotinsky was never extreme or dogmatic and certainly never intellectually unreliable. He understood and accepted the fact that the Arabs would oppose the establishment of a Jewish majority in the Land of Israel. He also understood and accepted the validity of the Arab claim to the country, but believed that it was less valid than that of the Jewish people. The Arabs, he said, would accommodate themselves eventually to the Jewish state; in the interim, 'an iron wall' would have to safeguard the Jews from Arab wrath. He rejected equally the idea of 'evacuating' the Arabs and that of creating a binational state with them. Time, Jabotinsky thought, would take care of the problem. The whole of Palestine was large enough, he declared, to contain 'a million Arabs and then a million of their progeny, several million Jews – and peace'.

As for myself, nothing I have learned since I was a young man in Poland has altered, or in any way lessened or diluted, my belief in the logic, the justice and, yes, the grandeur of the objectives, as Jabotinsky articulated them, of Zionist activism.

I must now touch upon a major development that took place in Palestine two years before I left Poland and which, because it caused a wound in the body politic of Zionism that is still not totally healed after all these years, also belongs in any account of that period in my life.

It happened in 1933. The Zionist Revisionist Party, which Jabotinsky had created at roughly the same time that he launched Betar, had grown substantially, constituting a serious threat to the old-established leadership of the World Zionist Organization, to its long-time President, Dr Chaim Weizmann (Israel's first President in 1948), and to David Wolfsohn, Weizmann's similarly minimalist successor. But despite the inroads they made and the appeal of their platform, the Revisionists were not able to achieve leadership, Their resolutions (including one calling for a Jewish state) were blocked, their anti-British stand and demands for an official Jewish self-defence force under the Mandate went by the board, Jabotinsky was always maligned, and in Palestine they were wildly accused by the Labour

Party and the Histadrut (the General Federation of Workers) of being strike-breakers and warned of meeting with bodily harm.

Zionist 'left' and Zionist 'right' seemed doomed to collide; the *Yishuv* (the pre-state Jewish community of the country) was on the brink of an upheaval in which, so it appeared to Labour, the Revisionists had to be crushed. Civil war? In Palestine? Among the Jews? Surely impossible, but little by little the Labour majority began to discriminate more openly against the Revisionists, denying them jobs, comparing Betar's brown shirts with those of the Nazis and becoming more abusive, both verbally and physically.

Then came a June evening in 1933 on which Dr Chaim Arlosoroff, a gifted young economist who was one of the Labour Party's most promising members, was shot to death as he strolled on the Tel Aviv beach with his wife Sima. In its grief and anger, the Labour Party pointed a finger at the Revisionists. The shock of the murder – and of the accusation – was felt far from Palestine. In Warsaw, alarmed Jews asked each other: how could it be? What had taken place? Who had done it? At first, some of the Yiddish papers, which I held with shaking hands, wrote about the case as though the questions were idle ones: 'obviously' Arlosoroff had been murdered in cold blood by fanatics belonging to an offshoot of the Revisionist Party.

Three men, Abba Achimeir, Zvi Rosenblatt and Avraham Stavsky, were arrested. I couldn't believe it. I read and re-read the news stories, hoping against hope for some explanation, some enlightenment, an announcement that none of it was true, not the murder, nor the reaction. The agitation in Betar was tremendous: for weeks we thought and talked about nothing but the Arlosoroff case. Years afterwards, when President Kennedy was assassinated, I relived for a moment that same stunned disbelief, that same feeling that something had happened after which everything would be different, and I remembered the way I had felt in Poland in that summer of 1933. Eventually, the tone of the reporting from Palestine changed; so did the news. Of the three prisoners, two were acquitted almost at once and one, while convicted, was later cleared for lack of evidence. An Arab confessed, then took back his confession. Mrs Arlosoroff remained firm in her accusations, but the number grew of those who assigned her a dubious role in the drama which was never quite forgotten in Israeli political circles.

The case returned to public attention fleetingly in 1982 – shortly before the war in Lebanon – when Menachem Begin, then Israel's Prime Minister, formed an official Commission of Enquiry to review it, presumably for the last time. The Commission exonerated, absolutely, the men already cleared half a century earlier, suggested that Mrs Arlosoroff's positive identification of the murderers may have been mistaken, and absolved the Labour Party, without naming names, of responsibility for a 'blood libel'. But there had been collective blame – and punishment; the reputation of the Revisionist Party had been besmirched and a probable shift of power (in its direction) within the World Zionist Organization warded off. In fact, this 'blood libel' determined the rise of Labour to the supremacy it retained until 1977. In 1935, Jabotinsky left this body to found the New Zionist Organization with himself as President.

As for me, I was already in Palestine. I had known for a very long time that I would make the move. The question was only when. Then one day, walking along a Warsaw street, I heard a newsboy shouting 'Special Edition' at the top of his voice. I bought the paper and, standing in the street, read the news: Dr Josef Goebbels, Hitler's Minister for Enlightenment and Propaganda was planning a visit to Warsaw. I don't know how other people in the street reacted, if at all. I only know that I asked myself, then and there, 'What are you doing here? Poland is lost.' There was no room for me there any more. The only place from which I could do anything now to help my people was the Land of Israel and, later that day, I began my preparations for leaving.

2

GOING UNDERGROUND

ALL TOLD, SINCE the founding of the state, some two and a quarter
million men, women and children have arrived in Israel to settle, or,
as is said in Hebrew, to become *olim* (from the word for 'ascent').
Some have not stayed long; some have taken years to adjust; others
have never really made the adjustment at all, essentially remaining
strangers in the land; and almost all at first found certain aspects of
the new life difficult, frustrating and disappointing.

Wars, chronic tension, unfamiliar climate and language, the under-
currents with, and the special problems of, a state committed to non-
selective immigration caused virtually each wave of settlers to suffer
hardship, to compile lists of complaints, periodically to feel deprived
and misunderstood – and then to turn, almost without noticing the
process, into *vatikim* (veterans), themselves now responsible for the
acclimatization of the next wave of new citizens.

But it was not so for me. From that winter morning in 1935 when
the ss *Polonia* – packed with Jewish students and young 'fictitious'
couples, typical of those years, consisting of a Palestinian Jew and
the 'wife' he briefly married so that she could legally enter Palestine –
docked in Jaffa, I felt completely at home, 'settled', part of the country
and at ease. I suppose this was due, mainly, to the years of my
Hebrew schooling, to having read, heard and thought so much about
the *Yishuv*, to already knowing almost everything about the way
people lived and dressed and what they ate. Nothing was strange to
me, not the street names, not the sights and sounds, not even the
strings of camels making their way along the beach. I walked around
Tel Aviv revelling in everything, above all in my good fortune.

Here I was, aged twenty, just where I most wanted to be; able,
ready and eager to take my place among the 400,000 members of
what was already a beleaguered community; all of us here because,
finally, whatever our personal vision of Zionism, our differing back-

grounds and habits, we shared a collective hope and a very long past. Even the weather, I thought, was miraculous; it was the middle of November and I was not in freezing Poland (already for me like another planet) but in the blazing sunshine of a land with cloudless skies and not a sign of snow anywhere. It was almost too good to be true and, though such words do not come often or easily to me, I can only describe my first few weeks in Palestine as joyful.

Joyfulness, however, was not enough; there was also a living to be earned and here, too, I felt that good luck had singled me out. I found work almost immediately. First, like many other new immigrants in the 1930s, I did physical labour – as a building worker. When that job ended, I joined the ranks of the unemployed, but not for long. I heard of a job available in an auditor's office, applied for it and got it. When the firm decided to open a Tel Aviv branch, I was it. Book-keeping wasn't what I had expected to be doing in the Holy Land, but I knew how to concentrate and I learned quickly. Within a year, not only was I still employed but I had even made enough money to be able to repay the debts my father had incurred on my behalf in Poland. And, most importantly, after office hours, I was now free to devote myself to what most mattered to me. As for the rest of my higher education, since in Poland I had formally begun to study law, in Palestine for a while I put in an appearance at the Hebrew University of Jerusalem, took a course or two in Jewish history, and even spoke at a couple of student meetings. Then I decided that academic affairs would have to wait. There were more pressing things to be done and I was filled by the desire to do them. Nearly sixty years later, however, I did acquire a law degree – thanks to Boston University, which, in November 1991, was kind enough to present me with an honorary degree. I haven't much liking for ceremonies, but that one was splendid and I was amused at the way some things work out, after all.

Those were the years of what the British chose to call 'the Palestine disturbances', but which were actually major anti-Jewish Arab riots intended chiefly to put a permanent stop to all Jewish immigration to Palestine. They lasted for three years, cost the lives of 2,000 Arabs (as always, more Arabs than Jews were killed by Arabs), some 500 Jews and over 100 Englishmen, and were accompanied by an Arab general strike. But the riots failed to frighten off the Jews; immigration never stopped, though it was to acquire various forms. Whom they did frighten were the British, who, from then on, did their best to appease the Arabs by consistently reducing the number of Jews allowed to enter the Land of Israel. And, from then on, immigration was at the heart of the Palestine problem and of the relations between the British and ourselves.

While continuing immigration was the most significant Jewish response to the Arab terror, it was in no way the only one. There was also the *Yishuv*'s urgent need to defend itself. In the first years of the Palestine Government, Jabotinsky had pressed for the creation of an official, openly acknowledged Jewish militia to function under British control with British assistance, while the established Zionist leadership, including the Labour Party and its affiliates, pulling in the opposite direction, opted for an unofficial, independent-of-the-British, if necessary even secret, organization. This was indeed created, becoming the Haganah (Hebrew for self-defence), which was sometimes clandestine, sometimes not, sometimes in favour with the British and treated as semi-legal, sometimes forced underground and badly harassed.

In the massacres of 1929, the Haganah had proved to be under-equipped, inadequately trained and too poorly organized to be effective. Not geared to taking the initiative or to reprisals of any sort, it was largely occupied with guard duty in Jewish towns, kibbutzim and other settlements, activities which, for many of its members, were, though important, neither enough nor appropriate. The feeling grew that, at the very least, the killing of Jews because they were Jews could not be tolerated in Palestine; that this must, at all costs, be prevented; and that if it was not always possible to prevent such deaths, they were to be avenged at once. By 1931, a deepening sense of limitation and rising criticism of the Haganah's ineffectuality led to a split in its ranks – and to the founding of Haganah B by Avraham Tehomi ('Gideon' was his underground name), who had been made Haganah commander in Jerusalem following the 1929 riots and who left its ranks in protest against its policies, especially its political involvement.

The Haganah policy of self-restraint (*Havlagah* in Hebrew), the official policy of the Jewish community of Palestine, was based on considerations that appeared to be practical, acceptable abroad, especially in Great Britain, and relatively fool-proof. If there were no retaliation, no counter-terror, no hand raised against the Arabs, then the British would not be able to hold forth, however much they might appeal to the hostile Palestine Administration to do so, about 'civil war' or 'Arab-Jewish disturbances', or use Jewish military action as a convenient excuse for stopping or cutting immigration or ending their grudging sporadic co-operation with the Haganah. Above all, the Zionist establishment feared that the great investment of effort, sacrifice and energy made by the *Yishuv* in the country's development might be imperilled if the Mandatory power were openly defied – or even seriously challenged.

As a policy, *Havlagah* was disastrous. It was short-sighted, self-deceiving and based on an inexplicable (to me) and unjustified belief that sooner or later, if we refrained from angering them, the British would keep the promises they had made to us (in the Balfour Declaration, etc.) and to the civilized world (through the League of Nations Mandate). Not only would Britain do this, but it would also recognize the error of surrendering to Arab blackmail and reward the *Yishuv* for good behaviour. This rationalization had become an article of faith for the Zionist leadership, along with the belief (in David Ben-Gurion's words) that 'The Arabs ... will be forgiven one day: whatever they have done will be forgotten. But this is not true for us.' Haganah B, on the other hand, represented the basic view that the Jews must respond to Arab attacks directed against them in such a way that the Arabs would indeed be deterred from further violence. This kind of response, seen as a historic necessity, would symbolize the revolution taking place in Jewish life – thanks to Zionism, i.e. to the understanding that Jews must defend themselves, no longer relying on the protection of foreigners. Haganah B also believed that by playing directly into the hands of the Arabs and the British alike, and encouraging the Arabs by leaving them the initiative, *Havlagah* turned the entire *Yishuv* into an easy target and each Palestinian Jew into a potential victim.

For a year or two, *Havlagah* remained in full force. Then, under intense internal and external pressure, the Haganah HQ slowly began to admit to itself (and to persuade the official Zionist leadership) that tougher measures were, literally, vital. It set about implementing a major change of policy that involved going on the offensive, engaging Arab gangs in combat and, to the extent that the British allowed, fighting for the land. But that is another story.

Eventually, some say inevitably, differences of opinion and clashes of temperament also developed within Haganah B. The organization split; some members returned to the parent Haganah, but more than half remained within the same framework. By 1937, Haganah B was known as the Irgun Zvai Leumi (Hebrew for the National Military Organization), of which I became a member.

It is not uninteresting, I think, to take a look at the political development of the underground organizations. The Haganah shifted from being an independent self-defence militia to being an army available to the Zionist institutions for carrying out their policies, and remained such until the Israel Defence Forces (IDF) were established in 1948. As for Haganah B (which had initially followed in the footsteps of the Haganah – emphasizing a few insignificant deviations), it turned into a combat formation made up of volunteers bound by a nationalistic and militant idealism whose central purpose, so its officers and active members came to believe, was to 'possess the country by force' if needs be, i.e. to constitute themselves into an entity capable of founding a Jewish state in the Land of Israel. This concept which, naturally, led to confrontations with the Arabs, and later with the British, made profound sense to me from the time in 1937 when I first read an electrifying article called 'We Aspire to Power'. In it, a young Palestinian Jewish poet, his *nom de plume* was Yonatan Ratosh, declared in fiery prose that we did not necessarily have to wait for our state until there was a Jewish majority as Jabotinsky, ever the legalist, had decreed, specifying that, of this majority, fifty-one per cent would have to vote in favour of independence. No, wrote Ratosh. We could first proclaim the existence of a Jewish government. That government would establish and develop the state, absorb immigration, settle the land and generally create the conditions required for the state's growth and early progress. I was fired by this concept and its implications and wholly committed myself to its realization. It didn't happen the way Ratosh thought it could and should, but the fact remains that when the State of Israel was established a little over a decade later, the Jews were indeed still a minority in the country – but it didn't take long for that to change. In the meantime, the Irgun Zvai Leumi became the spearhead of the struggle to implement this philosophy.

It must be noted at this point that the Arab riots of the 1920s, 1930s and 1980s are interconnected. Arab terrorism did not start with the founding of the Palestine Liberation Organization (PLO) in 1964. It is far older than that. Neither the mission nor the target has changed. The purpose has always been the disruption (at worst) or the prevention (at best) of Jewish immigration to and settlement in the Land of Israel. Nor have the Arabs ever kept this a secret. It is others who chose, for various reasons, to ignore or soften the loudly declared Arab war aims, dismissing them as Middle Eastern hyperbole. It is also noteworthy that Arab terrorism did not then have anything to do with the Arabs wanting to rule the country instead of the British – as we did, for instance. Not at all. The bloodshed was always directed against the Jews and had no motive except destruction. In 1936, when the Arabs turned on the British, it was only in relation

to the Jews, to Jewish immigration, to doing away with the Jews. It
was not to take over or to drive the British out of Palestine. Nor,
when the British did leave and the State of Israel was created, did
Palestinian Arabs attempt to assume control, or make use of, those
areas of the country that were not part of the Jewish state – such as
Judea, Samaria or the Gaza Strip – all inhabited exclusively by Arabs.
Arab energy and money were invested instead in endless and fruitless
bids to make life here unbearable for us.

The Palestine Government for its part seemed both unable and
unwilling to do anything about the riots. By demonstrating negligence, taking months to bring captured terrorists to trial and months
more to draw up suitable regulations, by combining idleness with
confusion, it gave the Arabs a sense of security; to the war-cry
'Slaughter the Jews', they confidently added the words 'The Government is with us', and no voice was raised from Government House
in disagreement.

In the end, it was London that lost patience with the Palestine
situation. A British general, with no special feelings about the problem
as such, restored order in four weeks. Working fast and refusing to
listen to any arguments, he imposed stiff collective fines and long
curfews, authorized immediate arrests and ordered the instant demolition of Arab houses wherever it was suspected that villagers were
hiding terrorists, storing arms or otherwise giving aid and comfort.
The terror subsided; the Arab general strike was called off; the country
calmed down. And why not? General Dill had his orders; there were
no television cameramen, no reporters, no media involvement. The
Arabs understood the message and, although the sub-war (which is
what it was) did not end, tentative peace came to Palestine for a
while.

In those days, secrecy in the underground organizations was not
what it was to become later. Whatever drama accompanied our
young lives at that stage – and there was little – was designed by
our elders to stress the importance of what we were undertaking. My
own Irgun 'initiation' is a good example. It took place one evening
in the darkened classroom of a Tel Aviv school – schools empty in
the late afternoons and evenings were indispensable to the underground for training that couldn't be done out-of-doors. The only
source of light was a gooseneck lamp beamed right at me to ensure
that I could not get a good (i.e. identifying) look at the three members
of the admissions committee sitting at a table in front of me. Someone
solemnly asked ritual questions: 'Are you prepared to make sacrifices

if called upon to do so?' 'Are you prepared to accept military discipline?' 'Are you aware that joining this organization may involve you in great danger?' Equally solemnly I gave ritual answers.

In fact, I had known for a week that my application would be accepted, but this didn't lessen my emotion when on one other evening, in another classroom, I repeated – after a man who spoke from behind a concealing sheet – the oath of allegiance to the Irgun Zvai Leumi: 'We swear allegiance to the Irgun Zvai Leumi in the Land of Israel. We shall be ready at any time to act in the cause of the rebirth of the nation of Israel in its homeland. To live and die for it. . . .' Each ceremony took less than five minutes, but the short formalities added a new dimension, and no small pride, to an already existing inner vow.

Afterwards I settled into a new routine: a book-keeping job in an office by day; at night either learning, or already using, the skills needed if the Irgun was to build up some sort of military capability, deal with the *Yishuv*'s attackers and make clear to the British that we were in Palestine as of right. We trained almost every night and all day Saturdays (in empty lots, orange groves and sand dunes long since vanished, their place taken by huge hotels and residential areas). I got used not only to managing on very little sleep, sometimes none at all, but also to the Irgun stress on military bearing, to standing to attention when an Irgun officer addressed me, to being assigned to serve in a quasi-military unit and having to familiarize myself with military hierarchy, of which there had been a modicum in Betar and for which I had not developed a taste even then. But military decorum, whether I cared for it or not, was not the point. What counted was that I learned to handle weapons, to understand something about explosives, to begin to think in terms of tactics and fairly soon to rise in the military hierarchy myself.

I think back now on those days as a sort of formative period, not particularly pleasant but certainly a learning experience. My first commanding officer, Aharon Haichman, was also the Irgun commander of Tel Aviv, which, since he didn't much like me, made him an awesome presence. I could see that he didn't think I would make much of a soldier, that I'd surely quit. But I didn't and, one day, in a discussion about discipline in the underground – which I said I thought ought to be much stricter than in an army – I noted, with some relief, that he seemed much less disapproving. In the end we got on very well and in later life met quite often.

From being an untried, almost invisible recruit, I became the Irgun equivalent of a second lieutenant. We were called *sganim* (the Irgun is long gone but the rank lives on in the IDF). I was attached to special units responsible for planning and executing reprisals, for Intelligence and also for training, and was put in charge of a youth organization called 'The National Cells'. I suppose that, in today's terminology, the high-school students with whom I worked would be labelled as members of a front organization. On the surface, it was just another of the *Yishuv*'s many youth groups, a club whose members were sufficiently interested in current affairs to get together for discussions after school, but in reality its activities were dedicated to preparing its members to become future Irgun fighters. We met once a week in a hut in the centre of town. We talked, listened whenever possible to one of the well-intentioned intellectuals whom I invited to speak on relevant subjects of their choice, and analysed again and again the Palestine problem, and what the Irgun was all about. Indoctrination? Education? Something of both, I imagine. What stands out in my memory about those gatherings are the attentiveness and intelligence of the boys and girls to whom I tried each week anew to pass on my own fervour. One of them was Eliahu Bet-Tsouri, who was to be executed in Cairo in 1944 for Lord Moyne's murder.

More importantly, when and where necessary, I participated in armed actions carried out by small Irgun groups, first against the Arabs, then also against the British – always immediately following upon either a murderous Arab attack on Jews or an outrage (torture, for instance) inflicted on Irgunists by British police in search of information. Sometimes such reprisals were timed to take place simultaneously in various parts of the country so that they would have greater impact. Our underground radio, 'The Voice of Fighting Zion', was quick to broadcast news of these executions, and background information was given wide and fast circulation through the distribution of explanatory posters pasted, usually in the dead of night, on to public notice-boards. There was no need ever for the *Yishuv* or the authorities to wonder who was responsible for any given retaliatory action – or why it had been taken. The Irgun immediately provided the full facts, earning for itself, among other things, a reputation for accurate communication with the public.

Let me not give the wrong impression: we were much concerned with the moral aspects of the way we lived, what we did, and the implications and aftermaths of our acts. Continuously accused, on all sides, of wantonly shedding blood, we were exceedingly sensitive to the charge, expended much time and effort on explaining that there was no other way, examined our motives and aims over and over again, and undertook no action blindly or automatically or for brutality's sake. Our goal – and in this, if not in other approaches, the Irgun, the Haganah and later Lehi (of which I shall write in detail) were in agreement – was not so much to punish as to deter, to warn and to raise the price of each Jewish life taken or damaged. Reprisals were not acts that called for, or elicited, celebration; they had to be, and were, part of the payment demanded from us for national survival, and I recall them as such, without apology or regret.

There were two outstanding figures in the Irgun when I joined it in 1939: its commander, David Raziel, and Abraham Stern, known as Yair. The story of the Irgun is the story of both of them. Often the dark of the underground, its peculiar challenges to endurance and ingenuity, the extreme discipline it demanded, and the solitude and danger in which its members, for the most part, lived and operated, combined to produce men and women of more than usual judgment and grasp of command. But sometimes, though rarely, people like that arrived into the heart of clandestine life, fully equipped in some extraordinary way for leadership; all of a sudden, everyone turning to them for guidance and instruction. It is the result of a natural aura of authority, of the kind of personality that, in close and never entirely safe quarters, one can respond to, but also absolutely rely upon. I knew and served, in that same dark, under these two men, themselves for years inseparable comrades-at-arms, who were both destined to die by violence long before the creation of the Jewish state for which they had so single-mindedly fought. Both of them I believe, had they lived, might well have altered the subsequent course of events, at least to a considerable degree.

Raziel's personal history was, I think, unique. He was born, in 1910, in Lithuania, into an Orthodox Jewish family and had lived in Palestine since his early childhood, attending a *yeshivah* and going on to study philosophy and mathematics at the Hebrew University. Increasingly, his attention focused on the rebirth of Jewish independence in the Land of Israel and, most especially, on the renewal of Jewish military tradition. It became impossible for him to continue with an academic career; nothing, he felt, should be allowed to compete with, or substitute for, his personal participation in the struggle and he opted – as so many of his generation did – for action and for resistance.

What particularly preoccupied Raziel was the building of foundations for a modern Jewish army that would bear, within itself, the heritage of the warriors of the Old Testament – with whose victories, defeats and tactics he was so familiar and which he obsessively analysed and assessed. He was not normally a talkative man, even by my standards, but he would discourse for hours on military matters, current or historical, in detail or broadly, with the enthusiasm and concentration of a true rabbinical student.

I knew Raziel's family (I lived for a while in a Tel Aviv room adjacent to a boarding-house run by his aunt) better than I ever got to know him. After all, I was a junior member of the Irgun, not in the least important, only getting a glimpse of him when he inspected one of my courses and asked abrupt, penetrating questions. My clearest recollection of him is his addressing the *sganim* course I had just completed at a 'graduation' ceremony which he attended with most of the senior officers of the Tel Aviv area – which was as unusual as it was risky since it could have been a major haul for the British – and at which, nervous because I knew he was present, I also spoke on behalf of the class. I remember how he stood there, more than half a century ago, talking to us about what it would be like when there was a Jewish army and describing the Jewish pilots and aeroplanes that would fly over Baghdad and Cairo one day. 'Everything will be different then,' he declared. I had never heard anyone talk like that before, but, although I was very moved by his words, I was also quite sure that what he was foretelling would really happen – as it did, though neither he nor I nor the other new officers could have known this. Raziel's contributions to the freedom of Israel were various, but possibly the most characteristic was the textbook on the use of small arms and training methods, the first of its kind in Hebrew, which he wrote together with Yair and which characterized them both and also their common cause.

In 1941 – Jabotinsky had died in New York and Yair and his followers had left the Irgun to form Lehi – one of the many ironies that punctuate Israeli history took place. The British, who had arrested and triumphantly imprisoned Raziel, now asked whether the Irgun would agree, in this second year of the war, to help sabotage oil installations in Iraq, a country then in the throes of the Rashid Ali pro-Nazi revolt. The request was slightly less amazing than may appear at first glance. With the outbreak of World War II, at Jabotinsky's insistence, the Irgun suspended its anti-British activities – despite Raziel's own repeatedly stated conviction that the *Yishuv* would be forced, in any case and sooner rather than later, to meet the British in armed encounter. None the less, always disciplined, he agreed to Irgun participation in the Iraq attack, taking it for granted that he himself would be among the attackers. In the turmoil of the abortive revolt, the fierce German bombardment of British bases in Iraq, and the lack of Iraqi affection for the British, nothing went as scheduled. David Raziel, aged thirty-one, was killed on the road to Baghdad even before his mission got under way, mourned by none more bitterly than Yair, who had once been his David.

The year in which I arrived in Palestine was the last year, so it seems to me in retrospect, that any intelligent Jew living there could possibly go on believing that the *Yishuv* might, after all, peacefully evolve into a state like others, its eventual independence taken for granted. By the same token, it was the last year that anyone could reasonably believe in a Jewish national home under British management, and the last year also of any British effort in that direction. Notwithstanding this, such was the position, for several more years, of the Zionist establishment.

Ecclesiastes, of course, was right: indeed, nothing is new under the sun. As long as fifty years ago, important spokesmen for the *Yishuv* and more important and experienced spokesmen for all-powerful Great Britain shared a naïve faith in the convening of conferences and the appointment of official commissions as effective means of securing peace in Palestine. If the Jews can be excused their wishful thinking because it was done under the shadow of the swastika, what can possibly explain British logic in launching so unpromising a series of attempts to remedy the deteriorating situation rather than showing some consistent firmness with the Arabs – and some measure of sympathy with the Jewish people? Instead, the British Government went on looking for a face-saving formula, for a solution that would neither upset the Arabs unduly nor finally slam the door in the face of the Jewish nationalism it was pledged to support. Despatching one commission of enquiry after another, it charged each in turn to report on what was 'actually' going on in Palestine and to recommend a solution that would be suitable, durable and not conflict with imperial interests.

One such commission, headed by Lord Peel, arrived in 1936. Its members travelled through Palestine under heavy guard, met with key Jewish personalities, resigned themselves to the Arab refusal to testify before them or to co-operate in any other way, and returned home to England, where, among other things, they heard Jabotinsky (long banned from Palestine for 'militancy') present his case for a Jewish state in all of Palestine. Declaring the Mandate unworkable, the commission recommended that Palestine be divided into a Jewish state and an Arab state, with a permanent British mandate over certain areas; the Jewish state, its population limited to half a million, being restricted to a territory of some 2,000 square miles. The reason for the commission's proposal, it was explained, was that, however hard it tried, it could see no compromise ever being made between the two nationalisms.

The reaction to the partition plan was no surprise to those concerned. It was rejected absolutely by the Arabs (at this point, sponsored both by Fascist Italy and by Nazi Germany); accepted in principle with foreboding and reluctance by the established Zionist leadership, headed by David Ben-Gurion, which claimed that, if nothing else, a Jewish state – however grotesque its contours and however vulnerable it might be – would make possible the rescue of some of the Jews of Europe; while a bloc of 'nay-sayers' – Revisionists, the Irgun, other non-Socialist, non-leadership groups, some Labourites and some extreme left-wing parties (objecting because they didn't believe in a Jewish state and pressing for a binational state, though they later abandoned this idea) – readied themselves to fight partition, denouncing it as absurd and useless. The dispute between those who believed in the immediate gain and were therefore willing to settle for the least and those who believed that they were responsible to future generations and bound therefore to hold out for the most was protracted, bitter and filled with tension. Those who participated in it felt the weight of centuries on their shoulders, and themselves to be the custodians of national destiny. Who could have guessed that this kind of situation would face us again?

Ten years later, when partition was once more on the agenda, circumstances had changed unimaginably. Six million Jews had been murdered; there was nowhere other than Palestine for the broken remnant of European Jewry. In 1948, a Jewish state came into being which was a far cry from that of which I had dreamed: a Jewish state from which much of the Land of Israel was severed. I have done all I could, in various ways, in the intervening years to help rectify this distortion to which I can never be reconciled, and to prevent others like it. But a great deal has happened since Lord Peel's visit. The borders of the Jewish state, however inadequate, bear no resemblance to the ludicrously non-viable plan of 1936 with which his name is linked. However of borders, the conflicts to which they have given rise, and the sacrifices made in their name, more will be said later.

What happened was that yet another British commission, going into the details of the Peel Plan, emerged from its meetings to state that not only did it consider partition unworkable but that the Mandate itself should be shelved. So Lord Peel's two states were put away in a Whitehall drawer where they belonged. In Palestine, rioting escalated. The Irgun's strength had grown, both within the country and abroad, and it had attracted international attention not only by its policy of reprisals but also by the hanging, in 1938, of the twenty-five-year-old Irgun member, Shlomo Ben-Yosef, sentenced to death by a British military tribunal for trying to avenge an Arab attack that killed two Jewish women and a child in a car travelling in Upper Galilee. The attempt came to nothing; no one was hurt and the bus shot at wasn't even damaged. But the Palestine Government insisted that the three boys involved be brought to trial for 'illegal possession' of arms. The trial became a cause célèbre. In a considerable miscarriage of justice, two of the boys were sentenced to death, but only Ben-Yosef was hanged – the first Jew to be hanged in Palestine – despite appeals from all over the world. He died, with Jabotinsky's name on his lips, to be mourned as the first 'casualty' in the Irgun's war of liberation. In 1942, a mine exploded in a booby-trapped Tel Aviv flat; three policemen who had been summoned there tried to force the door and the explosion of a second mine killed them. One was the police officer who had hanged Ben-Yosef. It had taken four years, but the account was settled.

Early in 1939, the Chamberlain Government invited Jewish and Arab leaders – and representatives of neighbouring Arab states – to a 'Round Table' conference in London in order to see once more what could be done along the lines of 'peace in our time' for Palestine. About peace-making attempts of this nature, I shall have more to say when I describe the peace-making processes of the 1980s and 1990s in general, and my own misgivings about international conferences in particular. If it is suggested that apart from far more realistic and graver considerations, somewhere in the back of my mind there still echoed the fiasco of 1939, I cannot deny it. The Jewish delegation to London then was the most representative ever to attend an 'international' conference; the Arabs sent important personalities, including the Jordanian Prime Minister, and there was also a delegation of Palestinian Arabs. The Zionists had been repeatedly assured that they were in no danger of having an Arab state forced on them, or of having Jewish immigration halted, or, indeed, of anything bad happening to them.

But, in fact, the British had already made promises to the Arabs regarding the permanent minority status of the Jews – and the freezing of immigration turned out to be a cardinal issue. The conference broke down before it started; the Arabs insisted on sitting at separate tables and not meeting or talking to the Jews, while the British tried talking to each side alone. The Arab 'minimum' demand was: a complete halt to all Jewish development in Palestine. The Jews refused to accept any plan based on curtailment of immigration. How could they have done otherwise at a time when thousands of Polish, Czech, Austrian and post-*Kristallnacht* German Jews waited for permission to enter what was now the Jewish national haven, some already arriving 'illegally', i.e. without British permission, in the over-crowded leaky boats that beached on Palestine's shores at night and were the best the underground organizations could supply? The conference accomplished nothing.

Those were already the years of concentration camps, of Nazi persecution, humiliation and terrorizing, of the plundering and the isolating of Jews, years before words like 'extermination' entered the Jewish lexicon and Jewish history. There was not a shadow of doubt in my mind, nor in that of most of the *Yishuv* for that matter, that by barring Jews who could still get out of Hitler's Europe from entering Palestine and doing so for reasons of expedience, the British were, in fact, sharing in the guilt of the Nazis. Afterwards, in the awful light of what we were to learn about the Nazi horror, that judgment had to be revised. But one thing, I think, cannot be refuted, even now: it was the British, by their decisions and actions on immigration, who ultimately determined the course of events in Palestine and who, because they refused to help save the Jews of Europe in the time of the great ordeal, earned for themselves the profound hostility of people like myself. It wasn't a question of hating. I am not, by nature, a hater: I have never felt hatred towards the Arabs. Not all wars require hating. But in that autumn of 1939, my thoughts, my very being, centred on the need for the Jews of Palestine to be rid of the British so that we could establish Jewish sovereignty in Palestine – before it was too late. It was now absolutely clear to me that there was an irreconcilable conflict between the British policy of appeasing the Arabs by not accepting the idea of an independent Jewish state in Palestine and the yearning, and need, of the Jews to make Palestine a Jewish state. So the confrontation was unavoidable. Not that the public, still believing in the alliance with the British, in the abiding validity of the Balfour Declaration and the Mandate, was easily persuaded of the truth, but reality had the last word.

Just four months before the outbreak of World War II, the British Government produced what it termed 'an alternate policy' for Palestine, contained in what is known as the White Paper of 1939. Its main provisions spoke for themselves: during the next five years, 75,000 Jews could settle in the Land of Israel; after that, in 1944 (how distant the date seemed then), the Arabs would decide whether and how many more Jews would be let in, subtracting all 'illegal' immigrants from the sum total. So much for immigration. As for land, only the High Commissioner would be entitled to 'prohibit and regulate' the sale of land by Arabs to Jews and this would, in any case, only be allowed in an area amounting to about 300 square miles. Beyond these, the White Paper decreed that within ten years, a Palestine state (predominantly Arab, of course) would be established, with the British reserving for themselves the right to postpone this step if and as they saw fit. Finally, a constitution was to incorporate 'safeguards' for the Holy Places, for whatever was left of the Jewish national home and for British interests.

The *Yishuv* was stunned. There were not many ways to express its despair. Everything seemed inadequate: demonstrations, hunger strikes, threats of civil disobedience, the intervention by influential personalities abroad. Nothing persuaded the British to change their minds. The Jews, they said, were hysterical, overstating as usual. Conditions in Europe were not nearly as bad as described and, anyhow, another conference would be called to see what might be done 'internationally' about the refugees. In the summer of 1938, President Roosevelt had called together at Evian, France, the representatives of some thirty-odd governments to find some arrangement for these unwanted people. At Britain's request, Palestine was removed from the agenda. Only one nation, the Dominican Republic, offered to take the refugees in. It is hard to put into words the way I felt. Nothing I did, not even my membership in the Irgun, breaking the law of the land daily, handling forbidden weapons and regularly participating in bloody reprisals, seemed an adequate outlet for the anger bottling up inside me. I had no taste at all for the political disputes. The quarrels of the Jews, the ill-feeling between the two underground organizations and the finer points of correct behaviour didn't interest me in the least. Should the Irgun join the rest of the country in demonstrations against the White Paper? Wouldn't it be both perilous and inappropriate for us to march through the city with banners and placards? Feelings ran so high on such issues that some people even left the organization for good, but I and most of my friends marched in a memorable Irgun parade of protest, by our presence each of us hoping to convey to the British, to the world beyond Britain and to the Jews who depended on us that somehow

we would bring them to Palestine, get them home, whatever the
cost. I imagine many of those who paced the length of Tel Aviv's
main street that night prayed as they walked that European Jewry
could hold out till something changed, till the peril was averted. But
there were also people like myself who took a private vow that the
British must be made to leave – even though there were few of us
and an empire full of them.

As for *Havlagah*, it was maintained by the Zionist establishment (and
the *Yishuv*'s national institutions, chief among them the Jewish
Agency) even in the face of British enforcement of the 1939 White
Paper and despite the pursuit and internment of 'illegal immigrants'
(some of whom died at sea attempting to break the British blockade
of the Mediterranean). None the less, within a few weeks of the
outbreak of war, in September 1939, 130,000 young Palestinian
Jews had registered as potential recruits for a Jewish Brigade to fight
with the British against the Nazis under the blue-and-white flag.
David Ben-Gurion, Chairman of the Jewish Agency and head of the
all-powerful Labour Party, helped the *Yishuv* to feel better about
the splitting national personality by coming up with a deceptively
reassuring equation: 'We shall fight the war as if there were no White
Paper', he said, 'and we shall fight the White Paper as if there were
no war.'
    What Ben-Gurion was telling the Jews of Palestine was that no
basic attitudes should be changed, that self-restraint was still the
order of the day, that an effort still could be (and was being) made
in the direction of immigration and settlement, and that those who
did not agree with him were to be considered pariahs. He labelled
them 'dissidents' and declared that they must be regarded as a
menace to the equilibrium that he was trying to achieve for the
greater good of all.
    Inside the Irgun, differences of opinion reached boiling-point; the
debates over the line to be taken began to sound a new note, harsh,
even offensive. Jabotinsky's guidance from abroad didn't help much.
He sounded not unlike Ben-Gurion. 'Our grievances against the
Mandatory Government are not forgotten but first the Nazi rattlesnake
must be disposed of – and afterwards our rights in Palestine and
elsewhere will be re-established,' he had said in one of his last public
speeches, though before the war he himself had completed the outline
of a possible military rebellion to be staged by the Irgun in Palestine.
It was a mild statement which managed not to address itself to the
question of what the Irgun should do. For some, it came as a bitter

disappointment. The war had altered everything, including the Irgun, now plagued by inactivity, indecision and fretfulness. The ban against retaliation and the absence of any move against the British took their toll and altered also the relationship between Raziel and Yair, who had worked together in such harmony. In September 1940, my life altered too, for I left the Irgun with Yair to enter the deeper underground from which Lehi fought our outlawed war against the British.

3

FREEDOM FIGHTERS

'WE ARE ALL recruited for all of our lives; only death can discharge from the ranks,' wrote Yair in his best-known poem. He called it *Anonymous Soldiers*, set it to music and it became the Lehi anthem. It put into short words the way we felt about that fight for freedom which history, as we saw it, made synonymous with a fight to the death against the Palestine Government. Parting from former comrades, leaving the Irgun, setting out on a precarious and lonely campaign – unaided, at times even hated, by much of the *Yishuv* – against forces committed to crushing us was not easy. That Lehi existed, that we never lost heart and that, until the Jewish state came into being, the organization endured despite these odds was due almost entirely to our continuing belief in Yair's credo. And when he was killed, two years after Lehi's formation, we were able to go on without him on the strength of what we had learnt from him.

Born in Poland (the part which was then Russia) in 1907, Yair settled in Palestine in 1925 and attended the Hebrew University. Like so many of us he was drawn to, and became active in, the Irgun Zvai Leumi and, in the late 1930s, was sent to Europe to contact the Polish authorities in the hope of obtaining their active co-operation in the Irgun's battle for Jewish independence in Palestine. He succeeded on two counts: the Poles agreed to help establish advanced Irgun training courses in Poland and to provide us with arms. One course graduated but another, in which I was to take part, never came into existence because then the war broke out. As for the arms, the Poles had intended to give us enough to equip a division – they thought they were helping to lay the foundations for a Jewish army – but only managed to supply a small number of machine-guns, rifles, pistols and some ammunition. Part of this was smuggled into Palestine, the rest was to be stored by the Irgun in Poland until it could be transported there. But that was lost. Why the 'generosity'?

To some extent it was due to Yair's magnetism, but also to the idea that assisting the Irgun would eventually serve to take more Jews out of Poland, thus reducing the dimensions of that country's 'Jewish problem'.

Yair made an ideal spokesman; he was exceedingly intelligent, erudite (he translated Homer into Hebrew), unusually good-looking, polite and very controlled. He spoke to people respectfully, seriously and calmly, and looked at them when he talked to them. He was also somewhat of a dandy, very well-dressed, always in a suit with a tie – even in Palestine, where the tone was set in those days by men in shorts, open-necked shirts and sandals. He sounded and behaved like a young university professor at some acknowledged European centre of higher learning, a man marked for distinction as a political scientist or philosopher – and, in fact, to some extent, he was both of these. But the subject matter of his discussions, reflections and reading, the conclusions he reached and lived by, and his over-whelming preoccupations could hardly have been further from the academic.

Above all, he was a true revolutionary, unable and unwilling to suffer any distraction from the main effort; wildly impatient for the Jews to be free. He believed, with that depth of conviction that is, I think, the outstanding attribute of all visionaries, that only the here-and-now counted; that the future would be determined in Jerusalem, not in Whitehall or Washington. He didn't want a better or more enlightened Mandate; he wanted none at all. He wanted the Jews to be sovereign in their country and, in 1941, he wrote a manifesto which he called 'The Principles of Rebirth'. In it, he declared, that the borders of Israel 'are explicitly stated' in Genesis 15:18; that the right of the Jews to the Land is one of ownership and cannot be rescinded; and that the fate of the Jews of Palestine lay in their own hands. He had no time or use for politics; he wasn't in the least interested in party platforms, or sectarian manoeuvring, or bickering about the advantages and disadvantages of Socialism and so forth. These issues didn't belong in the category of things that concerned or intrigued him. Nor did the spit-and-polish of the Irgun.

Creating Lehi, Yair did away at once with military trappings. We had no hierarchy, no GHQ, just a central committee; there were no officers and we didn't stand to attention or salute anyone or follow-the-leader, although discipline was extremely strict. Yair believed that people should think for themselves. 'Study, train and think,' he told us. He schooled us in the rudiments of covert life, including the art of camouflage: be inconspicuous, quiet, walk in the shade, be a little stooped, a little shabby, never preen or show off. Although he was a master of practical conspiracy, his craving for secrecy came out in unexpected ways sometimes. For instance, he wrote by hand, in capital letters, extremely quickly so that his handwriting would reveal as little as possible about him, be as anonymous, as impersonal as possible.

What Yair hoped for was that the Nazis, so eager to rid themselves of Jews, would help to bring the majority of Jews from Europe, through the British blockade, to Palestine, thus making havoc of British illusions regarding post-war control of the Middle East, facilitating Allied defeat and, possibly, if Britain knew what was afoot, even producing the withdrawal of the White Paper. Whatever the result, he reasoned, Jews would be brought to Palestine. He didn't make this plan public, but Lehi openly termed the world war a conflict between the forces of evil, between Gog and Magog, and made unmistakable its position – again it must be remembered that all this was in 1940 and 1941 – when it was reasonable to feel that there was little for Jews to choose from between the Germans and the British. All that counted for Yair was that this idea might, after all, be a way to save Jews about whom no one else, least of all the British, seemed to care. Nothing came of it, of course. By that time, though no one yet knew it, the Nazis were already at work on a very different solution to the Jewish problem. In the meantime, however, Lehi was not only feared and disapproved of by the *Yishuv*, but also suspected of Fifth Column activities by a public that went on believing – incredibly, in the face of accumulating evidence to the contrary – that the British would open the gates of Palestine to the anguished Jews and which refused to be weaned of emotional and political dependence on Britain.

It is not easy for me to write about Yair without sounding a melodramatic note because his personality and life were so dramatic. But it is a fact that he raised a banner only unfurled in Israel before by men like the hero whose name he took for his *nom de guerre*: Eleazar Ben-Yair, the first-century leader of the Zealots who, for three years, held out on Masada, the last outpost of the Jews in 70 AD, after the destruction of Jerusalem by Roman troops. The night before the final and victorious Roman assault on the rock fortress, Eleazar Ben-Yair spoke to the Jews: 'Never be servants to the Romans', he said, 'or to any other than God Himself.' Next day, when the Romans came, they found only two women and five children alive; all the others had decided to kill themselves. However, his choice of name notwithstanding, I am sure that Yair himself would not have regarded the saga of Masada as a model for the future of the Jewish people. On the contrary, when he spoke of the future it was always logically – and optimistically. That, I imagine, is what the founder of Lehi would have said and done had he been on Masada that night.

I was arrested twice and twice I escaped from my captors. In a way, those two arrests marked the outer limits of my life in Lehi. The first time was in 1942, in Tel Aviv. I had gone to meet one of our people in a flat the British found out about; they entered it, arrested him and, when I turned up, at once arrested me – and whoever else came there that day. My own room not far away was searched, and a home-made rubber stamp, used by us to forge identity cards and with which I forged application forms, was discovered.

In those days, it was standard procedure for suspected members of Lehi and the Irgun to be brought before experts of the CID's Jewish Section, most often to appear before one of that Section's stars, a Hebrew-and-Yiddish speaking British police officer, Tom Wilkin (later involved in Yair's death and shot and killed by Lehi in 1944). It was indeed Wilkin who interrogated me, revealing his awesome fund of information (including names and addresses) about the network of the Jewish undergrounds. The next step was my detention in Jaffa prison. All things considered, it was not too bad. I had no family, no obligations and was not displeased to find myself in one of those huge, dirty, by-now legendary rooms in which all the Jewish political prisoners sat together, on the floor, sharing rations and food sent in by families and spending their time arguing about local politics and planning ways of getting out. Of the dozens of figures that drifted in and out, I remember few, but the shrill daily arguments about the Soviet–Nazi pact indulged in by an earnest German Jew called Hans and an Arab secretary of the Palestine Communist Party (in which, for the first time I actually heard someone use the words 'Mein Führer') are the kind of useless detail that, somehow or other, has remained with me all these years.

For the most part, our Arab jailers treated us if not well, then without brutality, perhaps even with respect, some helping to smuggle in prohibited reading material for us or keeping us informed of events outside. My trial took place in Tel Aviv; the judge, who was a Jew named Shneur Zalman Heshin, was destined in 1948 to join Israel's Supreme Court, as did his son, but then was as far from that pinnacle as I was from being Prime Minister of a Jewish state. 'Why are you so cheerful?' he asked me, unreceptive to my plea that I had accidentally 'found' the false rubber stamp. It was not easy to be a

Jewish judge under the Mandate; only the most scrupulous jurists could have gone on weighing the scales of justice in the highly charged circumstances, always placing the law before personal loyalties, however profound. By so doing, they created a tradition that has withstood all criticism, even in a society as badly addicted as ours is to self-flagellation. At all events, he sent me to jail under the Emergency Regulations for a period of three months. The sentence didn't trouble me much because, in any case, I was under administrative arrest, something which then had no limitations of time. What upset me more was that, because of me, my Tel Aviv roommate David Orlovsky, was detained and remained in detention for years.

The first stop was the prison in Acre, the strongly fortified Citadel, dark, forbidding and crowded, in which Jabotinsky had been held in 1920 and where Ben-Yosef was hanged; the kind of prison where heads were shaved, shoes were rendered laceless and one wore the filthy stinking clothing of former inmates. I arrived on a day when a group of Irgun members who had been there for months were being released, reversing the process that I was just about to start, and, for a while, we were in a transit area together. They briefed me thoroughly, colourfully and, rather enjoying themselves, I suspect, also depressingly. Each prisoner had to be interviewed before going to his cell by the prison chief, Commander Grant. I remember how Grant stared at me as if to engrave my face on his memory for ever, and how an Arab trusty, standing outside the door, had said reassuringly, 'Go in. Don't worry. The *Mudir* [chief] will tell you something. Just say "*Na'am, Ya Sidi*" ["Yes, Sir"] to everything he says.' From that fortress, I was sent to a big detention camp at nearby Mezrah. Now I was free to think about escape, to talk and to read.

The Jewish prisoners grouped themselves naturally in accordance with the underground movements to which they belonged; the Irgunists apart from the Lehi members of whom, within a few days, I was put 'in charge'. What did we do all day? We did what prisoners do everywhere: walked round and round the camp's perimeter for hours discussing the past, the present and our ideologies. The atmosphere was very Middle Eastern and rather lax; the camp administration made few demands on us and there was virtually no abuse or ill-treatment. Under most other colonial regimes, prison life – though it might have been as easy-going on the surface – was basically different, with cruelty, persecution and provocation never far off. But this was not so, at that time, in Palestine.

This perhaps may be the place to point out that being a member of the Palestine Police Force or Prison Service, or just being a young Englishman in uniform stationed anywhere in the country then, was not particularly pleasant. There was no reward, monetary or emotional, for being so passionately disliked by both sides to a dispute which the average soldier or policeman didn't, by and large, understand, or for living in a land in which there was no servant class and where no 'well-bred' Moslem or Jewish girl would have anything to do with one. But whatever their feelings towards us, even in the worst of times, however anti-Semitic they may have been (and many were), we were better off, even arch-enemies like myself, than we would have been in the custody of almost any other nationals.

After a while, Nathan Yellin-Mor also turned up at Mezrah and, as he and I daily circled the yard, we came to know each other well, not dreaming, of course, that, along with one other man, Dr Israel Scheib, we would all too soon be taking over from Yair as the 'Troika' of Lehi's central committee. Yellin-Mor ('Gera', to use his code name) was an intellectual both by nature and by choice, an engineer by training and a proud Jew by faith. He had joined the Revisionist Party and Betar in Poland in the 1930s and was an enthusiastic supporter of the Irgun. I was to work very closely for years with him in the special intimacy and trust without which no conspiratorial society can hope to function, and came to respect, admire and depend upon his severe, practical and exceedingly logical mind. He was a born editor and formulator, less effective as a speaker than a writer but a good conversationalist whenever he felt like talking.

Much was to befall him, but more was to evade him when the state came into being. In the early days of the state, he was imprisoned for complicity in the assassination of Count Bernadotte (an event I shall return to in due course). Largely in order to free him, we founded a short-lived political party which we called The Fighters; on its ticket, Gera was elected to the first Knesset. Even before that, he had begun to turn leftwards, becoming increasingly extreme in his attitudes towards the Soviet Union and towards the Arabs. He told me once that a truly progressive man can only be judged by the way he feels about the Arabs, and he became preoccupied by the East–West clash and by the relationship of the US and the USSR. He was a man who had changed and yet remained the same; involved, sharp, dedicated but at home nowhere, hating the right-wing Herut, the political successor of the Irgun, and despising the Labour Party. In the last years of his life he was a marginal figure, possessing no influence. I know all too well that life does not operate in accordance with what is fair or unfair, but I also know that Gera deserved better than he got – or chose.

But for the moment, in Mezrah, we were both interned, cut off and apprehensive about the the news from home. It was not good. Collaboration between the Haganah and British Intelligence was leading to a joint war against the 'dissidents'. Lehi members not in prison (by now there were more of us in than out) were on the run, constantly spied upon, hounded, kidnapped and even tortured. However deep they burrowed, the British – aided by their informers from various elements within the *Yishuv* – tracked them down. The process of informing, delivering Irgun (or, when possible, Lehi) members into the hands of the British, which often required kidnapping them first, was a phenomenon known accurately, if horrifyingly, as 'The Saison', a word associated with the hunting season. It was the one great blemish, the one disgrace of otherwise heroic times and accounted, in its early phases, for the presence of many of the detainees at Mezrah, and for the suspicious and chilly relationship between the different underground groups represented there. The Saison came in waves, cresting and subsiding, reaching its peak in 1944 and involving, all told, thousands of people. Here, again, Lehi was in a special position; it was small, tightly organized, less vulnerable to infiltration than the Irgun and we made known that, without any hesitation, we would execute traitors, when and if we found them. It says much about Lehi that within its ranks there were none such. Not one.

The news of Yair's death came like a hammer blow, though it was not, could not be, a surprise; he himself had written: 'in death's shadow we march'. Lehi was in no way made up of suicide squads. We were not Kamikaze fighters; we valued life and strained the most meagre of resources to be sure that men returned from missions safely, that transport awaited them, that documents, clothes and safehouses were ready for the getaway. On the other hand, we were all well aware that our enemies vastly outnumbered our friends and that soldiers indeed die in action. I knew for a fact, because he told me this, that Yair had anticipated not only his death, but the way in which he would die – quite apart from the poetic acknowledgment of its occurrence that led him to write: 'Should we happen to fall in some building or street, to be furtively buried by night, thousands of others will rise in our stead, to defend and continue the fight.'

In a letter he sent me in Mezrah two months before he was killed, he described Lehi's deteriorating situation, the almost daily arrests and his growing sense of solitude. 'We are finished,' he wrote, 'unless the experienced people in jail break out and help me guide this small and endangered movement. I believe that the following must try to escape ...', and he listed some names, mine among them. His letter gave me no rest. It was as though, by writing this way, Yair was preparing us, training us in his own fashion to break through that final core of ego that makes so hard the sacrifice he knew would be demanded of us – and of him. All I could think of was escaping at once, not only because this is the duty of every captured soldier, every prisoner of war, but because the anxiety that Yair had expressed in those few lines was mine too.

The first attempt to break out of Mezrah failed, perhaps because it was too simple, but, amazingly, we managed to get back before anyone looked for us, and preparations could and did begin at once for another try – which was to work. But even before that, something unusual happened. One day a very senior British officer, Brigadier Ballantyne of the Middle East CID, called the Lehi prisoners together and addressed us:

You may never get out of here. We can do whatever we want with you. We can keep you here for ever or deport you so you won't see your families for years, or release you and even ensure you government jobs. Your future is entirely in our hands and we are prepared to be reasonable. Announce the dissolution of your underground, halt the terrorist activities, and we will treat you accordingly.

Then he added: 'I'll go even further. If you want, some of you will get permission to discuss this proposal with your comrades elsewhere and decide. If you agree, I promise that we will come to terms as to the specific conditions of your release.' And he went on to say that our political struggle per se could continue; it was the warfare, the armed attacks against the British, that must cease.

'It is an opportunity', I said to my colleagues, 'for us to talk to the people in prison in Acre, so we must tell Ballantyne's men that yes, thank you, we are interested.' It didn't take long for the British to bring six imprisoned Lehi fighters from Acre to Mezrah, and we sat down together to thrash out the pros and cons of the British proposal. From the moment that Ballantyne started to speak, I knew my own mind. We must do nothing, give nothing, exchange nothing – unless the British were prepared, now, to pledge the post-war creation of a Jewish state. Anything less than that, any informal unauthorized statement, was worthless; anything that did not derive from the British Government had no value and to agree to it would be tantamount to self-destruction. Not everyone shared my point of view; one or two people asked what merit there was to staying in detention, isolated and out-of-action, as the months and perhaps the years passed? How would this bring Lehi closer to its goal? And what if Ballantyne's offer was genuine, deriving not from the CID but from Whitehall itself?

In the end, we put together a counter-proposal, designed not to be accepted but rather to gain us enough time so that we could go ahead with planning our escape. We suggested that the British, at once, hand over to the Jews all civil authority in Palestine, including control of immigration, in exchange for which Lehi would not deny Britain the right to keep its armies in the Land of Israel for the duration of the war! There were a few other equally impossible provisos of which I remember only our stipulation that the British were also to supply us with the ships and other facilities needed to transport the Jews of Europe to Palestine. Ballantyne's spokesmen thanked us coldly and broke off further negotiations. What we learnt from the episode, however, was that the Mandatory Government, at last, was becoming worried about Lehi.

In February, I learnt of Yair's death from a Jewish policeman who stood close to me one morning and whispered: 'You know, they got Stern yesterday.' Later that day, members of Lehi sat in a hut somewhere in the prison grounds and I spoke to them, even for them, I felt, about Yair. It wasn't much of a send-off, but we were aware of what we had lost: the one man who connected our daily dealings, our fears, our self-doubts and our often failed plans to the mainstream of Jewish history, bidding us to see ourselves as part of a larger scheme of things, not as chosen but as having chosen; not as superior but as powerful.

His killing had followed a number of British attempts to do away with Lehi, once and for all. His picture had been posted with a reward, large in those days: £1,000, for his capture. Our printing press had been discovered and destroyed. The police, acting on an informer's tip, had broken into the apartment of a 'suspect' on Tel Aviv's Dizengoff Street and shot to death two of the four Lehi unarmed fighters who were there, seriously wounding the two others – obviously obeying 'shoot-to-kill' orders. Worst of all, a trap laid for Inspector Geoffrey Morton and for his ever-loyal officer, Tom Wilkin, took not their lives but those of another British and two Jewish policemen.

Other news reaching Mezrah in the winter of 1941 and the spring of 1942 was no better. With the rest of the *Yishuv* we followed the tragic voyage from Romania of the SS STRUMA and the 769 Jewish 'illegals' crammed in her hold. Thanks to the British, Turkish permission to land in Constantinople, which the *Struma* eventually reached, was refused her; the 48-foot boat was turned away from harbour and left to drift in the Black Sea. After a day, she exploded; only one passenger survived and the mystery of her sinking was never solved. It was yet another tragedy in a chain of events that made our involuntary inaction almost unbearable.

But the ultimate blow, of course, was Yair's killing. On 12 February 1942, a British police unit surrounded a building on a small street (today it is named Stern Street) in the busy south of Tel Aviv. Revolvers in hand, they climbed the narrow stairs to the roof-top flat where Yair was hiding. It belonged to one of the men wounded on Dizengoff Street and now in prison. Yair was living there in spite of the unwritten law that one does not shelter in a flat belonging to someone already in the hands of the police, but there had been nowhere else for him to go. He was dragged out of the closet in which he was trying to conceal himself and positively identified; then he was shot. As neighbours watched, Yair's body was dragged downstairs and rammed into a truck that was already standing by. The police issued a brief announcement to the effect that he had been shot trying to escape arrest. That night, his body was delivered to the burial society and buried in a Tel Aviv cemetery.

There was a postscript to his death. Years later, the details were confirmed in Morton's own book, published in the 1950s, testifying that Yair had been killed by Inspector Morton himself. Each year a brief memorial is held for Yair, on the Hebrew date of his murder, at his graveside. The building in which he died is now a small museum containing the Lehi archives. Each year there are fewer grey-haired men, like myself, who fought with him when they were young, but, increasingly, they are joined by younger admirers of his memory, including Members of the Knesset and of the Government, so there is continuity of a sort for him, for the other 125 Lehi fighters who lost their lives in some 300 operations mounted in the same cause, and for Lehi.

The plan for my escape from Mezrah, while not especially intricate, was fairly hazardous and involved crawling around in the dark, cutting or otherwise getting through the three-tiered barbed wire that encompassed the camp, somehow getting past the armed guards, their spotlights and patrols, and generally overcoming a variety of

obstacles. In addition, we could only defend ourselves, if anything
went wrong, with the 'weapons' we had managed, over the months,
to smuggle into the camp – all of two pistols. However, not trying to
escape was unthinkable. Besides, we now had one advantage: it was
still the 'thinking-over' period of Ballantyne's proposal and we were
fairly sure that the British would regard it as an unlikely time for us
to try to escape or for them to have to take special security measures.
Of the people chosen to make the attempt, I was obviously one;
another was Eliahu Giladi. Giladi was perhaps the only one of us
who was, by nature, an extremist, a fanatic, a man free of the fetters
of personal loyalties or ordinary sentiments, who found it difficult to
function within any framework or discipline but was fast-moving,
imaginative, daring and fearless. I thought these qualities mattered
more in the context of our escape than the theories he aired, at the
drop of a hat, about dealing 'effectively' with the *Yishuv* leadership
that had sold out to the British and so forth.

Anyhow, I promised Gera that if Giladi ever made a move in the
direction of unauthorized violence, I would deal with him quickly.
For the time being, he would make a good partner – which he did.
Later, after our escape, he became more restive, mocking our methods
of operation and even our goals. 'You don't understand,' he kept
saying. 'You must get rid of the establishment. Stamp it out and
begin all over again.' It began to sound as though he was losing
control of reality – and of himself. I remember some large anti-British
demonstration being planned in Tel Aviv and Giladi advocating its
exploitation for what he described as 'our purposes'. His idea was to
throw a grenade into the crowd so that the police would be called;
then trouble would start, the police would fire, and there would be
casualties that would produce in their wake a heightened hatred of
the British. I couldn't believe my ears. 'But innocent people will be
killed.' I said. 'That's the point', Giladi replied; 'that's what we need.'
On another day, he brought a list of Lehi members who must be
purged, removed from 'active service'. He became stranger, colder
and wilder; there were rows wherever he went.

Then the inevitable explosion occurred, which showed up one of
the great restrictions of a society devoid, as Lehi was, of its own
courtrooms, prisons, legal mechanisms and even the possibility of
conducting lengthy procedures of any kind. After all, we were not
an army, just people bound together by ties that could be loosened
at will. What happened was that one day a young Lehi member who
served as a runner for Giladi and for me did something to displease
him. Giladi got down from the old couch on which he was lying,

went over to the young man, cursed him very quietly and slapped his face. Then he drew his pistol and said, 'I am going to kill you.' I jumped up and stood between them, looking into Giladi's crazed eyes. 'Kill me instead,' I said. That night, however, it was our runner who killed himself. Sorrow? Anger? Most likely his grief over a god that had failed. Giladi was unfeeling and impenitent.

Then he developed a new *idée fixe*: Lehi should 'do away', as he put it, with the Zionist leadership, kill Ben-Gurion and clear the stage. He was not a traitor or an informer, but he was irrational. I waited for him to change, for the dreadful fantasies to leave him, but he went on, talking icily about the need to kill. I knew then that I'd have to make a fateful decision and I did. I decided that we couldn't go on like that; Giladi was far too dangerous to the movement. The circumstances being what they were, there weren't many people I could talk to freely, but I did speak to two or three of my colleagues and the next day the decision was made – and carried out. A day or two afterwards a letter came, via our special mail, from Gera in Latrun prison, begging me not to delay doing what had to be done. He, of course, had no way of knowing what I had decided or what had been done in the interim. Then I called together thirteen Lehi old-timers (including people who knew nothing of the situation with Giladi). We sat together in the sand dunes outside Tel Aviv and I reported to them in detail, telling them also that, since I couldn't consult them before, I took full responsibility for what had happened. If they thought that I had been wrong, let them say so – then and there. But no one took any exception to the decision I had made. The terrible crisis had come to an end.

I have often asked myself, over the years, had there really been a choice? Could I have acted differently? I tried to find out what happened in other underground groups, other resistance movements, but never found a parallel. It is my belief that I had no alternative – though it took its toll of me and cost me no small anguish.

But on the night of August 1942, all this was still ahead of us. Accompanied by the good wishes of our comrades, more advice than we could handle and considerable anxiety, Giladi and I set off for liberty – and the path that would, I hoped, take me nearer to doing what Yair expected me to do, i.e. to strengthen Lehi and keep it intact and active.

There were many spectacular jail breaks and escapes during those years including some that became famous, such as the 1943 escape of twenty Lehi men, headed by Gera, who broke out of the Latrun detention camp via a 76-metre-long tunnel that took nine months to dig. My own escape from Eritrea was, as I shall tell, quite a story in itself. But the escape from Mezrah, though not effortless, was not really in this category.

Commander Grant turned his camp inside out looking for us, personally inspecting the entire complement of detainees, fixing each one again with the same penetrating stare with which each had been received, searching his phenomenal memory to ascertain who was missing since the prison lists turned out to be in a mess. Then, so I was told, he asked for the whereabouts of two detainees, 'the man with the heavy eyebrows' (me) and 'that athletic type' (Giladi). The answer which no one gave him was that we were out of the camp and already on our way to Haifa. We walked and walked, slept for a while in a field, then near Haifa met up with a young man whose address had been given to us but who was astonished to see us appear suddenly as if from nowhere. I told him to go to Haifa and locate 'Elisha' (Yerachmiel Aronson), a man I was very fond of and whose eventual death in 1944 in a confrontation with the British I greatly mourned. We met Elisha in a Haifa park and he, in turn, led us for the night to the home of Eliahu Hakim's brother (away on holiday in Syria – a popular vacation-land for Palestinian Jews in those days), while the young man was sent to Tel Aviv to make various urgent arrangements there. As a result, Arieh (Anshel) Shpilman, today director of the Yair Memorial Museum and Archives in Tel Aviv, next day brought me the well-pressed uniform of an officer in the Anders Polish army (part of this force, organized to fight in World War II on the eastern front, had been transferred to the Middle East, so Polish uniforms were no rarity in Palestine then). At noon we drove from Haifa in an Arab cab to an orange grove in Raanana, near Tel Aviv, where Yehoshua Cohen waited for us.

Yehoshua Cohen was one of the many remarkable people with whom I was then associated. His father, a well-to-do observant Jew, was a man of strong principles, a man who practised what he preached. An orange-grove owner, he only employed Jewish labour – though it cost him more – and only bought Yishuv-manufactured products if at all possible. It was his way of demonstrating, and encouraging, Jewish self-sufficiency. Yehoshua was a gentle version of his father but in no way lacking roughness. At a very early age he first joined the Irgun and then went to Lehi. After Yair's death, in the time of troubles when almost everyone was in prison, he swore that he would never be taken alive. 'If the British kill us in any case,' he said, 'we might as well put up a fight.' He too practised what he preached. From then on – this was true for all of us – he bore arms.

The police looked everywhere for him, offering big rewards for his capture, but Yehoshua learned to live like a guerrilla fighter, a partisan, on the run – with his girlfriend Nechama, who was also his courier. He became a symbol of resistance at a moment when symbols were important. One instance was when he was training a group of fighters in the Jerusalem hills and was surprised by a British patrol. He immediately drew his revolver, forcing the patrol to the ground so that he and his men could get away – which they did. I think it was the first time that any member of Lehi had used firearms to evade imprisonment. Afterwards, he was among the first to settle in Sdeh Boker, the Negev kibbutz, then a solitary frontier outpost which was to acquire among its members David Ben-Gurion (who had resigned as Prime Minster) and his wife. They settled, lived and are buried there. Ben-Gurion and Yehoshua found a common language, became close friends, went on long walks together, and for the rest of Ben-Gurion's life, Yehoshua was his constant companion. He too is buried in Sdeh Boker.

Anyhow, we met him in one of the groves in which he had grown up, with which he was so familiar and which were now his and Nechama's hiding-places, and discussed plans for future activities. It was, I thought, a good omen that on our way, finally, to Tel Aviv, Captain Grant himself drove past us, jaw set, undoubtedly en route to his superiors to report the jailbreak. However, by nightfall, I was already immersed in Lehi problems, the months of detention no longer in my thoughts.

Certainly Lehi was not in good shape; some thought it on the verge of extinction. Only a handful of fighters were still free, still unknown to the police, but there had been some action on various fronts. A Lehi cell organized in Egypt had been able to send arms and ammunition to us and a number of new immigrants from Poland and Bulgaria had joined our ranks, all in their twenties, men and women used to having their ears to the ground, to wandering from border to border, to keeping alive on chunks of frozen bread and being too tired to sleep or talk. I knew that they would form the basis for rebuilding Lehi, if only we could direct them in the way they had hoped Yair would do.

Also we had developed some publications. Sitting in that orange grove, still in my incongruous clothes, only hours after the escape, I had looked at the first three Lehi leaflets that Dr Israel Scheib ('Eldad' was his code name, which he retained) had written for distribution, sparks flying – as they always did – from his pen.

Like Gera, Eldad was a highly educated, extremely literate man, a teacher by profession and a former Betarist. Born in Galicia and trained in Vienna, he had arrived in Israel only the year before and was soon considered the movement's intellectual leader. Like Gera, he never found himself in 'civilian' life afterwards, but his was a different, less sombre temperament and a different political orientation. Where Gera was to turn totally to the left in later years, Eldad was to become an arch-rightist, a believer in the Messianic aspects of the liberation of the Land and profoundly opposed to the return of any part of it to the Arabs. In the underground, we worked in total harmony, our endless notes to each other frequently expressing the same thoughts in the same words; on many levels, we understood each other. I had great respect for Eldad's ability and instincts. In old age, he has remained as alert, as bitingly critical and as committed to those views as when he was editing *The Front* each month and *The Deed* each week and helping Lehi to exert an influence far in excess of its means or numbers.

I suppose we were an odd trio; myself in the centre between these two strong-willed, brilliant men, having to learn to deal with their sharp differences of opinion, attitudes and personalities, having to avoid areas of acute disagreement and operate on the basis of consensus wherever it existed or could be brought into being. It was just as well that I underwent that training for the bigger, though not dissimilar, job of mediation that awaited me when I became Prime Minister in an Israeli Government of National Unity.

Incidentally, among his other exploits, Eldad was destined to be the hero of a famous 1946 escape, which, in many ways, was a precursor of the daring actions that have become a hallmark of the IDF. In 1944, trying desperately to shake off the police, Eldad, trapped on the third floor of a building, slipped from an outside pipe, fell and badly injured himself. He was caught, encased in plaster and held in detention for months, albeit being allowed, at intervals, to visit an orthopaedic surgeon in Jerusalem. The first attempt to free him was made while he was still in hospital – he was to be grabbed on his way to surgery under the noses of the accompanying police – but instead he was assigned to a prison hospital and the original plan discarded. His visits to the Jerusalem specialist were always made, of course, in a police vehicle under heavy guard. One day, a Lehi unit dressed in white coats burst into the doctor's room, disarmed the guards and formed a human chain while Eldad, long-healed, blithely walked to a waiting car, and freedom.

Although Yair's philosophy and injunctions remained in force, Lehi's modus operandi had to become more efficient, more money had to be raised, a training programme had to be inaugurated and the information services (including our broadcasting station) broadened. Within the central committee, we assumed our respective roles, on the whole, with ease: Gera and Eldad, between them, were clearly the people to share the sensitive and key areas that concerned ideology and propaganda, our ties with groups and individuals abroad, and the further development of publications that gave to Lehi the wide ideological base without which no other activities could have any meaning. They also gave interviews, though rarely, to journalists, who were led to them via elaborate, deliberately confusing routes and who were never allowed clearly to see the man to whom they spoke. As for myself, I was charged with overall organization, which also covered the detailed planning of major operations, though most critical decisions were taken jointly by the central committee – to the extent that the three of us were around at the same time, which didn't happen often. Behind locked doors I assessed candidates for crucial missions; from behind a screen I lectured at courses; in a room (the exact location of which no more than three or four people knew) I made, checked and approved the detailed plans for Lehi operations.

We were not many; never more than several hundred and there were months that even fewer than that were involved in Lehi operations. For most of the years between 1940 and 1948–9, our number never rose above 1,000 at the very most – and in this figure I include all of Lehi's active supporters. Towards the end of 1946–8, another 500 or so joined our ranks, but in the main the organization was minuscule, something that made possible its swiftness, effectiveness and secrecy. What is perhaps, in retrospect, most surprising is that we were able to divide and sub-divide in a manner that provided us with more or less adequate coverage of nearly all the functions that an effective covert organization requires: an intelligence section, with special units dealing with the CID, the Arabs, railways and ports, etc.; an operations arm (with its own manpower, instruction, transport and medical units), which also ran broadcasting; a recruiting unit, a financial unit (which dealt, among others, with stolen goods), a printing press and a youth section. In addition, we had overseas branches, including in Iraq, Czechoslovakia, Great Britain and the United States – though often these were cells of only one or two people. And, of course, we had workshops for the production of explosives, arms, spare parts and so forth.

It may be needless to state that one of our main worries was about

money. A few supporters were generous, but there were never enough
of these. To get back into action, we badly needed financial resources,
to build up bases, to buy arms, to pay for our broadcasts and
pamphlets, to keep ourselves alive. But raising funds from deep cover
is no simple matter. In view of the circumstances, our lack of
popularity and the real danger involved for contributors, there seemed
no alternative to robbery. My father would have called it expropriation
(as in revolutionary Russia); others called it confiscation; but in plain
language it was robbery – bank robbery. After all, where else would
one go for money? Not that any bank would do; we looked for banks
that were easy to enter and leave in a hurry, banks that were sure
to have large amounts of cash on hand and, preferably, banks insured
by British companies. Barclays made an ideal target in this respect.
Sometimes money was snatched right out of the armoured cars used
for delivering it. Many of the Lehi hold-ups were successful, but many
failed and led to arrests, and however essential the break-ins and
hold-ups were for us, they added markedly to public indignation and
lack of sympathy.

If nothing else, conspiratorial life has one great advantage: it is
tidier than most other styles of living; everything – rules, regulations,
proscriptions, discipline – is totally directed towards serving the cause,
doing things so that no trails are left, no extraneous information
accumulated, no clues scattered inadvertently and no exit left
unchecked. Communications, operations, relationships, everything is
pared, reduced to a minimum, made mobile, carried out as rapidly
as possible. How did we live? As best we could, as best suited Lehi's
needs, as the mood outside allowed. Like everyone else, I operated
from draughty shacks, from musty, rented rooms, from cellars and
attics, but sometimes I even hid for a day or two in the comfort and
security of a home belonging to some wealthy Lehi supporter prepared
to take the risk of being my host. I met those people I had to meet –
and never others – on street corners at noon or late at night, in
alleys or on park benches, whenever and wherever we were least
likely to be noticed, something that can be more serious than being
seen.

Our disguises were always simple, cheap, part of the local scene.
For months, stalked by the police, a tempting price on my head, traps
laid to catch me and my photograph adorning notice-boards, I walked
around when there was no alternative with relative impunity. A
black beard and a long, black coat turned me instantly into a vaguely
rabbinical figure. Certainly no one could have guessed that the fair-
haired, clean-shaven young man in khaki shorts, a cap jauntily pulled

over his eyes, was the same Lehi leader whose earlier appearance was in the rusty black garb of a Talmudic scholar. Yair's teachings proved themselves: imagination substituted for other resources; razors, wigs and borrowed clothes for the plastic surgery no Lehi member underwent, making it possible for me to avoid capture again until 1946.

Being invisible, unidentifiable, unknown had very high priority; no one knew or worked closely with more than one or two people at a time, aliases replaced all our given names, there were never any regularly scheduled meetings, nor were we ever together in any public place. No one rang doorbells or said 'May I come in?' No one phoned or used the regular mail. Messages by definition were urgent, so people in positions of particular sensitivity had runners; otherwise, usually an agreed-upon whistle of a bar or two of some familiar tune – La Marseillaise was one such – from below would bring the person you needed to some agreed-upon point always several streets away. Many messages were delivered by people walking in opposite directions, brushing against each other to pass a note or a whispered instruction. Written instructions, minute folded notes, were as terse as possible and were never accompanied by explanations of any sort.

Now is the time to say a few words about my own runner, Shulamit Levy, whom I married. Young, pretty, lively and intelligent, she had come in 1941 to Palestine from Bulgaria (where she had been a member of Betar), dodging the British dragnet for weeks on a boat so unseaworthy that the same number of people had to stand on both sides of the deck whenever the passengers were allowed up for a breath of fresh air. She was sent by the British to a temporary camp set up in Mezrah near where all the underground detainees were kept. Around the time that Giladi and I escaped from that camp, Shulamit, who had been moved elsewhere, joined Lehi. She was a perfect choice for the job of courier, new to the country and not known by anyone. Runners (or couriers) held a special place in the underground table of organization; it was Shulamit's responsibility always to know where I was, to fetch and deliver my mail, to make appointments for me, to buy food, to be a messenger, a switchboard and, inevitably, to a growing degree, a confidante. After a while, we fell in love. No one had been married in the underground; either people were already married or the ceremony awaited better times. A wedding in deep cover was unheard-of. But friends in Jerusalem put some pressure on us and even found the ideal rabbi to organize it. Rabbi Arye Levin, known to everyone then as 'The Prisoners' Rabbi', was the humblest, most righteous of Jews who ministered, like a saint, to the imprisoned men of the underground movements and who chose the rabbi that actually married Shulamit and me. Rabbi Levin and two Lehi members were present and a *minyan* (ten Jewish males who constitute the needed quorum, in Jewish law, for certain ceremonies) was gathered up in the street, though the city swarmed with detectives that day.

Marriage was one thing; if it wasn't ordinary domesticity, we were together – as we have been for close to fifty years. However, a family? That was something else. A baby in the underground? How long would the struggle last? I thought it might be for years, the duration of my lifetime in fact, before the British left and before the Jewish state came into being. And I also thought that life should be lived as fully as possible, whatever the circumstances, and that it was up to us to set an example, to show others that one could marry and raise a family and still carry on the fight – because all of these acts were natural and human. Of course, there were technicalities to overcome. I couldn't go to the hospital with Shulamit, whom we equipped with a fictitious husband for the length of her confinement, and I didn't attend my son's *brith* (the Jewish ritual of circumcision). But when in August 1945 he was born and named Yair, I felt I had contributed something, not only to my happiness and Shulamit's, but also to Lehi; indeed, later other babies were born, affirming faith in the future and hope in the present.

When Yair was a year old, I was deported and did not see him again until the end of May 1948, when I came back from exile, Shulamit came home from prison, and Israel came into being.

4

EXILE AND ESCAPE

DID LEHI REALLY believed that it could throw the British out of the country in the face of Haganah hostility and British determination to suppress and, if possible, uproot it? Yes, we believed this and I think we also succeeded – certainly to a considerable degree. Not alone, because by the time the British finally washed their hands of Palestine, other elements and influences in the *Yishuv* were out in full force. But it was Lehi that first served notice on the British and made good its warnings that nothing would be permitted to stand in the way of the achievement of Jewish independence in the Land of Israel, nothing and no one. Without doubt, the most dramatic and most publicized of these warnings came in the autumn of 1944 with the assassination in Cairo of Lord Moyne, Britain's Resident Minister in the Middle East. Books, articles and many speeches have described and analysed the 'deed' (as it became known thanks to Gerald Frank, an American writer who wrote a book about it containing many interviews, including one with me), and I am still sometimes asked questions about it by the media, here and abroad.

The idea was Yair's, born one spring evening in 1941 at a Lehi meeting in Tel Aviv. It was part of his total concept of how we should fight, not just the British in Palestine but the British Empire as such; to try to put out of action the people who made policy and moved the pieces on the Palestine board – such as the High Commissioner of Palestine or the British Resident Minister, headquartered in Cairo. Attempts on the life of the High Commissioner had failed, and Winston Churchill had appointed an Australian, Richard Casey, to the Cairo position. We had no quarrel with Australia and the idea was temporarily put aside. 'Still, let's keep track of that appointment,' Yair had said. 'Casey's successor is sure to be an Englishman.' Then Yair himself was killed.

But I knew about that plan and, together with my colleagues,

eventually decided to carry it out. Casey's deputy was Walter Edward
Guinness, Lord Moyne, Eton-educated, decorated for bravery on the
western front in World War I and a former British Secretary of State
for the Colonies. When Casey was sent to India, Lord Moyne became
the Resident Minister – and Lehi's target. He was, however, not only
a personification of British power; he was also a man who in all of
his capacities – Colonial Secretary, member of the House of Lords,
finally Minister in Cairo – had played a prominent role in the
enforcement of British policy in Palestine, making no secret of his
extreme opposition to Zionism or of his negative feelings about the
Jews. In June 1942, in the House of Lords, he had said: '... it is to
canalize all the sympathy of the world for the martyrdom of the Jews
that the Zionists reject all schemes to resettle the victims elsewhere,'
ignoring the fact that Eichmann's henchmen were already daily
'resettling' thousands of Jews in Nazi death camps. Later, he added a
bizarre footnote: since the blood of European Jews had intermingled
with that of Slavs, he said, only the Arabs were entitled to consider
themselves pure-blooded Semites possessed of a bona-fide claim to
Palestine.

Crude and bigoted as those comments were, they paled by comparison to his responsibility for the death of Jews. Turning a deaf ear
to all appeals, it was Lord Moyne who had ordered the Turkish
authorities to drive the *Struma* back to the Black Sea, where she
foundered and sank. And later, an even deadlier story was revealed:
in May 1944, when Eichmann sent an emissary to negotiate with
the Allies on the possibility of exchanging one million Jews for trucks
and other equipment, Lord Moyne's first response was, 'What would
I do with a million Jews?' Afterwards, that emissary, a Hungarian
Jew named Joel Brand, joined Lehi. But our decision had much less
to do with Moyne than with his status. It was neither easy to arrive
at nor easy to implement, its success resting on a hundred details
over which, in Tel Aviv, we had no control: on the cool-headedness
and courage of a handful of people in Egypt (our Egyptian cell made
up of Palestinian Jewish soldiers serving with the British army there),
on the goodwill and conviction of a few more, and, as always, on
luck.

Of the two young men we sent to Egypt, I had known Eliahu Bet-
Tsouri fairly well for several years as a member of a cell I headed. He
had not left the Irgun when I did, but later he joined Lehi. He
was twenty-three, fair-haired, green-eyed, fluent in various languages
including Arabic, and, given a pipe and a checked jacket, looked like
any one of the British soldiers on leave wandering all over Egypt in

those days. Eliahu Hakim was equally well-suited for the dangerous task. Born in Beirut and brought up in Haifa, he was bright, energetic and a crack marksman. He was also dark-skinned and dark-eyed and, on Cairo streets, indistinguishable from a native Cairene. Hakim, who came to me highly recommended by Yehoshua Cohen ('He is a man born for such actions'), had joined Lehi but given in to his family's pleas that he leave it. He volunteered for the British army and then asked Lehi to forgive him and take him back. I suggested that he be sent to Egypt several times to bring back suitcases filled with arms that the cell had collected, and he had done this with courage and intelligence. I knew that he would be proud to get the new assignment and that he would regard it – as both he and Bet-Tsouri did – as a mission of the utmost importance.

Slowly, carefully, working diligently and intelligently, the two of them, aided by the Egyptian cell, put together the file: where and how Lord Moyne lived, his daily routine, the exceptions to it. In September, the place and date were fixed: the garden of the Minister's Residence (not, as a rule, guarded) when he returned home for lunch, as he did regularly and promptly. Both were confident that no details had been overlooked, that there were no loose ends. We were in touch constantly and I followed every detail. Among the 15,000 Jews from the *Yishuv* who were stationed in Egypt, only about a dozen were Lehi members (three of them were girls), but Palestinian Jewish soldiers came and went all the time, our coded messages were taken and replies brought back; there was never a break in communication. I knew that the two Eliahus could be entirely depended upon, but there were things that worried me, in particular how they would get away. After some thought, it seemed to me that an ambulance would be the perfect vehicle for that purpose and I told them to have one ready. Much later, I learned that an ambulance had indeed been ordered but that it had broken down en route. It should be noted that while as few people as possible knew anything about any Lehi operation, all the details, all the instructions, all the pertinent information were always in the possession of at least one other person so that if anything happened to me (which was never unlikely), the organization could continue to operate smoothly.

On 6 November 1944, a few minutes before 1 p.m., Hakim and Bet-Tsouri ambushed the Minister's car as planned. They took care not to harm his secretary, who sat next to him, but when the Minister's chauffeur tried to wrest the gun from Bet-Tsouri, he was shot while Hakim fatally wounded Lord Moyne. A policeman who happened to be passing on a motor-cycle gave chase, but the two

Eliahus were under strict orders not to fire on any Egyptians, so they just shot at the motor-cycle to slow it down. In the end, they were caught and arrested, having tried to make their getaway on bicycles, something against which I had explicitly warned them, explaining that bicycles weren't fast enough and didn't permit sufficient freedom of action.

Their trial made Cairo, for a while, a centre of world attention. The international press crowded daily into the courtroom, reporters begging for interviews, even for autographs, from the accused. The British sent high-ranking CID and Intelligence officers from London and Jerusalem, hoping to learn more about the 'terrorists' of the 'Stern Gang'; and the Egyptians, packing into whatever space the press left them, listened with visible growing admiration and an increasing sense of identification with Bet-Tsouri and Hakim as they told the court how and why they had struck down Lord Moyne, declaring themselves to be soldiers sent to the front in a war that, one day, would result in the overthrow of the oppressors of their homeland – thus, for a few weeks, making Zionism popular in British-ruled Egypt. 'We did what we did,' said Bet-Tsouri, concluding his presentation to the court, 'and it was just. We do not fight for the preservation of the Balfour Declaration or for the "National Home" ... We fight for freedom, and the independence of our Land of Israel. Hakim too spoke of justice and freedom: 'We charge Lord Moyne and the Government he represented with the murder of hundreds of thousands of our brethren ... and the theft of our homeland,' he said. 'To whom could we turn for justice? We had no option but to see for ourselves that justice was done.'

Elsewhere, the response was otherwise. In the main, frightened of the British retaliation that was sure to come, the *Yishuv* reacted to the killing with panic. Only the news, when it came, of the death sentence given to the two Eliahus steadied the establishment's nerves; perhaps the British would be mollified by the hangings and the consequences of the Cairo assassination would not be as dire as feared. Dr Weizmann rushed to promise the British that Lehi would be liquidated once and for all and declared himself as grieved and as shocked upon hearing of Moyne's death at the hands of Jews as he had been when he learned that his son, serving in the RAF, had fallen in the Battle of Britain. The outpouring of repudiation, revulsion and, chiefly, fear – a chorus that even the Irgun joined – was relieved only by the pleas for clemency that came from abroad. For a few weeks, I thought that Bet-Tsouri and Hakim might be pardoned; the Egyptian defence lawyers, both distinguished jurists, managed to convey in their summations some of the warmth and the respect felt and expressed by the Egyptian masses for the young Jews who had attacked the common colonial enemy. But Churchill, a close friend of Lord Moyne, determined the outcome, insisting in Parliament that the Egyptians 'must implement the verdict . . . to serve as an example'.

Towards the end of March 1945, the two Eliahus went to the gallows. Each asked not be bound or blindfolded; each, independently of the other, explained that he was not afraid to look death in the eye; each sang the *Hatikvah* before the final order was given. I shall always remember the news bulletin on the radio and the details as I read them in *La Bourse Egyptienne*, then sold daily in Tel Aviv. The mission had been accomplished; Bet-Tsouri and Hakim had done the deed and died the death of heroes. Already Lehi faced new and crucial challenges; there was no interval, no pause in which I could properly grieve for the boys whom I had sent to Egypt, but the story did not completely end there. In 1975, when I was a Herut Member of the Knesset, the Egyptian Government agreed that their bodies be brought to Israel for reburial. Now the two Eliahus lie on Jerusalem's Mount Herzl, where lie the founder of the Zionist movement and the leaders of the state that he was sure would come into being. I received their remains at the Israel–Egyptian border and was asked by the IDF rabbinate to identify them. I recognized them at once, despite the years that had passed and the way in which they died. Their faces were untouched and calm; neither time nor the way they died had disfigured them. A chaplain told me that only the righteous are granted this privilege. I hope, and I believe, that this is so. At the funeral, the Government of Israel was represented and I delivered the eulogy.

In the months that followed the assassination, a concerted attempt was made by the *Yishuv* leadership to flush out the dissidents, to drag them into the open and turn them over to the British, thus punishing the criminals who dared disobey Ben-Gurion and who, by their recklessness and extremism, had placed the Jewish community in such jeopardy. However outraged and pained the British were by the lethal assault on Lord Moyne, nothing exceeded, or even matched, the wrath of the Zionist leadership. This phase of the Saison also held out the possibility, not to say the lure, of important political gains for the left wing, providing it with an opportunity for getting rid of those who threatened the existing power structure. Because Lehi was non-political and, at least in this respect, no menace, the 1944 Saison was directed mainly against the Irgun. Even so, a few Lehi members, among them my very close associate, Matityahu Peli, were kidnapped by the Haganah and held for questioning, sometimes for days.

As for me, I reduced my 'visibility' even further, barely leaving my room, talking to even fewer people, and relying more and more on Shulamit to keep open the essential channels. During those many hours alone, I found myself often thinking not only about Lehi day-to-day but also about the turn Jewish history had taken, the meaning of the crises through which we were living, the mistakes we might be making that could still be rectified or avoided, and how we and our struggle would appear, if at all, to the Jews of the next millennia. Would issues and occurrences of such importance to us be reduced, in decades to come, to a line or two in history books or, at best, form a paragraph in the total story of the Jews of the twentieth century?

I thought often, too, of the deadly conflicts that had flared among the Jews in the years preceding the fall of Jerusalem to the Romans and how – as I had learned in my childhood – fatal divisions had arisen between pacifists and activists, moderates and zealots, internal rifts which did not heal even when the Romans began their long siege of the city. Perhaps my only real fear in life, the only one at least of which I am aware, is of the injury we may do ourselves in this country in which intellectual vigour and the Jewish urge for self-expression turn so quickly into divisiveness. Nothing has ever mattered to me more, nor matters more now, than the unity of the people of Israel and the wholeness of their Land. So it was perhaps inevitable that when I was Prime Minister, I should strive so hard to form a government of national unity and as inevitable maybe that, back then in 1945, Lehi would propose to the Haganah and the Irgun the creation of a united resistance movement involving the entire *Yishuv*, at last, in armed conflict with the Mandatory power.

In the immediate wake of Matityahu's kidnapping, Lehi proposed a meeting. (In those days, despite the tensions between us, we used to meet now and then with Haganah representatives – they always sent their top men, Eliahu Golomb, Israel Galili, Moshe Sneh or Shaul Avigur – it being understood, naturally, that no one would be followed or hurt.) It took place in a school gym in Tel Aviv. At opposite ends of a long table, Gera faced Eliahu Golomb, a Haganah founder and a commander since 1931: two tough, experienced men, opponents, both patriots, Zionists and Jews. Without a word, Gera drew his pistol from its holster and set it down between them. Then he began to speak. He described what he knew might well await our kidnapped comrade, how the British might come across him 'by accident' (an accident prepared for them by the Haganah) which would lead him to torture, detention and perhaps even deportation.

They argued for a while about the Haganah's collaboration with the British, its purpose and its results, and Golomb came to understand that Lehi would not be passive in the face of a continuing Saison. 'We have means at our disposal too,' Gera said, and Golomb knew that it was so.

Then Gera proposed, as we had agreed he should, that the two undergrounds co-operate, work together without settling old accounts, begin afresh. Golomb didn't turn him down and the discussion went on all night. Gera arrived at my room at dawn. He wrote later: 'I found Michael pacing his room like a caged lion, sure that I had been taken by the Haganah. He was already at work planning reprisal.' To some, these lines may seem familiar, like moments from a film set in the wild West in the days of cowboys and Indians. But it was not like that at all. There were no desperadoes, no adventurers in the dimly lit gym that night; only serious men dealing most seriously on behalf of a nation and, in particular, of those Jews far away whose one remaining wish – still denied them – was to rebuild, in the Land of Israel, whatever was left of their lives.

The establishment's change of heart followed its belated dis-illusionment with the British at the end of the war. By now, there was no room left for self-deception. Most of the Jews of Europe had disappeared, turned to ash. It was this remnant (vaguely named 'Displaced Persons' [DPs] so that others would feel less guilty) that was then leaving the newly liberated death camps, trying to make its way to the only place, as far as any of them knew, where Jews were still alive and families possibly awaited them. But something else occurred that first summer after the war: the Labour Party won the British elections, the first since the outbreak of war. Initially, the *Yishuv* was beside itself with relief. Now the party in power in Britain was one that had sworn allegiance to Zionism for years and that, in hundreds of statements, speeches and manifestos, had condemned the White Paper as wicked and heartless. Given what the world was just learning about the gas chambers, the lime pits and the furnaces of the Nazis, there could be no doubt that the restriction of immigration, at the very minimum, would at once be relaxed, if not annulled. Lehi, need I add, had not joined in this outburst of hope and faith and I myself was certain that the awakening would be a very rude one indeed.

And it was. Britain's new Government, headed by Clement Attlee, and especially the new Foreign Secretary, Ernest Bevin, did not leave the *Yishuv* in suspense for long. Bevin's first speeches on the subject of Palestine made clear his anti-Zionism and revealed his particularly

coarse variety of contempt for, and dislike of, the Jews, whom he
described, among other things, as people 'who always push themselves
to the head of the line'. The British Government, he announced,
would make no changes whatsoever in the White Paper of 1939,
past pre-election pledges notwithstanding. Jews who were 'legally'
entitled to enter Palestine could do so; as for the others, the rest of
the DPs, they would have to find a place for themselves in Europe.
Bevin was so determined not to give way on the question of immigration that he even turned down the appeal of US President Harry
Truman for a one-time mercy allocation of entry permits for 100,000
'displaced' Jews from Germany and Austria. There can be no question
that had those certificates been granted, had mercy been shown, the
trend of events in the Middle East would have been vastly different.
But Bevin wasn't interested in striking bargains; he was out to show
us who was who and what was what, and he said 'No' to the United
States too.

Driven to despair by British callousness, unable to accept the
hopeless situation of the refugees – there was hardly a Jew in Palestine
who did not mourn close relatives murdered in Europe or long to
comfort those who had survived – Zionist leaders floated a desperate
idea: a deal with the British. One hundred thousand Jews would be
allowed to immigrate in return for peace and quiet, and all three
underground organizations would cease fire and end their battle with
the Palestine Administration and the British Government.

The proposal faced Lehi with a dilemma that touched on the core
of its ideology and posed questions bearing on its very existence. At
first, most members found the proposition unacceptable; we were not
fighting for freer immigration or any other concession. Lehi wanted
the British out; no bait, no compromise, no truce, no postponement.
The central committee, at that point Gera and I, argued otherwise.
It was, of course, very unrealistic, we said, to suppose that the British
would agree to the offer; apart from anything else, the Arabs would
keep them from doing so. But what if it were accepted, after all?
Should Lehi stand for ever accused, and with some justification, of
having stopped 100,000 Jews from entering the Land? Of course not.
So unhappily, we decided to say 'Yes'. But the British said 'No'. That
Lehi decision, and others like it, was not arrived at in a formal
meeting of any kind; no hands were raised or speakers heard. Notes
were passed; rushed conversations held; two or three people reported
on how members in other cities felt; it was democracy of a special
sort: clandestine, word-of-mouth and amazingly reliable.

The British 'No' served as a signal to the half a million or so Jews of the *Yishuv* that there would have to be a war, after all, and that, if war, then there would have to be unity. Together the Haganah, the Irgun and Lehi embarked on a major struggle ('*ma'avak*' in Hebrew) against the White Paper, a struggle that strengthened the *Yishuv*, transforming its national already largely autonomous institutions into independent bodies able, when the time came, to direct the Jewish thrust to sovereignty. The opening operation involving the three organizations and known in Israel as 'The Night of the Railways' took place on 1 November 1945. The British now faced a united front; all that winter and on into the spring of 1946, the United Resistance Movement (URM) held, Lehi's natural partner within it being the Irgun. It took time for us to get used to military terminology, to squads and companies, to the slackening of Lehi's formerly unbreakable rule of silence, to the not so totally covert life. URM operations varied from an extensive attack on CID headquarters in Jerusalem to the taking-over of a British military camp in Tel Aviv, from attacks against British airfields and the destruction of planes on the ground to the penetration of army installations and the 'confiscation' of impressive quantities of arms. The sound of detonating explosives and machine-gun fire was everywhere; once again, Palestine was a theatre of war, a war fought not for territory or glory but for immigration certificates for Jews.

Bevin remained adamant. In answer to President Truman, he angrily invited the Americans, since they claimed to be so concerned, to help solve the problem which he himself found so cumbersome. That same November, the appointment of an Anglo-American Commission of Enquiry was announced; its members, like their many predecessors, toured Palestine, heard witnesses and also travelled to the DP centres of Europe. Hope flickered again in many Jewish hearts (though not in mine) that this newest committee – on which was also represented the world's greatest power – would succeed in influencing the British regarding the hundred thousand. In its report, published in May 1946, the Commission indeed recommended that this number of Jews be admitted, that the land sale regulations be put aside and that the Mandate be extended – under a UN trusteeship. The British again said 'No'. The attacks in Palestine against them continued, including a sequel to 'The Night of the Railways' in which the Haganah blew up bridges and Lehi mounted a large-scale operation on the railway workshops – for which eleven Lehi fighters paid with their lives. It was ominous, I felt, that while Haganah fighters killed in that operation were accompanied to their last resting-places by a weeping crowd, the funerals of our men were held with only the burial society as mourners, as though Lehi was still an entity separate and apart. Nor were my forebodings unjustified. In the weeks that followed, the URM began to crumble, to fail, until it too was buried in December 1946. But, by then, a lot had happened, not least to me.

In the middle of August 1946, handcuffed and furious, I sat on the floor of the cockpit of a British Halifax bomber bound for Africa. My deportation order had been issued in accordance with Clause 15 of the Emergency Regulations, permitting the High Commissioner for Palestine to 'require said person ... to leave and remain out of the country ... in the interests of public safety and the defence of Palestine'. It further specified that 'said person ... be kept in custody, while being conveyed to Eritrea'. Not only was I in custody, chained like a bear in a Polish circus, but also isolated from everyone else on the plane, a kind of super-deportee, which in a way I was – though I felt otherwise: angry, frustrated and offended. How did foreigners dare deport me from my own country? The thought didn't leave me.

Behind me were eventful days. On Saturday, 29 June, less than a fortnight after 'The Night of the Bridges', the British – 100,000 soldiers strong plus 1,500 policemen – had gone into major action. The buildings of the Jewish Agency in Jerusalem were occupied by military units; leaders of the *Yishuv* and of the Zionist movement were taken into detention; arrests were made in dozens of kibbutzim throughout the country with tens of hundreds of settlers shoved into barbed-wire screening pens while the settlements were torn apart in a frantic British search for arms, oddly code-named Operation Agatha and known to Haganah historians as 'The Black Sabbath'. Three weeks later, the URM – fragile, barely functioning but still intact – answered the British with the Irgun-planned and executed blowing up of the south wing of Jerusalem's King David Hotel, which housed top British administrative and military personnel. The explosion destroyed the wing, but though the British had been warned to evacuate the building, they had refused. Close to one hundred were killed, British senior staff, Jewish officials and people who simply happened to be on the spot.

It was then that the Haganah, weakened and alarmed, found it had no more use for unity and not much for resistance, as Lehi defined it, and instead invested its energies largely in the collecting, transporting and delivering of illegal immigrants. But the British committed themselves to crushing the undergrounds for good, to catching every last man and woman on their 'wanted' lists, to smashing the *ma'avak* so that no one would ever be able to put it together again. This time they would not be stopped; they would not only comb the *Yishuv*, but they would also force it through a sieve. The British General Officer Commanding, Major-General Sir Evelyn Barker, roared that he would hang a terrorist from every lamppost in Palestine, directed that the Jews be punished 'in a way the race dislikes as much as any by striking at their pockets' and assigned 20,000 troops to Tel Aviv alone. It was one of history's smaller jokes that the residence of Israel's Prime Minister, the house I lived in for six years, is the house in which General Barker then lived.

It took a month to organize, but in the last days of July 1946 a four-day absolute curfew was imposed on Tel Aviv. The four days began in the middle of the night. People were ordered out of their homes and taken by trucks to various points in the city for checking and questioning, house by house, methodically. The city was sealed as hermetically as possible. Getting out of town was difficult, but Eldad, luckily, lived in Ramat Gan outside Tel Aviv and got there just before the curfew began; Gera and I stayed for a meeting and were stuck. Every detective in Palestine was at work; every empty lot illuminated; every warehouse opened and searched; every group of four interrogators equipped with albums containing photographs of underground members. I was still convinced that I could go on eluding capture in my economical and very effective disguise as a devout Jew, a black-coated, bearded, perpetual student of the Torah, when the house in which I lived was surrounded by CID officers and I was ordered on to the street. At the door, Shulamit silently handed me Yair; I took him in my arms and I walked outside. We stood there, a young rabbi and his baby boy, a little confused, bewildered by the noise, the lights and the English commands, blinking slightly, clearly not understanding what was going on. But one British officer, Sergeant T.G. Martin, looked at me hard, stared at my bushy eyebrows, was lost in thought for a second or two, remembered me, placed me and identified me; his memory, his concentration and the dossier he had built up all working for him together, at the same time. He had me, but those attributes of his, publicly displayed, made him a dangerous and thus a marked man, who was to meet with violent death in the autumn of that violent year.

Before my arrival in Asmara, I spent several weeks in solitary confinement in Jerusalem in the traditional tiny quarters that are truly confining. At first I slept for days on end, exhausted, glad to be able to catch my breath and to be alone. Once the fatigue lifted and I felt myself again, I had to inform my colleagues about what had gone on, making very sure that the information would not reach the wrong people. I wrote and wrote, again for days, in cipher I had learned by heart, until I wrote myself out. (I am sorry I have no copy of those voluminous notes which would certainly be useful to me now.) I entrusted them to an Arab courier and they arrived safely.

That is how it was; sometimes we won, sometimes we lost. In the Big Curfew of 1946, it was I who lost, I and other Jews hauled off for further investigation, I who was now being sent away. Deportation – whether used as punishment, deterrent or both – is, I think, the harshest of all measures, barring physical torture or execution, that society can employ against those who break or ignore its rules. Most prison sentences contain a promise of eventual release, the possibility of contact (however restricted, supervised and artificial) with the world outside, a continuity of family ties and communication – visits, local newspapers, radio, television. Except for the hell of solitary confinement, prisoners are rarely disconnected, but deportation disconnects; at one blow it removes liberty, privacy and community. Even under the 'best' conditions, total and enforced separation from home can damage men as hardy, as dedicated, as spirited as some of the people with whom I lived in the camp for deported dissidents at Sambal in Eritrea on the Horn of Africa.

All I knew about my destination was that the first stop would be Asmara, that some 251 Palestinian Jews had been despatched to Africa as early as 1944 from imprisonment in Latrun and Acre and were in British-run camps both in Eritrea and the Sudan, that others had been sent to join them from time to time and that on the plane with me (it was, I learned afterwards, the tenth such shipment) were six or seven additional newcomers. I was not only angry and offended; I was very worried about what would happen to Lehi in the aftermath of the Big Curfew and my capture and how Shulamit would manage. I was confident that she would do so and knew that she would be helped, but I wondered when we would meet again and what Yair would be like. I hope one day Shulamit will tell the full story of what happened to her and to our baby during the two years that we were apart. If she does, it will show another facet of life in Lehi, the demands that deep cover made on women, how brave and resourceful they were – though, to the unknowing eye, they often seemed, as did Shulamit, to be ordinary young women, not worthy of special note.

The house we lived in remained for a long time under CID surveillance, 'burnt', in our parlance. No one from Lehi came anywhere near it. Through the underground mail, Shulamit had received a letter from me, written just before we left Palestine, but for months that was all. We were no longer in touch after having lived in such proximity before, rarely out of each other's sight for more than an hour or two. One afternoon, on the street, a detective recognized and arrested her; she was sent to Jerusalem for extensive questioning and detained there for several weeks. When the CID refused to allow her to have Yair with her, she went on a hunger strike in such deadly earnest that her British jailers – not given to surrendering to hunger-strikers – moved her (in such a critically weakened state that she was close to death) to the hospital of the Bethlehem Prison for Women. There, on the twelfth day of her stubborn fast, the one man she always obeyed, Rabbi Arye Levin, gently persuaded her to eat, for the baby's sake and mine, and eventually she gave in. I had escaped from Sambal by then and in Djibouti, horrified, spotted a tiny item at the bottom of a newspaper page about the arrest in Palestine of an important female terrorist, Shulamit Yezernitzky. But there was still no contact between us. Then she was moved to Acre and, early in May 1948, released. We were reunited, the three of us, at the end of that month and, in 1949, our daughter, Gilada, was born. But all that lay far ahead of us on the day when 'my' plane made its first stop in Africa.

Eritrea had been developed, wherever it was developed, by the Italians, who had taken control of it at the turn of the century and in the 1930s made it their main base for the invasion of Ethiopia. In 1941, they were driven out by the British and, eleven years later, Eritrea was to become a part of Ethiopia. Surrounded by hilly, bare country-side, Asmara was very much an Italian colonial town; its few large buildings designed and built by Italians, Italian still a lingua franca. Sambal, a couple of kilometres away, had once been the site of an Italian boarding-school; what remained were the four long, low, stone buildings, turned into barracks, each of which housed some fifty or sixty Palestinian Jewish deportees; a few small rooms they 'reserved' for their younger colleagues (eighteen and slightly older); a mess hall and a cookhouse; and an additional structure used as a synagogue. Although there wasn't a Socialist in sight, life was organized along highly collective lines, apart from the fact that the deportees' committee – in the name of greater harmony – allocated barracks in accordance to underground affiliation: three for the Irgun, one for Lehi, with some autonomy granted each group. Our days were punctuated by various standard activities: lectures, drama group, football team, long stretches of monotony and homesickness (though

I myself was only there for a few months), and, more than anything else, the obsession with escape. We were gripped by impatience. Here we were, in the north-east of Africa of all places, while the *Yishuv* was involved in literally crucial events to which each one had personally contributed – the measure of his contribution being this exile, these wasted years. The urge to participate, the desire to be in Palestine, the need to return to the struggle, now nearing some kind of new climax, were overwhelming. Some impressively channelled their stress and disappointment into academic achievement: 150 deportees passed matriculation exams with flying colours; another hundred (including the present President of Israel's Supreme Court, Meir Shamgar) studied law, their results eliciting from the sponsoring British Council an unprecedented query as to exactly what and where this Camp 119 was, with its astonishing scholastic record!

'If I forget thee, O Jerusalem, may my right hand lose its cunning,' I wrote across the top of my first letter to Shulamit a few days after my arrival, telling her what solitary confinement had been like for me, about the plane trip to Eritrea (it was the first time I had ever flown) and describing my first sight of the country of my exile.

Perhaps [I wrote], it is, as everyone says, a beautiful country with a good climate – but, dear God, not for me. ... Everything in me cries out to be home, in the homeland; I long not only for those specific things with which, and for which, I lived in that homeland, but for its space, its soil, its skies and scenery ... conditions are not too bad ... the physical hardship means nothing to me. Even in solitary, I felt no pain. It is the lack of action that makes someone like me miserable. I used to think that if I were ever arrested, I would just sleep for days, without thinking or feeling. But I was wrong. I am not at all at rest here. I wake up very early for some reason and in the dark sometimes open my eyes and I see you and the little boy; your eyes wide open too, your lips and cheeks so pink, and the boy standing in his cot and shouting and laughing because his day is beginning ... and underneath him forms a small sweet puddle ... so, though I have been separated from all that is precious to me, much of my life and being continue to exist and to grow out there somewhere. It is as though I am only partially imprisoned.

Be strong; have no regrets. Don't think too much about me or about your own loneliness. It will add nothing, heal nothing ... one has to take the good and the bad and go on ... send me my son's pictures so I can look at him from afar; and write me all the details ... how you manage; whom you leave him with when you go shopping; how the neighbours treat you.

The prospects for escape from Sambal were not promising. All told, there had already been nine attempts, led by escape artists, as it were, from the Irgun; some twenty men were at liberty (in the end, a total of seventy made it), others had been returned and punished in various ways, among them confinement in a grim nearby fortress named after an Italian general. After each attempt, the British tightened controls and doubled precautions. The problem didn't end with managing to tunnel the way out of camp to freedom, though this in itself was a considerable feat, which involved crawling, or more accurately inching, through a tunnel no more than 65 centimetres wide, one of seven such tunnels dug by members of the Irgun and Lehi in the camps of Eritrea and Kenya. The digging itself – backbreaking, lung-burning, nerve-racking – occupied only a few people at any given time. The rest made passports (the first, which was Honduran, looked so good that when, years afterwards, its designers showed it to the Honduran Ambassador, he was most complimentary. 'Much better than ours,' he exclaimed), sewed the necessary uniforms complete with 'insignia' that, upon very close inspection, revealed the initials JRFE – not of a British regiment but of the 'Jewish Resistance Forces in Exile', pored over maps, planned routes, maintained vital contacts outside and dealt with the camp administration.

The burning question, however, given this abundance of talent for improvisation, was not just how to escape, but where to escape to. Africa was British, so no good; there was nothing, no transportation, no reasonable destination, that would not bring us, directly or otherwise, to the doorstep of the British. Eventually, however, a detailed plan was put together. I have been reluctant thus far to attempt naming many people – comrades with whom I worked during these years, upon whom I so depended and to whom I am bound by very special ties – but, now and again, a name crops up insistently, as does that of Yaacov Meridor. Commander of the Irgun after Raziel's death, later to be a partner of Menachem Begin in the formation of the Herut Party, a Member of the Knesset and of the Cabinet, Meridor directed and led some of the most sensational escapes from Africa, the last among those being the one that brought me too out of detention. On 14 January 1947, five people (I, the sole representative of Lehi) crawled at dusk through the tunnel, across a football field, between and under Sambal's fences and, on foot, reached Asmara – and shelter with the young Italian family that would hide us till we took the next step and with a Jewish doctor in town whose gentile wife offered to help us and did. Thanks to them, we stayed in Asmara for several weeks, well out of sight, while the British thundered that the Jews had evaded them again, one particular reason for their rage being the thought that Jewish freedom fighters were now on the loose throughout a dark and not especially pro-British continent. I wrote letters, counted the days and waited to learn when we were to move on to our next 'scheduled' stop, Addis Ababa.

It had been decided that Arieh Ben-Eliezer would precede the rest of us to Addis, making arrangements there for us to follow in two groups in a rented bus that would go back and forth. Arieh possessed a combination of warmth, practicality and the ability to communicate that I was greatly to appreciate on what turned out to be a tortuous voyage. He was a ranking Irgunist, had been in exile since 1944 and was to become a member of Herut and Deputy Speaker of the Knesset. Someone came up with another idea: never mind the bus, let's buy an oil tanker, have a special addition made to hold the four of us so that we can travel together, and, as for paying the driver, we'll give him the tanker when we're through with it. It sounded brilliant and everyone agreed to it.

Until then, until I entered that 'special addition', until that trip to Addis, I had never experienced real physical discomfort, never been ill or even weak. The eighty hours I spent in what Meridor was to call 'a moving coffin' were as near as I ever care to come to bodily torment. Doubled up, knees-to-chin, most of the time close to fainting, breathing only through minute airholes pierced in the lid of the special addition, we made our slow, agonizing way to Ethiopia. Like many such episodes, in the retrospective telling legends are created and there are always comic aspects, but there was nothing imaginary or entertaining about the pain we suffered; our only opportunity to take a deep breath was at night when the lid was partially opened, the container parked and the driver, to our fury, visiting 'as I always do', he explained, his native paramour. What should have taken hours took three days and three nights and, literally, almost drove the four of us out of our minds. But in Addis, Arieh met us, smiling, sympathetic and armed with information. He had rented a villa for a family of five; there, we would be able to work out some way of reaching the harbour capital of what was then French Somalia, Djibouti, where the British could, we thought, do little or nothing to us. The general outlook, however, had not improved: we had no passports, in fact no papers of any kind; and the British were intensifying their search for us – not too difficult an assignment in a town in which there were relatively few Europeans. But helping hands reached out to us – I recall a family of Jewish traders from Aden and a Jerusalem lawyer who had become the Emperor's legal adviser. Most were those of Jews or people with Jewish connections, but there were also others.

In the middle of April, Arieh and I left for Djibouti, where lay our one hope of getting home. In Addis it had been decided that only Arieh and I would go to Djibouti; the others would look for an alternative route. They stayed in Addis for a while, were arrested and turned over to the British, but even so Meridor got to Europe before I did. Djibouti was linked to Addis by railroad so the plan that took shape logically involved travelling by train. The idea was that we would be smuggled into a railway car – owned by another affluent Jewish trader – that weekly carried coffee beans to the port. Since it was a sealed compartment and a Somali Arab guard was perched on its roof for the duration of the two-and-a-half-day journey, it was not hard to arrange for him to open it up one stop before Djibouti so that we could walk to town without having to go through formalities at the main station. We should, I suppose, have known that things would go wrong; they had been going wrong ever since our escape from Sambal. But we were both confirmed optimists, the plan appeared foolproof and, anyhow, there weren't many other options. Instead, there were several surprises, none pleasant.

To begin with, there was very little room in the compartment; the space allotted to us between the sacks of coffee and the ceiling may have been half a metre but I think it was less; the train stopped long before the anticipated place – and didn't move again for another two-and-a-half days, during which time Arieh and I had very little to eat or drink or do, except count sacks of coffee and try to breathe. At long last, the 'extra' two-and-a-half days passed, the train moved and a breeze entered the car and our lungs. Then the train stopped again, the railway car was unsealed and opened, and an armed officer greeted us with the information that the police, informed of our pending arrival, awaited us. For the moment, because he was not quite sure what to do with us, he bound us over to the custody of Djibouti's rabbi, ordering us to turn up at the police station next morning.

At the Djibouti police station the Chef de Sûreté told us that the British Consul knew of our arrival and had asked the Governor of Djibouti to hand us over to the British, who had already despatched a 'delegation' to the border to receive us. We loudly protested, demanding to be allowed to talk to a lawyer, and after some discussion we were introduced to a French advocate who only spoke French, of which neither Arieh nor I knew one word. But the advocate, a quick-witted man, grasped the situation at once. He would act, he said, on our behalf with the Procureur Général. The Procureur duly declared that, according to French law, we could not be 'extradited' and even warned the Governor (who badly wanted to be rid of us) that by transgressing he might well be endangering his job. In the end, the French did not hand us over; instead, leniently they charged us with illegal entry into Djibouti. In the meantime, we contacted good friends in Paris and soon after were informed that we had been granted asylum, *'droits d'asile'*, as political prisoners. It turned out later that the Procureur had actually met the British 'delegation' that came to fetch us and was astonished that amongst them was a priest. There could be no reason for this, he thought, other than that they were going to execute us. From then on, he was sure that he had saved my life. And, who knows? Maybe he had.

I learned a lot in those months, close to a year, in Djibouti, not only because I read a lot (though that too), but mostly because, though I was still in Africa, the traditions, the culture and the language of France were all around me and I began to understand and admire them. Later, I was to live for months at a time in France, but my first encounter with it came then. My 'jail', for a while, was a private house, a villa buried in tropical vegetation, that belonged to the Governor of Djibouti and that Arieh and I shared with another ward of the French Government, Dong Bac Mai, a leader of the Viet Minh, later the Viet Cong. He was one of Ho Chi Minh's close advisers, an erudite French-educated revolutionary. Accused of murdering a number of Frenchmen in Indo-China, he had been advised to escape that country. The ship on which he was travelling had been boarded by French police and he had been arrested and detained at the villa. We spent hours, fascinated, listening to him as he told us about his homeland, about Russia where he had been enrolled in Comintern courses and about the Viet Minh, transporting us with each story to another world. I remember how sure he was that there would be a Jewish state – and soon. 'How do you arrive at that conclusion?' I asked him once. 'Through Marxist analysis,' he said.

He was candid about his hatred of the white man and about the need for ever-greater violence and brutality if the battle was to be won. He spoke like someone from the pages of the books I read in my youth, like an anarchist. He had no use for ethics; the end entirely justified the means; nothing mattered except independence and, after that, the revolution. He was unable to understand our revulsion at the idea of wanton bloodshed and I had the feeling that, as I tried to explain about my own activities, I lost face, that Lehi was not tough enough for him, not sufficiently ruthless – though outside that remote Garden of Eden, outside that paradoxical dialogue about violence, this was hardly the prevalent view. I also learned to enjoy fishing with a rod in the Indian Ocean and discovered how it relaxed the mind and aided thinking. Years later, when the media made fun of President Bush's angling at a time of crisis, I fully understood why he did so. Fishing is tailor-made for people who need to be patient. However, we were not in Djibouti to learn French, to analyse terrorism or to suspend re-entry into immediate reality. Each day our return to Palestine became more imperative for us, more urgent. Much had taken place during my detention in Sambal and protracted stay in Djibouti.

In February 1947, the British Government had referred the Palestine problem to the UN. Mr Bevin, at least for the time being, had had enough. A Special Committee on Palestine (UNSCOP) had been formed, which made the usual rounds, was treated by the British to the spectacle of the 4,500 Jewish refugees from Nazi camps aboard the ss *Exodus 1947* being forcibly penned and, at gun-point, returned to Germany, and came up with a report essentially recommending the solution first proposed by the Peel Committee, i.e. partition. A minority recommendation upheld by the three representatives of countries with large Moslem populations (Iran, India and Yugoslavia) opted for a federal Arab–Jewish state. History, more or less, repeated itself: the Zionists said 'Yes', calling for a rapid end to the Mandate; the Arabs said 'No' to everything and threatened that war would break out in the Middle East unless all Palestine became Arab; the British said that they would only help in the transition provided all parties were in accord – which meant that they would do nothing to aid the birth of the Jewish state.

But the United States and the USSR gave their blessing to the majority recommendation. On 29 November 1947, a UN Resolution was passed to partition the Land into a Jewish state, an Arab state and an international zone incorporating Jerusalem, and the first, if undeclared, stage of the War of Independence began. It was to last for over a year and a half, to cost the *Yishuv* 6,000 lives (one per cent of the Jewish population then) and to assure the existence of the State of Israel, which came into being on 14 May 1948. All those months I was away and useless, and that too I found hard to forgive.

Lehi and the Irgun had been very active, each British strike followed by a deadlier counter-strike. It was the twilight, if not yet the sunset, of the Mandate; a time for the British in Palestine of demoralization, vengeance and ineffectuality. Abandoning earlier patterns, however clumsy or (as in the case of the DPs) cruel, the military now launched new, more repressive measures. Imprisoned dissidents were flogged.

The Irgun responded by flogging British officers. The floggings ended. The British embarked on large-scale hangings. The Irgun hanged two British sergeants. The hangings ended. A British officer, Captain Roy Farran, and his friends were accused of torturing to death a sixteen-year-old Lehi member who was distributing leaflets and whose body was never found. Farran, though court-martialled, was acquitted and left the country. The letter-bomb sent to his home in England killed his brother instead of him. And so it went on. There were wars within wars and not all of Lehi's resources could be invested in battling the British or warding off its Jewish opponents.

There were also the Arabs, spurred on by promises of booty, of the rewards that they would harvest, in this world or the next, when the Jews were thrown into the sea in the Holy War that was about to commence. Easy prey, as always, for those who called them to combat – from a thousand minarets throughout the Middle East – they were certain that Allah would help them resist the creation of a Jewish state and, in their hatred for us, were willing to forgo the Palestinian Arab state offered by the UN at the same time. Where and when it could, Lehi struck at Arab infiltrators, detachments of the Arab 'Liberation Army' that entered the country from Syria, Iraq and Jordan, and at Arab military targets. The most controversial of these attacks took place in a village – the name of which was to serve Arab propagandists faithfully until replaced in speakers' kits by equally distorted accounts of what happened (in Israel's 1982 Peace for Galilee campaign) in the Lebanese refugee camps of Sabra and Shatilla. I refer to the village of Deir Yassin and the allegation that hundreds of innocent Arabs were killed there, in April 1948, by Jews.

Let me set down the facts, commenting only that considerable use of the operation was made also by the *Yishuv* establishment, which hastened to denounce 'the dissidents' with extraordinary disregard for what actually happened. Deir Yassin, in fact, is an early, and maybe classic, example of Israelis themselves bearing responsibility for sowing seeds of distortion and exaggeration that then, expertly tended by Israel's enemies, grow into the damaging myths that are so hard to uproot. In the early spring of 1948, Jerusalem – where one-sixth of the Jewish population lived – was under Arab siege, cut off from the rest of the *Yishuv* because the 40-mile-long mountain road leading to the coastal plain was controlled by the Arabs. Until that road was freed, no supplies could reach the Jewish section of Jerusalem which was living in a state of semi-starvation underscored by constant sniping from the Arab villages strung out along the highway. One such village was Deir Yassin, which, by the beginning of April, housed not only the villagers but also Iraqi troops and Palestinian Arab 'irregulars'.

It was decided, therefore, that Deir Yassin should be attacked by the Irgun and Lehi (at the time operating together) and that their forces should occupy the village. The Haganah did not join in the action, but made clear that it had no objection to it and stressed that the Irgun and Lehi would have to keep troops in the village afterwards to ensure that it didn't become a site for further infiltration. The village was stormed; the villagers warned by loudspeaker to seek shelter elsewhere; the purpose of the raid explained. Many of the local people did what they were told, but in the confusion most stayed where they were. The Arab positions opened fire, the fighting went on all day and over a hundred villagers died (despite the escape corridor opened by the attackers); some had fired on the troops after pretending to surrender and were killed, another thirty were Arab men disguised as women. There were no atrocities, no brutal excesses, nothing other than the horror of any warfare – which is bad enough but does not constitute 'a premeditated massacre' as the Arabs have referred to the attack ever since. There is more to be said about Deir Yassin and the Haganah's subsequent behaviour in regard to it, but I leave that to future historians of the War of Independence.

The attack on Deir Yassin took place about ten days before Arieh and I left Djibouti. For months, the problem of our leaving Africa and getting home had seemed insoluble. It was impossible for us to get to Europe by sea since all shipping had to pass through the Suez Canal, where it was liable to be searched by the British. Nor could we fly from Djibouti without having to land on British territory. Finally, in a gallant gesture, the French agreed to transport us aboard a small aircraft carrier (which the United States had once given to France) making its way from Saigon to Toulon. A special decision to this effect had been made by the French Government and, on 20 April 1948, we at last headed for home, or, at any rate, in the right direction. No one on the *Dixmude* knew about us: it had been a very quick stop-over; she sailed the minute we were on board. So the call may well have been just to pick us up.

I have two odd recollections from that voyage – on which Arieh and I must have walked the decks for hundreds of miles. One has to do with the handsome weather-beaten rear-admiral in tropical whites who listened with much interest while I answered his questions about the war in Palestine, and then said: 'I had no idea until just now that there are Jews who are not bankers or merchants or scientists.

I have never heard about Jewish farmers or soldiers before. Don't worry. If there really are Jews of the sort you describe, you will have your state soon.' The other concerns a note passed to me by the steward at lunch one day, with a booklet containing Jewish prayers. 'We don't know who you are,' it read, 'just that you are Jews. Please be assured we are ready to help if needs be.' It was signed 'Sailors on this ship'. Afterwards I watched the crew carefully, but never discovered the authors of that note.

In Toulon, the warmest possible reception awaited us on the part of the French Foreign Office. There were old friends from Lehi and the Irgun, and Arieh and I were given permission to stay in France for as long as we liked. But even the great courtesy shown us by the French did not preclude my inadvertent stay in jail, on my very first night in Paris, the result of a mix-up about a lack of passport and papers – from which Lehi people managed to 'rescue' me; nor the extremely polite request made to Arieh and myself that, during the visit to that city by the then Princess Elizabeth (now Queen Elizabeth II), we absent ourselves to avoid 'embarrassing' the British. Arieh went to Nice for a week or two, and I to Hendaye on the Spanish border. But the odyssey wasn't over yet; I still had to get home. Here too a solution was found. In those days, the *Yishuv* basked in the warmth of Soviet goodwill; Czech arms and planes were helping to make possible the survival of the new-born state already in the middle of a war. Prague was the one place from which I could fly directly to Haifa, Lod airport not yet being in Israeli hands. Air France conveyed me to Prague; someone handed me a used passport (not even changing the photo); a Czech policeman gave it, and me, a glance, nodded, and I was in flight again, this time aboard a Czech plane; an overnight stop in Athens put my failing patience to some final test; and then home.

5

FROM MOSSAD TO THE KNESSET

IT WAS THE 20th of May 1948, the State of Israel was six days old, and I was back, hardly able to believe that it was true. I walked around, those first days in Tel Aviv, as gratefully as I had thirteen years earlier: Shulamit, Yair, the Jewish state, the end of exile, the start not only of a new life for me but of a new historic era. I was filled with relief, with happiness and with a sense of accomplishment because by then, of course, the British had gone, although very soon, I knew, there would be not only daily responsibilities but also overriding anxieties. Could we stand fast in the face of the Arab invasion? Would assistance from abroad come in time? Did the fall of Jerusalem's Jewish Quarter to the Jordanian Arab Legion mean that, from now on, the city was in permanent danger? Israel had been recognized by the US and the USSR but was the Jewish state truly a *fait accompli* in the eyes of the world, or were other plans, under Arab and British pressure, still in the making? And Lehi, what of Lehi?

Within less than a week, I was back in action, Gera, Eldad and I reviewing events. Under Gera's guidance, a trend to the left had developed, a flirting with Socialism that appealed to some of the younger members and had first made difficult, then impossible, any union with the Irgun – though the strong theoretical differences between the two undergrounds had anyway begun to blur. In fact, however, with the new reality of statehood, the long day, or rather the night, of the undergrounds ended. At least for Lehi, the aims had been met: the occupier had gone, fled; the state had been proclaimed; the gates of the Land unlocked. Ben-Gurion, Prime Minister and Minister of Defence, was insistent on doing away with what he termed the 'private armies' as soon as possible, not only with the 'dissidents', but also, and for other reasons, with the Haganah's Palmach, the combat units that largely represented the left wing or the Labour movement and were already possessed of glamour, popularity and substantial autonomy. Whatever my other criticisms of him, to this day I believe that, in the specific matter of the disbandment of the undergrounds and the Palmach, his judgment was sound and of critical importance to the young state.

Towards the end of May, two Orders were issued by the Government of Israel: one authorized conscription in times of emergency, declared that compulsory enlistment would be instituted and that everyone serving in the IDF would have to take an oath of allegiance to the state, and prohibited the maintenance of armed entities other than the IDF. The second was an Order of the Day, signed by Ben-Gurion, announcing that the Haganah had emerged from the underground and become 'a regular army'. Used to obeying orders and eager to serve, ninety per cent of the members of Lehi at once enlisted; some ten per cent, it was agreed, were not to disperse yet, and then there were a few abroad. Also, since Jerusalem was not yet fully under Israel's control, Lehi units with transport and arms were to continue to operate there.

In June 1948, the UN enforced a cease-fire (it lasted for twenty-eight days) in the War of Independence. The terms were negotiated by the UN Mediator in Palestine, Count Folke Bernadotte, nephew of the Swedish King and head of the Swedish Red Cross, who had been appointed to the UN position by the Security Council. Not content with the demanding role of Mediator, the Count began to work on a 'peace plan' of his own, holding talks in London and Washington, doing his best to persuade everyone that his ideas would, at last, solve the famous Palestine problem. By the time the first cease-fire ended and the ensuing ten-day offensive by Israel was over, the Arab threat to Tel Aviv, Haifa and the coastal plain had been removed; the siege of Jerusalem lifted; nearly 700 square miles of Arab-controlled territory taken by the IDF; and over twenty per cent of the Arab fighting strength lost. Israel was alive and strong, but its borders were neither well-defined nor tenable, and the Negev was still under Egyptian siege.

When published, Count Bernadotte's Plan, to which an increasing number of influential people were giving their earnest attention, turned out to be a proposal for a new partition of Palestine. Jerusalem was to be internationalized, though originally the Count allotted it outright to Jordan, which also received the Negev; all immigration to Israel was to be subject to Jordanian agreement; all Israeli air and sea ports were to be supervised by the UN; and some 360,000 Arabs were to be brought back. It represented a disaster. What may appear in the late 1990s as absurd was not at all so in 1948. The Bernadotte Plan was a development that would have opened the way, without question, to putting an end to the Jewish state within weeks of its birth. The *Yishuv* was appalled; somewhere, it was thought, the British – with whom Bernadotte had close connections – were pulling the strings. At all events, Lehi believed that it was imperative for the plan to be shelved and Bernadotte removed from the arena. At first, he was warned: Lehi leaflets demanded that he leave his post, that he leave the country and that his Plan be publicly repudiated.

But Bernadotte was sure that with this Plan he was entering history and he paid no heed. On 17 September 1948, he was shot and killed in Jerusalem, the city he was ready to give away. Lehi took no responsibility for the deed; the idea was conceived in Jerusalem by Lehi members operating there more or less independently. Our opinion was asked and we offered no opposition. The assassination was attributed to a splinter group, 'The Fatherland Front'. Israel's Provisional Government acted quickly; it declared Lehi illegal, arrested all the members it could find and broke up the Jerusalem units; for a while it both prosecuted and persecuted us. Gera was imprisoned; Eldad and I went into hiding, outlaws again, back in the underground but determined not to fight the State of Israel.

What worried me most were continuing reports of discrimination in the army against Lehi members. I felt that this had to end; there had to be a point after which conspiracy ceased and that cessation had to be recognized by the Government too. I asked a well-placed colleague to arrange a secret meeting for me with a spokesman for the Government, someone in whom Ben-Gurion had complete confidence; a meeting was arranged, but it was no ordinary emissary who was sent to talk to me. Shaul Avigur was then Deputy Minister of Defence, I had been promised that I would not be followed or arrested and the man who drove me to the private house in which Avigur and I met was Yair's brother-in-law, so I felt secure.

'Lehi is through with its former role,' I said to Avigur. 'We may perhaps go into politics. Or not. Whatever happens, a new chapter will open. The decree of illegality must be annulled and Lehi members must be released from jail. If not, we shall never feel completely safe and the underground will never totally die.'

'I understand,' Avigur replied, 'but guarantees must be mutual. How do I know that this is not a trick so that Lehi can stay in business, protected by the Government of Israel?'

'Look,' I answered. 'Underground organizations can hide every-thing, conceal people, arms, safe-houses, but not their very existence.

An underground movement that does nothing, de facto, does not exist, does it?'

He listened, without comment, then asked me to give him the names of Count Bernadotte's assailants. Nothing would happen to them, he said, but he wanted their names on file. I said, 'No.' After a few days, Ben-Gurion cut through the tangle to proclaim a 'general amnesty' and the Provisional Government passed a special law so that all Lehi and Irgun members be released, including those already sentenced.

We held a sort of parade, the first and last. We had never all been together before; now people exchanged real names and addresses, openly dispensing with the safeguards of conspiratorial life, with the underground. We were not used to public speaking either, so not much was said, but I remember the way that men and women, with whom I had worked and been in danger, whom I had commanded and utterly trusted, looked at me that day, half-disbelieving that I was the 'legendary' Michael, peering, with the same curiosity, at the men who had for so long called themselves Gera and Eldad. No one orated, no one cried. The mood was quiet, a little sad; there was a sense of vulnerability, maybe even of fear. How would it be above ground, without the shields, without the discipline, without the bonds of that singular comradeship? We were about to move into the mainstream of so-called normal life, though, of course, Israel has yet to attain that fully. But we didn't know this. The vision that had motivated us and brought Lehi into being was essentially realized, and the question before most of us now was how each one would cope with the new life.

Blinking a bit in the strong light of ordinary life, I found myself – like thousands of other Israelis in the first years of the state's existence – a man arrived, as if suddenly, at his middle thirties, a family man with a wife and children to support, needing a decent place to live, regular employment and, beyond these, perhaps even more essential, an emotional and psychological substitute for the intensity to which we had all been addicted for so long. It was not nostalgia, nor a lingering over a past that appeared more glorious as it receded, nor that I missed the daily risk to life and limb. It was the whole-heartedness and the completeness of commitment to an ideal for which I hankered, the habit of service – however the word may embarrass in these more cynical days.

With its disbandment as an underground movement, Lehi had briefly metamorphosed into a short-lived political party we named

The Fighters Party, which made its debut in the February 1949 elections to the first Knesset, where it was represented by Gera, known once more as Yellin-Mor. In fact, the Party had been created almost entirely as an attempt to secure Yellin-Mor's release from jail (where he had been ever since Bernadotte's assassination), but the general amnesty accomplished this anyway, and, just as I had not especially welcomed or encouraged the Party's birth, so its end (it disappeared before the 1951 elections to the second Knesset) did not sadden me. I was not interested then, nor have I been since, in politics per se although I have dwelt so long in the political sphere. It was obvious to me from the start that now Lehi, its goals met, had no platform, nothing to say, its members, for the most part, not having much in common. In other words, there was no point in striving for continuity.

Regarding my own future, I was not so certain. The public and official climate in Israel, insofar as former 'dissidents' and known opponents of the Socialist parties were concerned, ranged from the chilly and suspicious to the openly hostile. My son, with no bitterness, even recalls attempts to set our home on fire and fights at school over my good name and that of Lehi. So I was not likely to find many doors, or arms, flung open to me. What's more, it was the era of Israel's austerity, of the mass immigration, up to the end of 1951, that had brought 684,000 Jews from all over the world straight to tent cities and tin towns from which they were expected to integrate into the frail economy of a state still not allowed to live in peace and still afflicted by a large-scale Arab boycott. There wasn't enough of anything: food, money, experienced manpower, or time to prepare properly for the flood of Jews.

On the other hand, I had a profession: book-keeping. I wasn't enthusiastic about it but I had done it before and fairly well. I applied to the State Comptroller's Office for a job only to be told bluntly that I was 'not reliable' enough. Later on, an order was issued which put an end to such judgments by decreeing the destruction of the dossiers of all 'dissidents' – and instructing government offices to treat them like everyone else. Then I thought perhaps I should put my by-now not inconsiderable organizational experience to work, this time for my personal benefit. I toyed with the idea of trying my hand at business, but the vital motivation was simply not there. The illusion that, having 'succeeded' in the struggle against the British, I could become a captain of industry was not unique to me. It was shared by a number of my former comrades, some of whom discovered that they liked the other world and had the necessary talent to survive in it, going on to combine making money with helping to develop Israel. But there were more like myself and it was with these, inevitably, that I joined forces to set up or manage a variety of endeavours of which the best that can be said is that, like The Fighters Party, when they vanished, it was quickly. I took on a couple of 'executive' jobs, managing an association of cinema owners and, later, a small public works contracting company. But nothing I did had much flavour or purpose. If Shulamit had been more demanding or less understanding of my restlessness and discontent, life would have been intolerable. But she settled down in the little flat we took in the middle of Tel Aviv, decided to stay at home with the children, even if it meant (as it did) making do with less, and never complained about anything. Even so, I couldn't adjust to feeling, for the first time I could remember, that I was useless, that I had become a bystander rather than a participant, uninvolved in what was going on around me.

Then, one day in 1955, the tide turned. A friend who had been a member of Lehi told me, in confidence, that he had joined Israel's security services. It was right after a major Israeli 'mishap', later known as the Lavon Affair (Pinchas Lavon was then Minister of Defence), which involved the nation's military and security estab- lishments, the Government headed by Moshe Sharett, and David Ben- Gurion who had retired to Sdeh Boker, and which simmered until the 1960s when it boiled over. Anyhow, in its wake, there were shake-ups and shifts of personnel and new people were being sought by the Mossad. 'If you agree,' said my friend, 'I will find out if there is room for you too.' Well, why not try, I thought, though I didn't take his suggestion very seriously. But after a few days, he phoned: 'They are very keen. The head of the Mossad told me so himself. He wants to meet you.'

The Mossad (translated exactly, its official and full name means 'The Institution for Intelligence and Special Tasks') came into being with the state as its central intelligence facility, authorized to gather information, undertake research and carry out special covert missions beyond the borders of the state but not within them. That responsi- bility lies with the General Security Service. For years, the Mossad was run by Isser Harel, who had, characteristically, come to the conclusion that since bygones were bygones and had to be so, it would be a good thing if the Mossad availed itself of some of the special abilities acquired by such formerly 'wanted' men as myself. I imagine that he also may have calculated that this would ensure my remaining under surveillance for somewhat longer! We met at his home. It wasn't a long talk. Although we had never spoken before, we knew quite a lot about each other and got to the point at once. 'Are you prepared to join us?' he asked. 'Can we trust you?' When I said 'Yes' to both questions, Isser told me that he, for his part, had no reservations and that no strings whatsoever were attached to the offer. 'Just be frank with me. If you are ever asked to do anything that is against your principles, tell me about it at once.' I liked that, and him, and instantly agreed to this too. I was to spend the next ten years in the Mossad, most of them working closely with Isser, and we were to talk about many things, but that conversation was the only one we ever held on the subject of my coming to work for him – and for the State of Israel – and it changed my life. Entering the Mossad returned me to working on behalf of the state.

I felt at home very soon; I had returned to an atmosphere, behaviour, incentives and points of view that were, in many ways, familiar to me. At first, introduced to relatively few people, I asked only specific questions and refrained (luckily this came to me naturally) from speculating about whatever was obviously being omitted from my otherwise most thorough 'tutoring'. For about half a year, I was what might be called a free-lancer, moving from sector to sector within the Mossad; then I was allowed to set up a unit of my own and made responsible directly to Isser himself. I knew, of course, that somewhere my dossier was on file, that I was surely rubbing shoulders with men who had tried, not so long ago, to hunt me down and had done so, moreover, at Isser's instruction. But it didn't bother me. I too felt that what had happened before the state was proclaimed was one thing; everything after that was something else and, in time, I also brought in new people, men who had served with me in the underground and for whose courage, stamina, intelligence and loyalty I could vouch.

Although this is a subject upon which, by law, I must not write in any detail, let me explain that the spectrum of Mossad concerns is very broad indeed, ranging from recruitment of sources and collection of information on matters directly concerning Israel's security, through to projects that are peculiarly Israeli. Among these are: the protection and defence of Jews abroad, the bringing to Israel of Jews forbidden to leave their countries of origin or, for instance, the capture of Nazi war criminals, as in the case of Adolf Eichmann, whose presence and public trial in Israel taught our children more forcefully than anything else could have, or did, the unspeakable facts of the Holocaust and was, for many Jews abroad – and for Israel's enemies – an unforgettable object lesson in the reality and reach of the Jewish state. Some of the operations undertaken in the period of my Mossad service which became public knowledge included the controversial exposure of the effort being made in Nasser's Egypt of the late 1950s by German scientists and technicians to develop non-conventional weapons – a clear threat to Israel; or, in another direction altogether, the safeguarding of the paramount status of the law in Israel (and avoidance of heightened tension between religious and secular communities) when six-year-old Yossele Shumacher, kidnapped from the country by ultra-Orthodox extremist groups in defiance of a court order, was eventually tracked down in New York and brought to his parents in Israel.

This range of activities (I have only hinted at the scale) is, and has always been, the responsibility of remarkably few people from whom a great deal is demanded, not least the ability to direct others, fluency in a variety of languages, and possession or acquisition of often highly specialized crafts and competences. That the Mossad has earned an international reputation for effectiveness is due to the fact that these few are people of unusual calibre: genuinely patriotic; able to accept the discipline of absolute truth within the ranks while living lives of deception outside; willing to disregard, and sometimes act contrary to, their personal interests; frequently keeping families in one place while they operate in another; relaxing only in the company of their co-workers and therefore, more often than not, exceedingly lonely. They are, of course, paid civil servants like all other government employees, but what is so demanding about their daily work is that it routinely combines the ordinary with the unusual, the obligatory with the need for singular devotion, all under the considerable constraint of an anonymity that precludes any public appreciation. Not that these attributes are exclusive to the Mossad or to Israel, but the circumstances of our lives are such that everything is more complicated, more dangerous, more crucial than it would be if our survival were not still a cardinal issue. But since it is, it would not surprise me to learn that the charge laid on the individual men and women who work in, and for, the Mossad is indeed heavier than that governing the work of their counterparts elsewhere.

Isser was a very stern taskmaster, prepared to forgive mistakes, even rather serious ones, but never lies, disobedience, a defaulting of any sort (whether money or even marriage was concerned), talkativeness, inaccurate reporting or any manipulation of fact. Since I was used to such strictures and approved of them, I had no trouble with them. Some time ago I came across the Mossad's credo, something that permeates and expresses the fundamental attitude towards it of those who work for it – at all levels. I thought a line or two from this plain mimeographed sheet might be of interest:

Honesty ... moral standards ... awareness of personal responsibility are what direct us along a path of simplicity of behaviour and secrecy ... into our ranks we accept only the best and of ourselves we give only the best, encouraging initiative, creativity and daring. ... Leadership in the Mossad demands of those who claim it the assumption of responsibility for command ... personal example ... the ability to delegate authority and to inspire. ...

My Mossad background, I think, had a great deal to do with the harmony in which, as Prime Minister, I worked with the various branches of Israeli security and which themselves, by the way, work together in almost total harmony, something that cannot be said of all its counterparts abroad, including in the United States, France and Britain.

Because it is responsible directly to the Prime Minister, in recent years I visited the Mossad annually to see for myself, and hear about in some detail, new developments (these days, mostly technological and startlingly inventive), meet with department heads, speak to them briefly and answer their questions. Not so long ago I stood alone for a minute at the small corner set aside in Mossad headquarters to honour the memory of Mossad personnel, those who have died over the past four decades – and those who fell in the line of duty but cannot be commemorated publicly lest their names reveal connections that Israel does not wish to or cannot disclose. It is a modest memorial for each member of that company who passed away, a plaque, a photograph, a few lines of tribute to a good soldier, some place at last to which families can come – the least such families deserve.

My own family got used to the hours I kept, to my being abroad, to the people who turned up at the house without notice. From Shulamit, the children learned the unspoken rules: not to be curious, not to ask about the visitors they saw and not to disturb me when they came – and there were always such 'visitors' in our home. Some were ex-Lehi members with problems to be solved or quarrels to be settled, and I used to think of my father's house and how he, too, had listened and counselled and sent people away feeling better. Some were Mossad workers who came to talk quietly, sometimes urgently, where no one would overhear or intrude. Strangely enough, the only family revolt broke out when I was posted to France for a year or two and, of course, we went all together. Both Yair and Gilada pined for home, for Israel's sun and blue skies, for the freedom of Tel Aviv streets, for their friends, for Hebrew all day long and, I suspect, for their own last name instead of the cover name (Barzilai) they were forced to use but about which to their credit they never once made a mistake. In the end, it seemed unfair to keep them abroad and we let them go back. But for me, the romance with France that started in Djibouti became full-blown in Paris: the scenery, the way people looked, the food, the wine, Piaf. I felt my tastes change and expand.

I was only in the Mossad for ten years ('only' because, by Mossad standards, that is not long), ten years that influenced me and during which I learned a lot. Afterwards, as Prime Minister, and before that as a member of the Cabinet, I had to work hard to summon up impartiality where the Mossad was concerned. As is true in other democracies, Israel's secret services are frequent victims of media exaggeration and impatience, never more so than when, as is unavoidable, errors are committed and the press feels free to go on the sensational offensive, knowing that the services cannot fight back openly or adequately explain themselves. They cannot even point out that mistakes and miscarriages of justice are very rare, that these have never stemmed from greed for money or power, that inevitably there are failures, sometimes reprehensible, to find adequate solutions at the right time for discrepancies that exist between the law and the requirements of security. The possible pitfalls are countless; not everyone who enlists in the Mossad necessarily manages to cope under all conceivable circumstances. But Israel has every right to be proud of its covert agencies, of their humanity, of the extent to which no one is regarded as expendable, and of the effort made to lavish compensation and attention on those who have suffered injury or bereavement. Nothing is done in the name of revenge and a great effort is made to see that the families of the worst of the state's enemies are not endangered, though the price paid by Israelis for this is often horrifyingly high. And, I must confess, I am proud of having been not only the first of the 'dissident' underground leaders to cross the threshold of that Holy of Holies – by invitation – but also the first Mossad employee eventually to be at its helm.

There were many changes within the Mossad when Isser Harel left in 1963 – due mainly to a major policy dispute centring on the work of the Germans in Egypt and differing assessments of its gravity insofar as Israel was concerned. I stayed on for a year or two, trying to accommodate myself to his successor and to new ways, and then departed, not to come in from the cold but rather, or so I felt, to return to it once more. Again I had to get used to life above ground, to finding a job, and to searching for an outlet for my need to engage in something more than earning a living.

A cause presented itself which at once took hold of me: the struggle of the Jews of Russia against the tyranny of the Soviet regime and the attempted obliteration of Judaism in the Soviet Union. Not that the fortunes of this great Jewish community have ever been good. Like most Jews of Eastern European origin, and of a certain age, I had long followed, with horror and pain, the Communist attempt to finish off what the Tsars had begun – when it came to Zionist and Jewish cultural activities. The persecution of Jews, the accusations and mock trials that led to the execution of hundreds of thousands, the Government-directed anti-Jewish campaigns that let hooligans loose to pillage, desecrate, torture and kill, the murder of Jewish leaders, writers, doctors and poets sent to their deaths on absurd charges or imprisoned and subjected to brutality, were not items I merely read in the paper and sighed over. They were wounds within me: Hebrew and Yiddish, languages that the Soviet Government tried so barbarically to erase, and for the teaching of which men were sentenced to hard labour in the frozen reaches of Siberia – these were the pillars upon which my childhood had rested, the languages I spoke at home, and through which my family had expressed love and intimacy. And in the same way, for me, the Jews of Russia had always held a special place: they had been among the first Zionist pioneers to come to Palestine between 1882 and the start of World War I when it was under Turkish rule, had founded many Jewish settlements and towns, and their numbers had included Israel's first President, its first Prime Minister and many members of the first Knesset. Without Russian Jews, I cannot begin to imagine the Zionist movement, the fight for the Jewish state or Israel's early years.

So there was never a time that I was reconciled to the separation between us and them, to their enforced isolation, to their captivity (because, in terms of Jewish life, that is what it was), or accept that nothing could be done, that the odds were too great and that the curtain obscuring our view of each other was too heavy to be raised. There was a moment – tragic in its wasted intensity – in the autumn of 1948 when Golda Meir went to Moscow as Israel's Minister to the USSR and, standing in front of that city's Great Synagogue on the eve of the Jewish New Year, was overwhelmed by a throng of cheering, sobbing Jews demonstrating their joy at the establishment of the state and their longing to be part of the miraculous event. Of course, the Soviet Government saw to it that this 'disloyalty' was punished; the Jews were pushed back into the grimness and misery from which, for an hour or two, they had emerged so bravely to declare themselves.

But in 1967, news of the IDF's victories in the Six Day War, of the unification of Jerusalem, and of the liberation of Judea and Samaria penetrated the Iron Curtain. Although the Soviet Government broke diplomatic relations with Israel (its role in the onset of that war is another story), the Jews signalled that they were desperate to join us and began to apply for visas to emigrate to Israel – and were, of course, refused and penalized. In Israel, two schools of thought developed: one, that whatever we did must be done discreetly, with quiet diplomacy, without unduly angering the Soviet Government, for otherwise we would only be further harming the Jews. The other, with which I agreed, called for a highly visible, very audible, unremitting effort that would embarrass and pressure the Soviet Government and leave no question in the minds of the refuseniks as to our determination to help them get out. I remember walking along a Tel Aviv street one day while all this was happening and suddenly thinking to myself, what indeed if we had all spoken louder in the 1930s and 1940s? It was a thought which didn't leave me for a long time.

The first time that I met some of the Russian Jews who had endured and prevailed and won the exit permits that made it possible for them to come, at last, to Israel – I think at once of Yasha Kazakov, Dov Shperling and Lydia Slovena, who became close friends – they stirred me as few people have done. I felt them to be heroes from an epic: spiritually intact despite everything they had lived through and suffered. Nothing of their yearning for Israel, of their pride in Judaism or of their essential personalities had been lost or distorted on the long road they had taken in order to join us. But the bond that developed between us was based on more than my admiration for them or their joy in the warmth of the reception they received. We related to each other on the level of people who knew about the workings of an underground, who had experienced the constant threat of exposure, who had been tracked by persistent authorities out to destroy that which lay at the core of their being. Everything we talked about for days, everything they told me about their clandestine activities, the secret seminars and lectures, the defiant samizdat publications, not only affected me but was also familiar. We were humans and Jews, activists and freedom fighters, and we understood each other.

It meant much to me that I was able to aid their effort – through people abroad and in ways still not to be revealed – both concretely as well as with judgment and advice, and that something of my past both in Lehi and the Mossad could be invested in this urgent cause.

My father, Shlomo Yezernitsky, head of the Jewish community in Rujenoy, opening a summer camp for poor children, 1930s.

My sister Miriam with her husband, Mottel Skalevich, 1930s. Both were killed in the Holocaust.

My sister Rivka Pitkovsky in the late 1920s. She was also killed in the Holocaust.

On my graduation day at the age of sixteen, Rujenoy, 1932.

Shulamit on her graduation day in Sofia, Bulgaria, 1940.

With a group of friends on a Tel Aviv roof-top, 1938.

Underground fighter, 1940s.

'Yair' – Abraham Stern.

British police 'Wanted' poster. I am at the bottom, extreme right; beside me is Nathan Yellin-Mor; and Menachem Begin is at the top, extreme left.

Exiled in Djibouti, 1947.

Shulamit with Yair in 1948, when I was in exile.

Back home, 1948.

Lehi leaders after emerging from the underground, 1949. Left to right: Matti Shmuelevitz, Nathan Yellin-Mor, myself and Israel Eldad.

With Shulamit, Tel Aviv, 1950s.

At the Western Wall after the Six Day War, 1967.

Menachem Begin, Anwar Sadat and myself, as Speaker of the Knesset, during Sadat's historic visit to Jerusalem, 1977.

Newly appointed Foreign Minister with Prime Minister Begin, 1980.

With President Sadat in 1980.

With President Hosni Mubarak after Sadat's funeral, Cairo, 1981.

My first Government, October 1983.

My first day in the Prime Minister's Office, October 1983. Left to right: Yehiel Kadishai, Matti Shmuelevitz, myself and Uri Porat.

I took my concern for Soviet Jewry – and my efforts on its behalf even since the late 1960s – to Herut in 1970 when I joined that Party, thus beginning my political career, as unaware that I was doing so as of the massive changes that would alter Russian history and the fate of thousands upon thousands of Russian Jews. To write about this, however, requires me first, if only in the most general terms, to write about Menachem Begin.

Like many others, perhaps more than most, I always hoped that one day, even from the seclusion into which he retired in 1983 – most of the time only a stone's throw from the Prime Minister's residence he occupied for six crucial years – Begin would decide to record, analyse and comment upon the great events in which he was involved and those which he initiated. I know he wanted to write at least one book about the Holocaust, but didn't. Certainly no serious study of modern Zionism, of contemporary Israel or of the Middle East in this second half of the twentieth century will pass him by, because his was a major impact, a leading role in the shaping, both literally and otherwise, of the Jewish state as we know it today.

It is both strange, and sad too, for me to find myself referring to Begin in this commemorative way. Even in his still-unexplained isolation, to all intents and purposes a recluse, on the surface he was surprisingly unchanged. When I visited him, we talked about the news, discussed latest developments and sometimes chatted about people. He was glad enough, I think, to see me, but neither of us were men to ask personal questions or intrude. I never tried to find out how he really felt about the way he lived or his abrupt withdrawal from society – and he never attempted to tell me. There were other unspoken agreements between us: I never asked for his advice (though there were times when the temptation to do so was very strong), nor did he ever proffer it. He selected a path that led him away from any active participation in or even the most theoretical responsibility for any aspect of national affairs. Abdicating in September 1983, he left behind him – to an extent few men could do, I think – the public personality that had made him commander of the Irgun, the all-powerful head of Herut, the brilliant leader of the Opposition and, in 1977, at last turning Israel's establishment inside out and upside down, the first non-Socialist Prime Minister and the first to make peace with an Arab state. His intellect, his keen mind and his curiosity remained unimpaired by the tragedies and depressions that apparently made life, as he had once lived it, unbearable for him.

I was, of course, acquainted with Begin long before I joined Herut. I had met him in Warsaw when I was studying law and he also a law student, had already made a reputation for himself in Revisionist circles. Jews talked about his 'oratory', the fervour of his Zionism and his influence within the Betar leadership. When I left for Palestine in 1935, I stopped at the Betar office to say goodbye and we exchanged a few words. It wasn't until the days of the underground, until after, in Poland, he had been arrested by the Russians, imprisoned in an Arctic hard labour camp and joined General Anders's army which brought him to Palestine in 1942, that I came to know him at all well. We had much in common: we were both born in Poland, about the same age, products of warm, traditional Zionist households (Begin was a more observant Jew than I), brought up to be proud of our Jewish heritage, militantly to demand equality and liberty for the Jewish people, and to have our adult lives, and thus many of our attitudes, permanently affected by the Holocaust. We understood each other, liked each other, and could and did work together.

But the differences in our personalities were no less significant. Begin was much concerned with form, with *hadar*, courtly gestures and ceremonies, while I felt these had no place either in the underground or, afterwards, in the governing process. The public's attitude towards him, the nature of his contacts with it, his perception of himself as reflected in the responses he evoked, mattered tremendously to him; like an actor, he drew strength, even inspiration, from the approving roar of a crowd or the applause of audiences. I wasn't a particular admirer of Begin's famous speeches; I felt them often to be filled with pathos and overstatement – though who could remain unimpressed by their power, their sarcasm and careful architecture? I was impatient with his deference to titles, his being awed by generals or professors, and I disliked his acceptance of flattery and fawning and wished, always in vain, that he were not so hungry for popularity. In fact, it surprised me that Begin had survived as he did, quite undiminished, the months he spent in the underground, in deep cover, deprived of such stimulus.

More importantly, he hadn't approved of, or understood, Lehi's modus operandi; he opposed all assassination. Going to war when there was no alternative was all right, but the singling out of one person, even of an informer, for execution was morally wrong in his eyes. He wanted courtrooms, trials, validation; cautious legal procedures that were impossible in the underground. Even there he cared, much more than I ever did, about what people said or thought. Like Jabotinsky, the idol, whom in many ways he emulated, for much of the period of the struggle against the British he went on believing in the primary importance of the political effort and its priority over armed conflict. 'Do you really think you can create a state with pistols?' he asked me once before he became commander of the Irgun, before we were both disguised in our rabbinical blacks. But when the time came for open warfare, he was interested in co-operating with Lehi, even in the creation of a united underground with us – provided that we acknowledge Jabotinsky as our authority and mentor, which, of course, we could not do. So there was never a formal union between the Irgun and Lehi, only a measure of co-operation that waxed and waned.

It was as the leader of Herut after independence that Begin's skills as tactician, his acute political sensitivities, his Parliamentary presence and his flair for the dramatic, all flowered – nourished by the attention and admiration not only of those in his immediate vicinity, but also of the Israeli masses and many of his opponents. Recognition, compliments and the appreciation of outsiders made him feel accepted and respectable, no longer an outlaw. That Moshe Dayan, whom he made his Foreign Minister, thought highly of his patriotism and gentlemanly qualities, and crossed over from the Labour benches to join the Likud-led Cabinet of 1977, pleased Begin inordinately even though he must have known that his pleasure in such dazzling 'outside' acquisitions often hurt and offended people inside Herut. I suppose that I, too, was a kind of acquisition from outside, that Lehi was my 'calling card', and in this respect, in his eyes, I was also a 'catch'. He was delighted when he learned that I was interested in the Party, did whatever he could to help me acclimatize within the new environment, and nothing to hinder me from rapid ascent – though he also did little to promote me.

During those years, there were stretches when we spent much time together. One such was in the course of the trouble in which the Party found itself over the Tel-Hai Fund. This had been established by Herut in the early 1950s as a private company engaged in commercial transactions and fund-raising to pay off debts incurred by the Irgun in 1947, and which became involved in a number of scandals because it took loans and couldn't produce capital upon request. Begin was distraught; the idea that Herut's name, Jabotinsky's name, his name should be linked with dishonour and failure maddened him. I promised to help him get the money back, and for months sat, literally, besieged in the Party headquarters in Tel Aviv, staving off debtors while Begin travelled the world, sparing no time or effort in his search for donations. He got them somehow; supporters rallied, someone lent us $1 million in cash, and by the end of 1977 everything was paid back. It took nearly four years but Herut was saved, though I sometimes thought that it was the Tel-Hai débâcle that first ruined his health. From then on, sickness, accidents, depression and sorrow followed, each in turn taking its toll until even his accomplishments and world fame couldn't sustain him. There were disloyalties that pained him more than he chose publicly to reveal; the limited war in the north, designed to bring peace to Galilee, turned into the long, cruel Lebanese war; his wife, Aliza, died while he was reluctantly abroad. It was all too much, so he went home and stayed there.

Of Begin's invitation to Anwar Sadat, Sadat's historic visit to Jerusalem, Camp David and its sequels, Begin's Nobel Peace Prize, most people know – and I shall return to some of these topics later. What is less known, perhaps, is Begin's role in the difficult, essential, not-yet-finished work of integrating the thousands upon thousands of Jews who came to Israel during, and after, 1948 from the Arabic-speaking countries of the Middle East and North Africa and bolstering their sense – in a way that no one else in this country did – of their own worth and rightful place within the state. Politics? Yes, of course, to some extent. But how astonishing that this Jew (Begin was fluent in nine languages, but not Arabic), whose natural 'constituency', now perished, had been in Poland, Russia, the Baltic states and the Balkans, found his way alone to the so-called Oriental Jews in the misery and starkness of the transit camps, listened to their tales of woe, spoke to them about their problems, and won their hearts and allegiance. He was in no position then to make promises or to improve their situation, but he knew that the immigration of the North African Jews was different from most others, that they were Zionists from birth, not needing to be taught the love of Zion, or spiritually or psychologically readied for the great move. They had always, naturally and unwaveringly, felt the Land of Israel to be their homeland. Brought up like that generation after generation, they needed help and support only in the actual mechanism of getting there and finding their place in the new society. They hadn't even had obstacles placed in the way of their emigration by the rulers of the countries in which they lived, or been punished for wanting to be part of the return of the Jews to their Land. There were some exceptions, very few: a tiny percentage of North African Jews, assimilated into French culture, chose to settle in France or French-speaking Canada. But overwhelmingly North African Jews yearned for Israel – as did the Jews of the Middle East, though the roads these had to take to reach us were harder, by far, to travel.

Drawn to Begin, by the imagery and passion of his speeches, his burning love of the Land and the enduring centrality of Jerusalem – which echoed their own deepest emotions – and by his sharing these with them in person, he won their hearts. And when the 'upheaval' of 1977 took place and the four-party conservative–liberal Likud bloc he headed came into power, those new immigrants to whom he, but not Ben-Gurion, had come in the time of their trouble, voted for him. Many Likud members today are the children of those newcomers, better equipped than were their parents to see to it that the social, economic and educational gap between them and other strata of Israeli society closes completely, however belatedly, and it is they who streamed, unsummoned, from all over the country, in their multitudes, to attend Begin's simple funeral in Jerusalem in March 1992. They had loved and trusted him, and no one could have, or has, taken his place for them. It must also be recorded that it was directly due to this identification with Begin that first through Herut, and later via the Likud bloc, this 'second generation' of new immigrants entered the Israeli establishment as holders of extremely important civic and national positions within it, thus contributing immensely to the totality of their communities' absorption and integration.

One other insight into Begin's uncanny political instincts – in some respects, and certainly in Israel, they were unique – can be gained by noting that he also turned, at the same time, to the political centre, to the urban-educated, bourgeois sector, bringing Israel's Liberal Party, so long a stronghold of staid, enlightened Western European Jews, into the Likud structure. In fact, there can be no doubt that if there is a true 'nationalist' movement in Israel, it is Begin's doing, and I believe therefore that on this score too the State of Israel is indebted to him.

It was fascinating and highly instructive to watch Begin with non-Israelis who were often awed, baffled, annoyed or otherwise affected by him but never, to my knowledge, indifferent. He often met the US Ambassador Samuel Lewis, whom he called Sam, always a sign of cordiality because, when he was angry with someone, he restricted himself to surnames. But at particularly tense moments 'Sam' too was 'demoted' to 'Mr Ambassador'. At such times, Begin would become very sharp-tongued. Lewis came one day with a special emissary despatched by the US President to 'discuss' the Knesset law of December 1981 applying Israeli law, jurisdiction and administration to the Golan Heights. In the middle of the conversation, Begin suddenly lashed out at the two Americans. 'Tell me, do you by any chance think this is a banana republic?' They were stunned into silence by his attack.

I witnessed another occasion when Begin's response left his important listener speechless – though this time he was being both his long-winded and his witty self. It was at a meeting with President Carter at which the significant question of the participation of the Arabs of East Jerusalem in the elections to the Administrative Council (to be created in the autonomy, according to the Camp David Accords) had come up – and Begin had heatedly repeated his strenuous objection to what he rightly regarded as a possible loophole for disputing the legality and status of united Jerusalem, this being, by the national consensus, permanently and totally a subject closed to discussion or negotiation. 'Yes, I know,' Carter said patiently, 'but don't say "No" at once. Think it over.' 'Well,' Begin said, let me tell you a story, Mr President.' Carter, who did not especially like Begin, was visibly astonished when Begin launched into the sad tale of Rabbi Amnon of Mainz, a legendary tenth-century figure, under much pressure from the local bishop to convert. 'Think it over,' said the bishop, so Amnon asked for three days so that he could do that. But he didn't turn up on time, his conscience having greatly pained him. Contritely he proposed that his tongue be cut out for not having said 'No' at once. 'Not your tongue, but the legs that didn't bring you here,' said the bishop, who ordered the Rabbi's arms and legs to be amputated and salt poured into the wounds. 'So you see, Mr President, what can happen if one thinks things over.' Carter was in a state of shock; the story itself, its moral and the speed with which Begin produced it were too much for him. Even I was a bit taken aback; and when talks began again, it wasn't about the Arabs of East Jerusalem and the autonomy.

At other times, he annoyed non-Israeli listeners (and, come to think of it, many Israelis too) by adopting a very didactic manner; 'preaching' to people who felt no need of being preached at, certainly not about the Holocaust, which Begin, unjustly, was often accused of using as an oratorical 'gimmick'. He felt it his obligation to history to remind gentiles, in particular, of what had happened and to whom, and he didn't care that he was charged with demagoguery or that he frequently risked making his audience squirm.

What could be called 'my apprenticeship' in Herut was not only short but also relatively uneventful. Within the Party, founded by Irgun veterans, mine was not a new face; my name stood for something and, after all, Lehi and the Irgun had shared a common past. By then, too, most veterans of both undergrounds knew and accepted the fact that the original split had not been necessary, and that the parting of ways between Yair and Raziel had contained no element of spite or personal grudge. Besides, these were other times and other challenges. Also my sponsors, so to speak, were impeccable: founding fathers of the Irgun's so-called 'Fighting Family'. Arieh Ben-Eliezer, Yaakov Meridor and Haim Landau were among Begin's closest advisers, and all of them wanted me in the Party. Ben-Eliezer had shared Djibouti with me; I had known Meridor in the early days of the struggle; and Haim Landau was active on behalf of Soviet Jewry, in which context we had met. Since Herut had already set up a unit devoted to this campaign and the Party's voice was the most penetrating of those raised in Israel, it made sense for that area to be the starting-point of my Herut activities. The topic became identified with me. I talked about it at meetings, kept it in the forefront of people's attention, and dealt directly with the many Russians who came for advice and help to Party headquarters.

Then came the one-man insurrection of Ezer Weizman. Ezer, a sabra, well-born in Zionist terms (a nephew of Dr Chaim Weizmann), an ex-RAF pilot, a founder and a former commander-in-chief of the Israeli air force, was chairman of the executive committee of the Herut Party in the days that preceded the creation of the Likud bloc. In the 1970s, he was a favourite of the press and of a large section of the public that regarded him as dashing, even glamorous. I did not share this view of him; I thought him to be politically a lightweight, excessively ambitious and unreliable. Not surprisingly, he didn't particularly like me either, nor did he welcome my presence in Herut. When he made a bid to take over the Party and reduce Begin to a figurehead, together with other colleagues (chiefly Haim Landau) I helped to put down the 'uprising'. A new executive was formed. Among those who left in the wake of Weizman's failed putsch was the man who had directed the Party's Organization Department, which Begin now asked me to head.

My daily schedule lengthened beyond recognition. I was representing an investment company in a plant located not far from Tel Aviv, rose before dawn and was at my desk before anyone else. Around 3 p.m., I would go home, eat the lunch Shulamit left me (she had taken an afternoon job in a travel agency), and went off to Herut headquarters, where I often worked (of course, on a purely voluntary basis) till midnight or later. The days seemed to have no end, but I was never tired. The activity stimulated me; I was getting to know another Israel. I enjoyed being with people and, above all, felt that what I was doing mattered, not very much perhaps, but somewhat – and that, in itself, meant something to me. Herut was Israel's second largest party with branches throughout the country and thousands of members, all of whom wanted to feel that, however isolated they might be in their Negev development towns or northern villages, they were still an integral part of a political mechanism that had its say in the way that Israel was run and that could, and did, represent their interests and express the ideology in which they believed.

The subjects raised at the branch meetings I attended were not primarily local problems, but rather the state's complex geopolitical and demographic dilemmas: the future of Judea, Samaria and the Gaza Strip, our relationships (or lack of them) with the Arab states and so forth. I used to return home immensely encouraged by the spirit, calibre and intelligence of the so-called average Israeli which said much, I thought, about the sources, the roots, of Israel's ability to withstand and survive.

In the aftermath of the Weizman episode, I found myself called upon to fill a variety of roles that involved helping to put the Party together again. That threat to Begin's leadership had not been the first, but it was among the most serious, and he was more than usually cautious about who occupied key positions and the extent to which the 'plasterers', summoned to repair the cracks, could themselves be trusted. In 1973, I became a Member of the eighth Knesset on behalf of Herut. I left work and, at the age of fifty-eight, turned into a full-time politician. The Knesset was more than a stepping-stone, or even a platform, for me. I was, I felt, at the centre of Israel's life as a democracy; not prominent, not a party leader, still I was nearer than I had been since the days of Lehi to having a voice in national affairs, no longer on the sidelines, and I regarded this as a privilege and a welcome duty. Here and there, I was even noticed. I served on the Foreign Affairs and Defence Committees, proposed the establishment of a committee for Jewish affairs to strengthen the bonds between Israel and the Diaspora, and was amused to see recently that I had been singled out for praise even by the Parliamentary reporter of the *Jerusalem Post*, Israel's English-language daily, which rarely, until the 1990s, found kind words for me.

Describing a typical debate on the administered territories and the new settlements in Judea and Samaria, the *Post* wrote: 'Mr Yitzhak Shamir is a clear, vigorous speaker,' and quoted a statement that might, I realize as I re-read it, have been made only yesterday – though this was in the autumn of 1974:

The dominant element in the Israel–Arab relationship is that those Arab groupings which do not recognize our right to live in the Land of Israel [i.e. the entire historic area] also do not recognize our right to live in part of the Land of Israel. ... And the enemy to whom these proposals [to return some areas] are directed, repeats stubbornly that he is willing to take back the areas but peace – that not. What is the point of one-way deals?

The correspondent then went on to write: 'Mr Shamir also said it was time we learned to believe our enemies when they say that they wish to destroy us. Who, after all, believed Hitler when he wrote in *Mein Kampf* that he would destroy all the Jews of Europe if he ever got the chance?' Not enough has changed since then. How tragic that is.

Despite my daily journey to Jerusalem, we decided not to move from Tel Aviv; our friends, our children's friends, our natural habitat were there. We lived as usual very quietly, seeing a few other couples, chiefly from Lehi, on Friday nights; going for long walks along the beach on Saturday mornings; and each Tuesday evening my son Yair and I would meet over snacks that Shulamit prepared for us, and talk – not so much about personal matters, but more about Israel, the world, what was going to happen, talks that were to be continued in the form of Friday night phone calls, a tradition he and I established when the move to Jerusalem finally took place. The 'highlight' of our social calendar was always a party on the eve of Independence Day with the friends closest to us and a walk together through Tel Aviv in the earliest hours of the next morning. Like young parents, annually we celebrated yet another year achieved by the growing state, watching it become ever stronger, though still never entirely out of danger.

6

THE UPHEAVALS

NINETEEN SEVENTY-SEVEN WAS the year of the great 'upheaval'. On 17 May, in the general elections for the ninth Knesset, the Likud gained the largest number of seats and, on 7 June, Menachem Begin was invited by Israel's President, Professor Ephraim Katzir, to form a government.

It was inevitable that this would happen. In fact, for years I had been sure, and said so, that a transfer of power would take place, the question being only when. The jubilation of 1967 – the joy that accompanied the swift victories of the Six Day War, the unification of Jerusalem, the liberation of Samaria and Judea that created new settlements throughout the Land of Israel, reaching from the Golan Heights in the north to the southernmost tip of the Sinai Peninsula – had died down. The old–new contours were taken for granted by most people, fiercely upheld by others, and even more fiercely disputed by those to whom the problems posed by the then one million-odd Arabs living under Israeli control in those areas was paramount.

A National Unity Government had been established during the war and Begin sworn in as a minister without portfolio, a position he occupied until the summer of 1970. That year, he and five colleagues of the Herut–Liberal bloc had resigned over Prime Minister Golda Meir's acceptance of a US proposal (the Rogers Plan) for peace negotiations with Egypt and Jordan, which was based on an Israeli withdrawal from the 'administered territories' and described by Begin as the Middle Eastern version of Munich. However, the fact that the nationalist camp had participated in the governing process and that Begin had won the approval, even the admiration, of circles traditionally and violently opposed to him and to what he represented, became increasingly important as time passed.

The Yom Kippur War of 1973 had been traumatic; it had destroyed long-standing mythologies, showed up the establishment's unwarranted complacency and, to put it bluntly, given the people of Israel the feeling that the country was in the wrong hands. The dramatic hijacking of a French airbus by German and PLO terrorists and the breathtaking raid and rescue of its passengers by a special IDF unit at Entebbe in 1976 cheered the nation up and, for a few days, lessened the depression and tension of a grim post-war period, but didn't change anything – or save the Labour Party. Furthermore, Labour, having done a bad job for years, was now exposed not only as incompetent but also, in large measure, as corrupt. One disgraceful revelation followed another: there were bankruptcies, jail sentences, suicides. Even years later, major Histadrut companies continued to collapse and close for lack of proper management, to be charged with 'unreliable' financial reporting, gross negligence and unprofessional behaviour, and thousands of trade unionists were thrown out of work as plants shut and insolvent factories locked their doors all over Israel.

The public, shocked and disillusioned, registered its emotions at the first opportunity, the elections held after the Yom Kippur War. At those 1973 polls, the Labour bloc lost some seats, the Likud gained some, but most significantly a protest vote had emerged that was to prove decisive four years later. In 1977, a new party, the Democratic Movement for Change (DMC), led by the late Professor Yigael Yadin, the noted archaeologist, author and second commander-in-chief of the IDF, took enough votes away from Labour to make the Likud Israel's largest party – although the DMC goal had been to punish Labour and teach it accountability rather than to hand laurels to the Likud. The DMC (opposed to withdrawal to the pre-Six Day War borders but willing to negotiate with the PLO if that infamous body recognized Israel) was a passing phenomenon: by the 1981 elections it had ceased to exist. Its role, however, had been crucial.

Begin was not well during most of the 1977 campaign (he had suffered a heart attack) and barely took part in it. But Ezer Weizman, accomplishing a return to the fold, was energetically in action, eager to do well as manager of the Likud's bid for success. The public was fed-up, and proved it. But that didn't mean that in press rooms, on campuses, within the crowded ranks of the Labourites on the one hand and those of the free professions on the other, the idea of a Likud (or Likud-led) government was not anathema. There were even people who proclaimed that they were not sure whether they could go on living in what, they were certain, would from now on be a Fascist state. But, after a while, Herut and its associates in the Likud were shown to be flesh and blood and Begin's Cabinet reassuringly included known and respected personalities: Yigael Yadin, who became Deputy Prime Minister; Ezer Weizman, Minister of Transport; Ariel Sharon, initially responsible for agriculture and settlement; and Moshe Dayan as Foreign Minister. Not all these reputations stood the test of time and Begin's weakness for generals was very apparent, but so were his timing, his integrity and his stubborn belief that peace could be achieved – despite the daunting fact that no Israeli Prime Minister had yet received an affirmative response from any Arab leader to the peace initiative each one had repeatedly suggested.

Considering the war so doggedly waged for half a century or more against the nationalist camp in its various forms, the suspicion and maligning to which all conservative and right-of-Labour enterprises and persons were subjected, and the horror for many in seeing those who had governed for so long with such confidence in their political immortality now occupying the benches of the Opposition, the dust settled quickly – and I found myself embarking upon responsibilities of the sort I could never, in any flight of imagination, have foreseen. In 1975, I had been elected chairman of the Party executive, in which capacity I had worked during the election campaign, conducting long, complicated negotiations with Herut's partners in the Likud bloc, mainly the Liberal Party; soothing hurt feelings, attempting Solomonic judgments and dealing with branches and centre alike. Internal nomination and election procedures within the Party had already been much streamlined and democratized, but not sufficiently. I organized a committee charged with recommending to the Party's nomination committee a new system for choosing candidates for the Knesset, in groups of seven, that allowed for sifting, correction and re-sifting, and was considered very progressive, though later its usefulness wore out. Its most striking 'fringe benefit' was that it brought to the Likud's Knesset faction an outstanding group of bright, attractive, involved young people, among whom some – later to be known as the 'Likud princes' because they were the sons of prominent right-wingers – went on to become ranking ministers in my Cabinets.

After the elections, Begin asked me to become Speaker of the Knesset, and I agreed. Was it enough? Was it what I wanted? Should the offer have been a Ministry or at least a Cabinet seat? My friends and the family – Shulamit, Yair and Gilada – all certainly thought so, and told me that I had been wronged and shouldn't accept the proffered 'crumb'. But I didn't see it that way. I would have liked a policy-making role, to have a hand in the political changes that Herut would now bring about in Israeli society and that were of such interest to me, and that were bound to be of critical importance. But it was psychologically impossible for me to lobby for myself, to campaign, to try in any way to 'sell' my purported abilities, though I knew that this was acceptable procedure. My inhibitions, I think, stemmed largely from my upbringing, from the emphasis at home on modesty, the abhorrence with which my parents regarded any self-serving and their contempt for people who 'pushed' themselves to the fore. And partly, I was too proud or old-fashioned or puritanical to ask anything of anyone – and I have never done, or needed to do, so. I knew that while in terms of protocol the Speaker's position was a lofty one (in terms of hierarchy second only to the President of the state), in reality it usually marked the end of the incumbent's career, but I didn't think that this was inevitable or that being Speaker automatically precluded all other opportunities. And, indeed, in my case, it certainly didn't. In fact, I actually created a precedent in that respect. I also thought that the Knesset would be an ideal place from which to study the mechanics of statehood, to learn the details of democracy in action, and how other political parties and personalities interacted, traded, connected and separated in the manoeuvring for control which is the essence of Parliamentary life, and I withstood all arguments to the contrary that were presented to me.

My installation took place in the middle of June 1977. The family, including my small grandson Dror, was present in force and, I think, despite their initial high feelings on the matter, quite excited. So, however business-like and matter-of-fact the procedure (and my own behaviour) was, I found myself moved by the brief ceremony, by the price that had been paid – in various currencies – so that there could be a parliament of a Jewish state and wished my parents could have been there. It would have made them happy.

Early that morning I had remembered that I would need to say something and wrote down a few words. After I was sworn in as a Knesset Member (together with the other Members present – there are 120 in all), I talked for only a minute or two. I started out with generalities, thanked the Members for the honour paid to me and mentioned, obliquely, the special character of the ninth Knesset. Then I made a personal statement:

Allow me, from this seat [I said], to express some fraction of what I feel as I recall to memory the anonymous heroes of the underground, those who gave their lives in the fight for Israel's freedom and thanks to whom all of us – and I – have come this far and reached this day. It is for me as though they sit here, on this dais now, in these minutes, watching and listening, and their souls sing with joy, and shine with a light like the glory of the firmament.

I spoke of all those who had fought and died for independence, but in particular for the people who had fought with me – and those who listened to me knew this though, among them, were some who still disapproved.

The two-and-a-half years I spent as Speaker of the Knesset opened up a whole new world for me – a world of rules and regulations, of observing not only Israel but also, to some extent, human nature as such, from angles that were fresh to me. They involved me in the never-to-be repeated experience of Sadat's visit to Jerusalem; and, mostly through television, familiarized the Israeli public with my name and face. Thus they also changed Shulamit's life, confronting her with protocol, the entertainment of important visitors, rounds of diplomatic parties and official travel abroad. One of the first of these trips included our visit to Great Britain as guests of the Speaker of the House of Commons (then George Thomas), in which past associations went, for all concerned, largely unnoticed though I had a chance at an official banquet to declare – only half-believing it was really I who spoke – that '... we did not always enjoy good relations with British Governments, but that never stopped us from admiring your Parliamentary heritage'. I also met with Prime Minister Margaret Thatcher, who saw to it that not the past but the present, i.e. economics, formed the topic of our talk. 'Imagine', Shulamit said to me on one of those days, 'those months and months in the Bethlehem prison and here we are, surrounded by honours. The circle has closed.' Correct as the British were, the climate was even warmer across the Channel in France, where we were hosted by Senate President Alain Poher. Later, I visited Strasbourg as head of a Knesset delegation to the European Parliament, whose distinguished and charming President, Simone Weil, a frequent visitor to Israel, greeted us with special warmth and all the members – except the Communists – rose to applaud us. There were journeys to Scandinavia, to the Far East, again and again to Europe; everywhere there was a lot to learn and much to see.

I also declared war on the unrestrained freedom of speech, and often of manner, displayed by the Members of the Knesset. When the gavel and reproaches were not enough to quell the fervour and the noise, I used harsher methods: first silencing the microphones on the Members' desks and then having them removed altogether ('The Speaker has taken the first step to liquidating Israeli democracy,' shouted the spokesman for one left-wing party), and employing other such autocratic tactics. Of course, there were extenuating circumstances: the Labour bloc was adjusting to a distasteful secondary role; the inexperience of the new ministers who had never handled an Opposition before; the vehemence with which Israelis tend to express themselves on most subjects; and bad habits acquired over thirty years. But after a while, my insistence on raising the level of debate, both in the plenum and in committee, bore fruit. I was also determined to uphold and, whenever possible, contribute to the Knesset tradition of impartiality where Arab and Druse Members were concerned – and made a consistent effort in this direction.

What interested me more than vigilance over the Members conduct were such activities as the 'Inter-Parliamentary Union' (IPU) which met once a year, was the most senior of all existing international organizations, but lacked a real purpose. Its membership was then made up of over 100 countries of which less than a third could lay claim to being democracies and which were grouped into all kinds of blocs: Warsaw Pact, Islamic, Non-Aligned, African, European Community, American, etc., into none of which Israel could be fitted. I thought that the voice of real Parliamentarianism should be heard, that the democracies, Israel among them, had much to say in their own right, especially since the UN in those days no longer constituted an appropriate forum for them, and that the IPU would make an eminently suitable substitute as well as justifying its existence. Everybody I spoke to about this said, 'Good idea,' but no one was prepared to take action. I believed also that this organization could collectively strive to provide answers to problems not restricted to given nations but that trouble contemporary society in general: how to preserve state secrets without imposing censorship; how to prevent freedom of expression from deteriorating into anarchy; how to combat terrorism without resorting to emergency regulations. I found other intellectual distractions in the Knesset's fine library and reference facilities, with their pleasant staff and thousands of books and periodicals. For the first time since I was a very young man in Warsaw I indulged in reading, in tranquil hours between sessions and sittings, the historical and political literature, mostly non-fiction, that I liked best, and laboured at my English, which was almost non-existent and which I thought the Speaker should know well – though some of my predecessors had managed with an interpreter.

Then there were the people who took to dropping in to my handsome office (far larger and more impressive than any other I was to occupy). Among my guests there were the Knesset Members who wanted to resign, for whatever reason, and came to give formal notice. Regardless of their political affiliation, I always regretted these visits. I felt a little like the manager of a club whose members were drifting away. I remember in particular two Members coming to make the sad announcements; one had been Minister of Justice, the other Minister of Education – men of considerable calibre. They had become useless, they explained, each one separately; they had no influence, nothing to do. I understood them then – and perhaps even better now, though my days are still very full – and I thought to myself that the Knesset would be poorer, greyer, without them and that a way should be found to retain their experience and knowledge. There were the Communists, mostly Arabs, who came constantly to argue at length over the most delicate shadings of what they took to be possible infringements – however minute – of their right to free speech; and the members of Agudat Israel, most orthodox of the religious parties in the Knesset. In plenary sessions there were no Members as vociferous as they were, for ever on their feet, protesting, demanding, warning, but in the Speaker's Office they were the politest, most deferential visitors, always impeccably groomed from beards to shoes, always apologetic about disturbing, but none the less eager for prolonged discussions with me on budgetary matters. And there were the regular callers who had no real business, but came by to air opinions over a glass of tea or a cup of coffee. One such was Israel Yeshayahu, who had been Speaker before me, and was the doyen of Israel's Yemenite Jews and a loyal Labourite, who liked the chance, now and then, to complain about colleagues and to talk wistfully, in his wonderful musical Hebrew, about Ben-Gurion and the way it used to be. It was he who so ardently championed the idea of an Upper House for, he explained, more reflective, less pressured consideration of vital issues than was currently possible. It would be a good thing for the Knesset and for Israel, he said, and he may have been right.

Certainly the most momentous event to take place in the Knesset – not only while I was Speaker but, in all probability, ever – was the visit of Egypt's President, Anwar Sadat. Forty-eight hours after his plane landed in Israel on the evening of Saturday, 19 November 1977, a new era began in the history of the Middle East. For the first time, Israelis were able, seriously, to entertain the possibility of almost immediate peace – real peace, that is, not some theoretical academic arrangement contrived for activating at a distant moment, given such-and-such circumstances, but peace that would alter individual lives, reflect itself in the absence of danger and open up new vistas, figuratively and otherwise. The sheer drama, the suddenness and the magnetism of Sadat's physical presence not only allowed but compelled the public to take hope again and to imagine what it would be like when one-time and recent enemies at last became good neighbours – that vision which, ever since 1948, Israel had held up to the Arabs and which they had so consistently rejected.

Nearly a decade and a half have passed since the intoxication of Sadat's visit; many of the central players have left the stage, and the stage itself has darkened. Many Israeli expectations raised in the course of that astonishing encounter, and for months after it, have been dashed, raised, dashed and raised again. There have been disappointments and a graceless lack of symmetry between the form and content which we have judged suitable in the new relationship and the grudging guidelines set forth and adamantly maintained by Egypt. Nor have the terms of the Treaty of Peace signed in Washington in March 1979 between the two countries yet been fulfilled in their entirety by Cairo, though Israel has kept its promises, however difficult it has been. But that which moved Sadat, which fired him and induced him to risk not only his life but also Egypt's standing in the Arab world, that promise of 'no more war' the words he repeated so often in the brief remainder of his life – *that* has survived, and so his efforts were not in vain, not for Israel and certainly not for Egypt.

I can find no better word than 'earthquake' even today to describe the sight of Sadat descending from his plane at Tel Aviv airport, bedecked with Egyptian and Israeli flags, shaking hands with Begin and Katzir, the Cabinet, the Chief Rabbis, Ariel Sharon (who had led the Israeli counter-attack across the Suez Canal in 1973) and Moshe Dayan, and smiling at people like Golda Meir whom he had never met but instantly recognized. The public and press were beside themselves: newspapers put out special editions welcoming Sadat in Arabic; wherever he went, men, women and schoolchildren stood for hours to catch a glimpse of him, cheering and sometimes weeping with joy, excitement and the momentary quenching of an over-whelming thirst for peace. Nothing I write about the yearning with which Sadat was received here can be exaggerated, nor about the subsequent apprehension and growing chill with which I listened to him in the Knesset.

Inside the Knesset, however, elation had to make way for an organizational effort of the scope generally reserved for national emergencies. We had two days – the Knesset, of course, being closed on Saturday – in which the Clerk of the Knesset, his staff, the political factions, the Knesset Guard, the caterers and I had to be deployed, instructed and rehearsed, protocol learned and observed, arrangements made for security and for the never-satisfied media. Even the name of the other country involved required a command decision:

was it 'The Arab Republic of Egypt'? Or would 'Egypt' do (it
did) in the many and various formal salutations and invitations to
be readied? And none of these considerations could compete with the
tension of compiling invitation lists to meet even minimal requirements.

Despite midnight predictions to the contrary, Sunday, 20 November, dawned. Sadat attended early morning prayers at the El Aksa
mosque in Jerusalem's Old City, visited Yad Vashem, Israel's memorial
to the Jews murdered in the Holocaust, and arrived at the Knesset
gates, where I received him and watched as he reviewed the Guard
of Honour and placed a wreath at another memorial, this one to
Israel's war dead. I looked at the flame of its Eternal Light, at the
solemn guest in a dark suit standing silently before it, and wondered,
as I suppose most Israelis must have done, about his thoughts, but
Sadat's face gave nothing away. In my office we made small talk ('I
too was a Speaker for a long time. A hard job,' Sadat said) and, at 4
p.m. sharp, entered the hall.

Certain general similarities between Sadat and Begin came out, it
seemed to me, in their speeches that afternoon – apart from the
common search for peace: both were religious men, their intense
nationalism derived from a sense of mission that, in turn, was rooted
in the scripture in which each deeply believed and, therefore, in the
spirit of their forefathers. They spoke, each in his own fashion, easily,
and often, of God, quoting from the Koran and the Old Testament,
each ending his speech with similar words, Sadat proclaiming 'Love,
right and justice', while Begin's closing words were 'Love, truth and
peace'. Sadat made sure that there could be no misunderstanding of
his intentions nor of the cost of peace: Israel's complete withdrawal
to the 1967 borders was the *sine qua non* of any further *rapprochement*.
'There is no peace that could be in consonance with . . . the occupation
of the land of others', he declared firmly (and incorrectly for, of
course, there are many historical precedents). The tone of Begin's
address was more conciliatory, less unequivocal. He spoke of issuing
a similar invitation to the President of Syria and to Jordan's King
Hussein, and of opening up both countries to free movement; he also
talked about the Holocaust and the history of the Jews. He was only
really militant in denying that Israel had occupied 'the territory of
others'. 'No, sir,' he thundered. 'We took no foreign country . . . we
came back to our homeland.' But, he said, 'we shall conduct these
negotiations as equals, no victors and no vanquished; all the peoples
in this area are equals'. The third speaker was Opposition Leader
Shimon Peres, who, since the Opposition did not oppose peace, could

only urge that the negotiations, whenever and however they took place, not fail.

The Israel–Egypt Peace Treaty was finally signed on the lawn of the White House in March 1979. The Camp David Accords on which the Treaty was based were at the heart of Israel's hopes for the future and, though far from ideal, were the most feasible and promising formula available for the achievement of peace, possibly even of normalcy, if not with the entire Arab world, then at least with its largest, strongest and most influential member. The tortuous negotiations that had been carried on so tenaciously, painstakingly and solemnly by Begin, Sadat, Jimmy Carter and their teams (the Israeli delegation including Moshe Dayan and Ezer Weizman, then Minister of Defence), lasted for sixteen months, beginning immediately after Sadat's visit to Jerusalem.

What exactly are the much-publicized Accords? Let me try to summarize their essence, apologizing in advance to readers who already know all this. Entered into by Egypt, Israel and the United States, their name deriving from the US Presidential retreat at which the major stipulations (in the form of two 'framework agreements') were hammered out from 5 to 17 September 1978, the Accords provide guidelines not only for peace between Egypt and Israel but also between Israel and those of its Arab neighbours who are prepared to negotiate on the same basis – thus attempting to offer a specific, far-reaching solution to the so-called 'Palestine problem'.

The 'Framework for the Conclusion of a Peace Treaty between Israel and Egypt' calls for 'the full exercise of Egyptian sovereignty' in Sinai up to the 'internationally recognized border between Egypt and Mandated Palestine' and the withdrawal of Israeli armed forces from the Peninsula; goes into some detail regarding the stationing of UN military forces in various border regions; declares that the terms must be implemented between two and three years after signature; bestows on Israeli shipping the right of free passage through such international waterways as the Suez Canal, the Tiran Straits and the Gulf of Akaba; allows for construction of a highway between Sinai and Jordan with 'free and peaceful' passage by Egypt and Jordan; and for 'normal and friendly relations' to be established between Israel and Egypt, including full recognition, diplomatic, economic and cultural relations and the mutual protection of citizens.

The 'Framework for Peace in the Middle East' is vaguer, leaves more room for negotiation but places greater responsibility on, and clearly demands the larger sacrifice from, Israel. Most importantly, it lays the theoretical groundwork for a self-governing authority (administrative council) for Judea, Samaria and Gaza for a transition period of five years – during which the residents of these areas (i.e. Palestinian Arabs) run their own lives and administrative affairs; and the withdrawal of the IDF, making way for the redeployment of remaining Israeli troops in specified locations. The negotiations on the future of those autonomous areas are to determine their final status, to conclude a peace treaty between Israel and Jordan, and to be conducted by representatives of Egypt, Israel, Jordan and 'elected spokesmen' of the inhabitants. And so forth.

Reading the actual text of the Accords is illuminating; among other things, they are, perhaps unavoidably, written in a style which reveals nothing of the past, as though the conflicts referred to were equally the fault of all sides and recent. What, however, does emerge with depressing clarity is that the concessions made by Israel directly to Egypt in the Peace Treaty, most especially the return of ninety per cent of the territory administered by Israel since 1967 (with all that this implies in terms of the investment of Israeli energy, money – and hopes), were not enough. For Israel to receive the guarantee of peace – surely a minimal birthright – it was required also to veil heavily, if not deny altogether, the abiding Jewish claim to the Land of Israel, a thought worthy of attention today. A variety of Appendices, Annexes and Articles were added to the Frameworks in the months of talks before the Treaty signing, but the above represents the kernel, the heart of the agreements as brought by Begin to the Knesset for its approval.

Not yet a member of the Government, I was not party to the Camp David deliberations nor kept privately *au courant* regarding the many various setbacks – and less frequent gains. In fact, I was abroad in Denmark (heading a Parliamentary delegation) and thunderstruck to learn that we had agreed, pending Knesset approval, to Israel's total withdrawal from Sinai – including, naturally, from the northern Rafiah Salient with its flourishing young Israeli settlements and the model town of Yamit that the Israeli Government had helped to build, had consistently backed and that had literally flowered in the desert. It was difficult for me to imagine that Begin had accepted even the possibility of these Jewish settlements being uprooted, and, in great suspense, I waited for confirmation of a decision that I regarded (and have never since ceased to regard) not only as wrong in itself but also as a disastrous precedent. When it came to the Knesset vote, I had no alternative other than to abstain – though I knew it would anger Begin – not because I was opposed to peace (how stupid such allegations are), nor because I was intrinsically against the

Frameworks (or later the Treaty itself), but because to abstain from voting in favour of the enforced removal of Jewish settlements was the least I could do and remain at peace with myself. I would vote that way again if the situation were to be repeated or any version thereof.

I have been asked what I would have done in Begin's place. It is idle to speculate but, in this case, maybe not entirely irrelevant. Perhaps I would not have gone as far as he did to secure the Treaty or held out for longer, however irate the US President, however demanding the Egyptians, however pragmatic and pressing my own advisers. Not impossibly, on the question of the Rafiah settlements, the Egyptians would have given way in time; as a matter of fact, even at Camp David that issue was not completely settled. But who knows? Conjecture is pointless; so is post-factum criticism. Beyond the principles we hold, there are our personalities, the way we interact. I knew the main actors in that drama, Begin and Weizman, very well, Dayan less so; I had seen Sadat close-up and in action, and was to meet President Carter and feel for myself his coolness towards us, his annoyance with our hesitations, his greater ease with the Egyptians, who, because they asked for everything, made life easier, while the Israelis debated and analysed each word of every clause, knowing all too well from past experience the cost to Israel, and to the Jewish people, of faulty, misleading punctuation, ambiguous phrasing or the slightest difference in the interpretation of text.

Not that the Camp David Accords were minor for any of those concerned, but there were substantive differences for each participating nation in their respective importance. For the Americans, the Accords represented not only the strength of US influence in the Middle East, with its many global implications, but they also heightened and deepened the personal prestige of a tireless and driven President. For Egypt, they held the gift of those ties with the United States which Sadat so profoundly hoped would deliver his country from its awesome poverty, and restore lost pride and self-confidence to the militarily vanquished. Only for us could the outcome directly, radically, even permanently affect existence itself, and the tiring bargaining involve survival.

Like the negotiations, the Knesset debates on the Accords had been heated, difficult, sometimes bitter – and protracted. I had called the House (which was in recess) into special session on 25 September; legally it was not obligatory for Begin to obtain Knesset approval for the Frameworks, but politically it could not be otherwise. The day before, the Cabinet had given its approval to the proposals solidly though not unanimously; the Resolution now before the Knesset provided for endorsement of the two Frameworks and approval of the evacuation and resettlement of the Sinai settlers – assuming that all other facets of the Accord with Egypt had been satisfactorily worked out. The session was held over two days: eighty speeches were delivered in the course of nearly eighteen hours with eighty-four Members voting in favour of the Frameworks, nineteen against and seventeen abstaining, all 120 Members having voted. Hardest of all for me was neither the length nor the inevitable repetitiveness of many of the opinions voiced, but rather the knowledge that, outside the House, Jews – demonstrating against the settlers' removal – were being held at bay, as was both proper and necessary, by the police, while I, inside the Knesset, its Speaker, could only give vent to my innermost feelings with a negative syllable in a roll-call of votes.

On 13 March 1979, a special session of the Knesset had been held with the participation of President Carter. Thwarted by deadlock in the negotiations, by the lack of cordiality between Begin and Sadat, and by what he termed Begin's 'obstructionism', Carter took matters into his own hands, travelled to Israel and Egypt, and, embarked on shuttle diplomacy, was in Jerusalem to speak to the Knesset himself. It was the House's second encounter with a foreign President; the wheels were now well-oiled; the protocol learned; the session begun with all official amenities smoothly observed. I escorted President Carter and Israel's President, Yitzhak Navon, into the chamber, which was packed with invited guests: Mrs Carter, Mrs Navon and Mrs Begin already in their places in the Presidential box; in the VIP gallery, members of Carter's entourage: the affable US Secretary of State, Cyrus Vance, one of the 'stars' of Camp David; US National Security Advisor Zbigniew Brzezinski, Ambassador Samuel Lewis and others. There was even a trumpet fanfare formally to welcome Carter to the Knesset as he took his seat to my right. The chamber was very tense; so was I, hoping that the Members would at least allow the President of the United States to finish his twenty-minute speech with no interruption – which they did – though this courtesy was not granted either to Begin or to Peres, the only other speakers.

Listening to President Carter, I could sense his impatience with Israel's (and Begin's) rigidity and his iron determination to implement the US design for peace in this part of the world. From the words he chose, the distribution of praise he meted out respectively to Egypt and to Israel, the guarantees and pledges he gave, it was apparent to me how little he understood, emotionally, the fateful dilemmas facing Begin on Israel's behalf or the magnitude of our doubts. These included various aspects of the projected autonomy, the connection ('linkage' it was called) between that and the Peace Treaty, our need for a binding statement that the Treaty would have priority over Egyptian commitments to other Arab states in any possible armed conflicts with Israel, or the depth of the anxiety aroused by Egypt's request to open a liaison office in Gaza – with all that this might bring in its wake. For Carter, these reservations were examples of Israeli quibbling, pointless worries raised only to delay and evade. For Begin – as a lawyer, a nationalist and a Jew – each was a dangerously loose stitch, which, given a tug, might well unravel the whole cloth. Their interpretations of the Accords were sometimes so at variance that it was as though they had signed different documents. Later, I saw them work together: everything was disputed, argued over, their incompatibility barely concealed or contained. I am sure, in retrospect, that had he served another term, Carter would have hardened his position – and his heart – where Israel was concerned, and what that would have been like I myself was to learn later when I became, both symbolically and actually, an obstacle in the way of another similarly determined US President.

It was perhaps unfortunate that, in his evident mood of disaffection for us, Carter should have been treated to a full-blown display of heckling by some of Israel's 'elected representatives', who barely permitted Begin to utter two consecutive sentences, despite my growing severity and eventual anger. Nor was embarrassment lessened when Begin turned to Carter with a smile: 'You see how beautiful is our democracy, Mr President.' Perhaps he was glad Carter could see for himself that others too had grave misgivings about the Accords. The President smiled back broadly enough but he was not an amateur smiler, and I doubted that he thought it 'beautiful' when extremists on the left yelled in his presence that autonomy was 'a mask for the continuation of conquest', castigating their Prime Minister for haggling over land at the expense of peace, or when those on the right shrieked at Begin that 'Sadat is fooling the whole world. He doesn't want peace. And you, Begin, know it. Tell the truth!', or when Geulah Cohen (in 1981 a founder of the small Tehiyya Party) tore up a piece of paper (after I called her to order for the third time) shouting, 'This is what will become of the Treaty. There won't be peace. ... Munich is what there will be!'

At 4 o'clock on the morning of 22 March, the Knesset concluded its debate on the Peace Treaty itself – the longest debate of its history. Spread over two days, it had lasted for twenty-seven hours, giving an opportunity to the 118 Knesset Members present (only two were not) to hold forth for ten minutes each on the merits, or otherwise, of the agreement. An excess of democracy? Is there such a thing? By the end of the marathon session, grey-faced and spent, I was no longer sure of the answer. On the other hand, the only functions left to Israel's legislators, insofar as the Treaty was concerned, were indeed to talk and to vote – everything else had already been decided. The debate had gone on and on, speakers often talking to a virtually empty hall, everything telecast live – though I couldn't help wondering, around 3.15 a.m., who was following the seemingly interminable oratory.

Finally, they voted: ninety-five Members raised their hands to approve the Peace Treaty; eighteen voted against; two abstained (one being myself); three had announced that they would not take part in the vote and two were not in the building – one was in mourning, the other in jail. Counts were taken; the results proclaimed; one of the ministers said: 'There's been a mistake in the counting.' But I knew that there had been no errors and I had had enough. 'This session is closed,' I said, banged my gavel twice and went home, grateful to have been a peripheral participant in the sessions, grateful that they were over, unreconciled to, and pessimistic about, much of the Treaty, and having not the faintest notion that within a year my involvement with it would no longer be so peripheral.

At the end of October, Moshe Dayan resigned as Israel's Foreign Minister and Begin named me to take his place. From then on, the Camp David Accords were to play a major and pressing role in my life. But I did not leave the Knesset behind me; I had entered it with some hesitation but now parted from the Speaker's Office with some regret. I had come to love the Knesset, its lights and shadows, angularities, dissonances and cohesiveness, its devoted staff and its growing awareness of itself as the workshop of Israeli democracy. Whenever I returned to it, it was with pride, affection and pleasure in seeing my portrait among those of its former Speakers, and I am glad that I am a Member of the Knesset, as my public life nears its close.

7

FOREIGN AFFAIRS

THE 10TH OF March 1980, my first day as Israel's Minister for Foreign Affairs, as a member of the Cabinet and as the successor to a world-famous and notably dynamic personality – a daunting combination of circumstances. Again, I was embarked on a new 'career', this time presiding on unfamiliar terrain over a senior staff of diplomats, almost all of whom had been born and bred into an ideology which I opposed and in whose eyes, I thought that morning, there might actually be no way in which I could be acceptable: not politically nor from the point of view of diplomatic expertise (though the Knesset had been a good school), nor as the personal choice of a Prime Minister still regarded, in this stronghold of the Labour movement, with suspicion and discreet disapproval. Never mind my distant past; the recent past was ominous enough. However effective and 'respectable' I may have been as Speaker of the Knesset, the fact remained that I was an acknowledged 'hard-liner', a man who had abstained in the 1978 vote on the Camp David Accords, and again in 1979 in the voting on the Peace Treaty with Egypt, and who, many believed, would probably have voted against both agreements had he felt free to do so. Hardly a recommendation for a Foreign Minister, now that those Accords and Treaty were a cornerstone of Israeli foreign policy.

I too had doubts. Was the Foreign Ministry in the heart of Jerusalem really the right place for me? Had I made a mistake in leaving the comfort and relative privacy of my Knesset office? Nor did I particularly look forward to my initial encounters with Ministry people or, for that matter, with the international diplomatic corps. Friendly sources had already informed me that my appointment had raised eyebrows also in those circles and was seen, on the whole, as further evidence of Menachem Begin's disdain for public, in this case meaning world, opinion. But the reality, as so often, turned out to be otherwise. The Ministry's apprehensions – and mine – were groundless: the diplomats quickly calmed down and were eventually even complimentary; and I found myself working with men and women of competence and experience who could hardly have been more helpful, more outgoing, more generous with their time and talents and who, it evolved, were, on the whole, relieved by Dayan's departure.

His high-handedness, brusqueness and what they had sensed as lack of real interest in the Ministry's far-flung workings had alienated them. Besides, four months had passed since Dayan's resignation; no Ministry can operate efficiently without a Minister to represent it in the Cabinet, to set guidelines, to assume ultimate responsibility. If senior Ministry officials were not delighted by Begin's choice, they were at least delighted to be needed – and need them I certainly did. Within weeks, thanks to the staff's co-operation – including that of the then Director-General, Yosef Ciechanover, who resigned but agreed to carry on and did for a long time – I no longer felt myself to be a stranger in their midst, the new boy in class. What perhaps also helped to make for harmony, and maintain it, was that I brought no people of 'my own' with me – I had none, in any case. And, possibly even more, that only a handful, if that, of indisputably superior newcomers entered the Foreign Service at my specific rec-ommendation, while various top people who had either come with Dayan, or been taken on by him, stayed – several of them not only working closely with me in the Foreign Ministry but moving with me to the Prime Minister's Office in 1983, where they were to form the circle of my immediate advisers.

Ciechanover was one; another was Elyakim Rubinstein, a brilliant young lawyer who had served as Dayan's aide and bureau head, been indispensable to him throughout the Camp David negotiations (about which he probably knows more than anyone in the world), and who agreed later to become head of my bureau. An observant Jew and extremely erudite, he was by way of being a prodigy, and I am not surprised that though he worked so long and intimately with me, he was appointed co-ordinator of the Israeli delegations to the negotiations with the Arabs following the elections of 1992. I myself saw him often in action with the Palestinian and Jordanian del-egations and was always impressed anew by his ability to deal with people, to work hard and to get to the heart of the most complex situations. It was he who recommended as his successor (to head my bureau) Yossi Ben-Aharon, who also moved with me in 1983 to become head of the Prime Minister's Office, so he and I worked together for some ten years. There was also David Kimche whom I knew from my Mossad days and who was to head the Israeli delegation to the Lebanon talks of 1983. Avi Pazner, eventually Ambassador to Rome, also accompanied me to the Prime Minister's Office, where he served as my press adviser. I cannot imagine that any Foreign Minister or Prime Minister, for that matter, could have had a more gifted or trustworthy group upon which to rely.

More expectedly, I became the recipient of bitter complaints from disappointed Herut stalwarts, who had taken for granted Foreign Ministry jobs now that a Herut man was in charge and who accused me of letting the Party down when I didn't see to it that they joined me. The Ministry staff, for its part, was unfailingly loyal, even though my policies (and the phraseology that went with them) were not what they were accustomed to, liked or could easily identify with. But on this score, too, they won my admiration and gratitude, for the way in which they went ahead as good civil servants should, did their jobs and helped me do mine. I studied hard, getting to know the intricate network of Israel's foreign relations, its component parts and activities, its methodologies and personnel. I read everything that landed on my desk: cables, position papers, intelligence reports (these with a special relish I never lost), letters, memos and clippings, believing in the need to accumulate as much knowledge as possible if I was to be a useful Foreign Minister – not just a figurehead for state visits abroad or cocktail parties at home. I listened with great concentration to department heads, to ambassadors back on brief visits, to whichever staff members could add to the total picture. And at night when I tired of reading, I often walked for an hour or so in the quiet of sleeping Jerusalem, trying to think through each separate problem on the next day's agenda, to see this or that crisis in context, pondering alternatives, short-cuts, potential mine-fields, always aware (to use Begin's words in the Knesset debate on my appointment) that 'a Foreign Minister has no foreign policy of his own ... his task is to carry out policy decided upon by the Government'. But even for this I needed time, perspective and facts, so I disregarded the pressures, and sometimes the panics, of others, took my time and did not even change the pictures on the walls of the Foreign Minister's office for months, never having seen any merit in change for change's sake.

I was also much on the move, travelling and talking. A naturally untalkative man, I now talked incessantly – at the UN, throughout the United States and South America, in the Far East and Africa, in the capitals of Western Europe, interpreting, explaining, trying to enlighten old friends and recruit new ones, to the best of my ability presenting Israel's current assets and needs.

Representing Israel abroad from the shadows as I had done in the Mossad, or as an honoured but essentially uninfluential guest as I did as Speaker of the Knesset, was not like doing so as a Foreign Minister. Now, whenever I travelled, it was with a shopping list in my pocket, for ever wanting or needing something, never sure that what I had to offer in return would meet the bill. What made such missions harder and more unpleasant than necessary was that almost wherever I went, the Arab states, their Third World friends and an unsavoury collection of their anti-Semitic helpers seemed to have been there before me, 'preparing' the ground.

Nothing I had to sell to would-be customers, to put it bluntly, could compete with the Arabs' wares, which included oil, gold and UN votes – and when and if these failed to win them friends, there were always the threats, and the realities, of the Arab boycott, of economic blackmail and of terrorism to fall back on. After all, how can one compare Arab power with the infinitely lesser potential, in all respects, of a small country like Israel whose one main resource is the motivation and brightness of its manpower? We couldn't buy anyone; we weren't out to menace anyone; and though we had staunch friends of our own, they didn't do our bidding blindly. So we never stood much chance of support or help from governments whose greed or fear were easily activated.

Even so, I was disheartened to learn for myself that this sort of expediency was at work even in the most advanced of European capitals, though the argumentation presented there for turning us down was more elegantly expressed than in less sophisticated societies. A notable instance was the blatantly one-sided Middle East resolution adopted in Venice in 1980 by the nine leaders of the European Economic Community, calling for Israel's total withdrawal from Judea, Samaria and Gaza and declaring that the PLO 'must be associated with any negotiations ...' though only days earlier this organization had once again defined its aim as the liquidation of the State of Israel. Unfortunately, this surrender to Arab extortion was far from being unusual.

Nothing came simply or easily. In Europe, as opposed to elsewhere, there were also black recollections and painful moments of truth. My first trip to West Germany was such. I hadn't expected it to be so harrowing, or perhaps I had chosen not to think much about how it would actually be, but one thing I decided at once: I would not visit Bonn as though it were merely another major European city, a seat of government like Stockholm or London. There would have to be some acknowledgment of where and who I was, and of what and whom I represented. Not for the sake of the Germans, nor to teach anyone anything; only for myself and my colleagues because we were Jews in Germany on official business for the Jewish state and could not enter that land without first paying tribute to the memory of the Jews slaughtered by the Nazis. So we began our stay in Germany at Dachau, near Munich, the first Nazi concentration camp that served as a model for all the rest, through which hundreds of thousands of Jews passed in the 'death transports' that hauled them eastward, and where thousands more died of hunger, cold, disease and despair.

Full diplomatic relations between Germany and Israel had been in force then for fifteen years, and German aid to Israel had taken many forms: the exchange of academics, professionals, artists and tourists was already a regular feature of Israeli life and Israeli shops were filled with German goods. There were still Israelis, Begin himself was one, who could not bring themselves to speak or listen to the German language, to welcome a German visitor, to travel to Germany or knowingly buy anything manufactured there. But by the early 1980s, they were a minority. It was necessary to find some way of handling the totality of our relationship with Germany so that while essential topics relating to the here-and-now could be and were dealt with efficiently, it would be obvious that the Holocaust was profoundly imprinted on the collective memory of the people of Israel. By the same token, it was no less important for us to make sure that the people of Germany remained conscious of the terrible responsibility they had incurred towards the Jews. It was, in short, no simple matter – for us or for them – to find, and maintain, a balance between the demands of the past and those of the present.

The Germans were well aware of our dilemma but not unanimous in their reaction to it; some accepted the guilt but claimed there was no connection between that and the new Germany; others responded with more subtlety, with deeper understanding. Foreign Minister Hans Dietrich Genscher was one such. We met often, mostly at the UN, and I came to regard him highly and to value his support of Israel in the Common Market and his wariness with the Arabs. People listened to him when he spoke and when he told those in his own Ministry to 'be careful not to push Israel into despair', they listened very attentively. He resigned as Germany's Foreign Minister in April 1992 and I wrote to convey my 'profound feelings of appreciation and admiration after so many years of understanding between us ...', and was touched by his reply – '... I was impressed by the clarity of your judgment and your willingness to engage in open dialogue' – not because of the compliments it contained but because of what it signified in terms of the intellectual and emotional efforts we had both made in an extraordinary cause.

In Dachau, reciting the *Kaddish*, the ancient Jewish prayer for the dead, I cried, pierced by sorrow for the perished multitudes – and my family – feeling for a moment that the weight of the memories was almost too much to bear. But the brief ceremony over, the inadequate acknowledgment to history made, we went on to Bonn. I met with Chancellor Helmut Schmidt and Genscher, discussed the issue of the moment (West Germany's stand on the EEC's Middle East initiative) and, at dinner, clinked glasses and did not permit myself to think about Dachau till I was alone.

Both the Germans and we became adept at balancing acts, they much better than us, measuring how far they could go in their dealings with the Arabs, how prepared Israel was, at any given time, to forgive and forget, and how likely we would be to release them from, or at least reduce, moral claims made in the name of the six million. It was inevitable, against the background of the past, that even in a climate of reconciliation, of fresh starts, we, and they, should sometimes topple from the tightrope we walked.

A typical crisis broke out in 1981 when I was told that Helmut Schmidt, visiting Saudi Arabia, had declared Bonn to be 'also morally committed' to the Palestinians, saying that West Germany would review its policy of not selling arms (actually tanks) in 'areas of tension' (actually Israel's enemies). In Bonn, Schmidt reassured me of undying friendship, swearing that the media had distorted his words. But along with his cordiality and demurrers, I detected an antagonism towards Israel and was sure that, although the sale of German tanks to the Saudis would indeed be held up, as it was, Schmidt, busily competing against the French and British for Arab favours, was fashioning some 'special relationship' of his own.

Not that Schmidt was the only German statesman seeking to reject or, at the very least, put behind him the burden of German history. For Chancellor Helmut Kohl, the Holocaust is history, long over, an enormity that happened when he and his generation were young or not yet born and thus not guilty, not to be blamed, not emotionally involved. We spoke more than once, Chancellor Kohl and I, about the grim connection between our countries; even when he talked to an elderly Jew from Poland like myself it was impersonally, his eyes and voice expressionless, though he was unfailingly correct and very careful not to criticize Israel or debate Israeli policy. He came to Israel for the first time in 1983, immediately after Begin's resignation (some said that the thought of the pending visit was the last straw for Begin in his depression), so it was I, as Prime Minister, who received him. But I doubt that his stay in Israel brought him nearer to that acceptance of the truth without which the chasm can never be closed, or truly bridged.

There would never, by the nature of the relationship, be any time during the years I held office that, one way or another, we were not closely involved with Germany. One bitter moment – it came as a considerable shock to young Israelis – was during the 1991 Gulf War when the East German-Iraqi connection regarding the training of Iraqi terrorists in the technique of nerve-gas warfare and the building by West German companies of poison-gas factories for Saddam Hussein were disclosed. This, ironically, while hundreds of thousands of Israelis nightly relied on the German gas masks obtained to protect them should the Iraqis, as they threatened, attack Israel with chemical weapons. But more about that war when I come to it.

In between airports, limousines, hotel rooms, assembly halls, press conferences, receptions, official, semi-official and (now and then) secret meetings, I looked around me and tried to take in some of the atmosphere of new places, promising myself to return, one day, to this city or that land for a longer stay. Sometimes Shulamit came with me; more often not, though later, when I was Prime Minister, her presence made my travelling much easier and she accompanied me more frequently.

My trips tended to be intensive; preparations, as in Jerusalem, beginning before the sun rose when I could concentrate on 'home-work', try to anticipate queries and make sure my answers would be accurate. Slowly I felt my way into the job, learning to narrow gaps, to stay away to the extent possible from rehearsal, for its own questionable sake, of facts and attitudes bound a priori to be unpalatable, to avoid polemics and get to the point.

I had taken over the Ministry at a period when, though the Treaty with Egypt was signed, other frontiers were still sealed; nowhere else in the Arab world was there any progress in the direction of peace or even recognition. African states that broke or suspended diplomatic relations with Israel in 1973 as a result of the Yom Kippur War still adamantly opposed us – not only at the UN, but whenever other forums offered themselves for this purpose; the UN General Assembly had passed, by a depressingly large majority, a set of anti-Zionist Resolutions that were also finding their anti-Semitic echo in unexpected places.

In many quarters, Israel's popularity, always fluctuating, was at a nadir, not improved by the precision of the 1981 Israeli air-force destruction of Osirak (Iraq's nuclear facility built near Baghdad), or the Knesset's decision to apply Israeli law, jurisdiction and admin- istration to the Golan Heights, though neither event endangered world peace or, at any time, bore any implications beyond those having to do with Israel's self-defence – though a decade later, for varying reasons, both acquired new prominence. So, like all other Israeli Foreign Ministers, official representatives or even ordinary travellers, I got used to answering the same hostile questions over and over again – as briefly and persuasively as I could – even when I felt their tone or wording to be offensive, frequently more suitably posed in a courtroom than in their actual settings.

I realize that, reading these words, someone is bound to think them prime examples of Israeli 'paranoia', of our so-called persecution complex. The fact is that I personally cannot imagine my asking citizens, much less official spokesmen, of other countries (except, of course, declared foes) to account for their nations' behaviour, reac- tions and aspirations with the rudeness and arrogance that many of my interlocutors abroad, Jew and gentile alike, permitted themselves. I sometimes even suspected that those who tried hardest to trip Israelis up with leading questions and inaccurate statistics were unconsciously revealing the way they themselves felt about Jews – or about being Jewish – rather than about the State of Israel or the Middle East as such.

Certain moments, certain people, snatches of certain conversations stand out. My first meeting with Ronald Reagan is one. I had, of course, expected courtesy and the mandatory small talk that precedes substance on such occasions. Instead, I was struck by the warmth with which Reagan spoke about Israel, his admiration for our refusal to yield to terrorism and the feeling that he identified with what the Jewish state represented. Almost at once I felt sure that he would be a friend – as, indeed, he proved to be – even in the worst of times (and some were very bad) that followed. In the course of the years I saw and heard Reagan at what well might have been his angriest – at various stages of the war in Lebanon when he charged us, erroneously, with atrocities, or during the serious disturbances (the intifada, the word derived from the Arabic for 'shaking off') that broke out in the administered territories at the end of 1987, when he berated us for what he had been informed was the unacceptable harshness of the IDF – but even then his fury was without coldness. He disagreed, he censured, he was very stern, but I never sensed in him a turning away from Israel or from those who governed it, nor ever found him cynical or indifferent. Almost all the Presidents of the contemporary United States have backed, advised and assisted Israel, but none more than Reagan. Of his eight years in the White House, I was Israel's Foreign Minister for three and a half and Prime Minister for nearly four, so I feel competent to testify to his significant contribution to the deepening and expanding of the bonds between Israel and the United States.

Nor was it coincidental that during those years the United States signed a pioneering Strategic Co-operation Agreement with us (leading to the establishment of a Joint Policy Co-ordinating Committee) and a Free Trade Agreement, and substantially increased its total aid package by turning the allocation for military purposes into grant money rather than, as in the past, a loan on which we paid (and still pay) interest. Since those innovations US aid to Israel has risen to some $3 billion a year. By any standards, this is a great deal of money, given not only because of the Administration's and Congress's knowledge that Israel is a reliable ally for all seasons, but also as an appreciation, perhaps peculiarly American, of Israeli ideals, of our faith in the future, of the fact that we share an ethical code and, on many matters, a point of view. If the admiration is mutual, it is because, as the century fades (though not the memory of its disgraces), it can be said – and I believe this to be so – that the American people are more committed to improving the human condition in general, to peace on earth, to civil rights, to equal opportunity and the pursuit of happiness, and, in the main, try harder to live by moral precepts than most of the peoples of Europe.

Not only have I never lost this appreciation of the basic character of American democracy but in the years when, as Prime Minister, I was so often faced by misunderstandings in the relationship between Israel and the American Government – sometimes unfortunately even between the US President and myself – at no time did I ever doubt the goodwill of the American people or hesitate to turn to Washington for help where the fate of human beings was concerned. Nor was I once disappointed in this regard.

I felt at home in the United States instantly, liked the people I met and responded to their directness and candour, qualities that typified, among others, two of the statesmen I came to know well who were important in Israel's current history: President Reagan's Secretaries of State, Alexander Haig and George P. Shultz. Haig made no pretence of neutrality where the Middle East was concerned; he perceived Israel as a natural partner in the fight against international terrorism (hoping also that we would play a role in opposing Soviet aggression).

A wartime general, former NATO Commander, once President Nixon's closest associate, a hard-headed tough man who was not among those that strongly condemned either Operation Peace for Galilee or the IDF's subsequent destruction of the PLO headquarters in Lebanon, Haig was very popular in Israel and his departure in 1982 from the State Department came as a blow at a difficult time.

George Shultz's appointment in his place was viewed with nothing less than alarm. People in Israel's Foreign Ministry and in the Prime Minister's Office who were especially familiar with the United States warned that since Shultz was the President of Bechtel, the giant concern so active in Saudi Arabia, he wasn't likely to be much of a Zionist or very friendly to Israel in his new role. When I met him (I confess, with some anxiety), I was much taken by him, by his business-like manner, his frankness and his modesty. Shultz told me at once that he knew how upset we were about his Bechtel connection but that it had nothing to do with his attitude towards Israel. He had visited this country and he knew the history of the Jews and their state. He would do the best he could for us. Then he asked: 'Do you believe me?' 'Every word,' I answered – and I did. 'Well then,' he said, 'we have a lot to talk about.' So we shook hands. On the way home I was reminded of that first meeting years before with Isser Harel, though perhaps Shultz would not relish the comparison. But both encounters concerned trust and in neither case was it betrayed.

A great deal has occurred in the world, including the Middle East, since then, but I can imagine no situation that could alter the esteem in which I held Shultz – though we were not always politically attuned to each other, to say the least. His wisdom, patience and genuine goodwill towards and interest in Israel were always at my disposal, most especially in times of crisis when solutions had to be found for acute problems. We disagreed on certain cardinal issues – Israel's borders, the status of Jerusalem, how and when we should end our military rule in Judea, Samaria and Gaza – but this never interfered with our collaboration. He became as familiar with Israel as I was becoming with the United States, and the dialogue between us benefited both of us accordingly, or so I think. And I was particularly grateful for his actions on behalf of Soviet Jewry.

I found the same spirit – concern with justice and appreciation of the potential of a strong democratic Israel – almost everywhere I went on those early visits to the States; nowhere more vividly expressed than by members of Congress, many of whom had not only accompanied Israel in the state's struggle for survival, but had also been veteran Zionists for decades before its creation. In the making of an independent Jewish state, in the guarding of its independence and in the provision of many of the means for its advancement, dozens of US senators and congressmen have proven invaluable friends. And, of course, there was the process of my discovery of the extraordinary Jewish communities of the United States with whom I dealt as though with members of a family – and who frequently spoke to me that way too! In the second half of the 1980s, we came to know each other better and I shall write about that interaction when I come to those years of my Prime Ministership. Not that I ever forgot a comment made by Henry Kissinger on my very first day in Washington. He was no longer in government service, could and did speak freely, and wanted to help. 'There's something you must bear in mind all the time,' he said. 'Take my word for it. You don't know anyone yet but I know them all, and well. Everyone – Congress, the Senate, the media – wants Israel to withdraw from the "administered" territories, to return to the borders of 1967. Not everyone will say so to your face now but that's what everyone wants.' He may have overstated, but, on the whole, it was a sound warning. I bore it in mind and concentrated on concrete ongoing matters – economics, security, culture – keeping the major controversial problems on a separate track that I mostly reserved for my talks with the Secretary of State and Congress.

It was not only Americans whom I met in the United States. Each autumn, the Foreign Ministers of most of the nations of the world gather at UN headquarters in New York for the opening of the General Assembly sessions. For me, those meetings were a further chance to broaden horizons, to meet counterparts on safe ground – neither mine nor theirs – to send and receive signals. I preferred, even at the UN, to work behind the scenes and talk discreetly with foreign delegates. One Foreign Minister I wanted to meet was the USSR's Andrei Gromyko. He was briefly to become President of the Soviet Union and, in 1989, he died, but in 1981 he was the only diplomat still active to have taken part in the 1947 UN Assembly in New York at which Israel was voted into being. He had made an impassioned plea then on behalf of the establishment of a Jewish state and, in 1948, the USSR had been the first to grant the new state de jure recognition. The Zionist world was overjoyed; what harm could befall the state if the USA and the USSR, masters of the twentieth-century world, stood together at its cradle?

During the War of Independence, the Soviet Government had actively helped Israel to acquire arms and ammunition from Czechoslovakia for use against the invading Arabs, but during the next two decades the benign attitude altered: the Russian godparent became increasingly hostile. In the East–West struggle for the Middle East, Israel, ungratefully in Soviet eyes, opted for Western support. Worse yet, when the USSR entrenched itself in Egypt (and, to a lesser degree, in Syria), the Arab armies that it equipped and trained so generously were, on several occasions, totally defeated by the IDF, each Israeli victory representing, in effect, a Soviet débâcle. In 1967, the USSR finally broke relations with us. The situation of Soviet Jewry, of course, was not improved as the USSR libelled and opposed Israel at all possible levels.

A meeting between Gromyko and myself was finally arranged – at my initiative. We met in the offices of the Soviet delegation in New York at night. Below us shone the lights of New York. 'You know, no one else in this entire city is working at this hour,' Gromyko said. 'Only we, two people with strong convictions, meeting to talk business.' Then he said, 'You will have to accept a small Palestinian state, you know,' his thumb and index fingertips making a sign for 'small'. I asked: 'Tell me, Mr Secretary, in Soviet terms, what is "small"?' We both laughed. I probed a little: why the abnormal relationship with Israel? Surely it wasn't connected to our form of government. After all, the USSR had a 'normal' relationship with the United States, for instance. He thought for a minute. 'Yes,' he said, 'you have a point. But the Middle East is something else.' He listened while I proceeded to charge the Soviet Union with active support of anti-Israeli terrorism and the supplying of arms to those who sought to destroy us. Gromyko denied the accusation. 'We are against personal terror,' he said, adding that the Soviet Union had always opposed this. 'Of course at the very beginning we too had such an organization. I can't remember its name.' 'I can,' I said, 'Narodnaya Volya'. He seemed very pleased. 'Yes, I know you are familiar with our history.'

Before we met, I had wanted to check his last conversation with a representative of Israel and to ascertain whether the question of Soviet Jewry had been on the agenda. It turned out that the last Israeli with whom Gromyko had talked had been Yigal Allon, who had served as Foreign Minister in an earlier Rabin Government. I was surprised to learn that no, the topic had not been raised and I decided I would bring it up myself. So I did. I asked Gromyko about Russian Jews. He answered with annoyance, not to say anger. 'That's an internal Soviet matter,' he said, frowning. None the less, I proceeded to prod him, so he responded with a few words about the 'equality' Soviet Jewry was enjoying within Soviet society as a whole.

When we met again three years later, Gromyko made no effort to evade the subject. He had obviously prepared himself for our encounter with a variety of clarifications.

The meeting took place at the time of our National Unity Government: Shimon Peres was Prime Minister, I was Deputy Prime Minister and, once again, Foreign Minister. I told Gromyko about Lebanon, about the PLO and how it had made life intolerable in the north of Israel, and explained that Operation Peace for Galilee had been a war against a terrorist 'state within a state' operating against us on our own border. I also brought up the matter of renewed ties between Israel and the USSR, stressing that there was no conflict of interest between our countries and that all and any improvement in the relationships between the Great Powers was of major importance and benefit to our own security, and added that we had not forgotten the vital aid given to us in 1948. 'This hand,' Gromyko said dramatically, lifting his right arm, 'this is what was raised to help create the State of Israel.' 'What went wrong?' I asked. 'Israel's aggression,' he replied. It had 'upset' the Russian people. All those conquests; taking territory that wasn't ours. And he went on in this vein for a while. Then he said, 'You people like to quote the Bible. Well, let me tell you that it will be a miracle if the Arab world ever accepts this situation.' When I brought up the urgent matter of letting more Jews go, he dismissed part of what I had said as 'propaganda' and denied that any obstacles had ever been placed in the way of the would-be immigrants. 'As for those you define as your brethren living in the USSR ... what do you expect, another miracle? By now whoever wants to go has gone. Let's face it, they don't yearn for the motherland in the way you think ...' 'Why don't you set up direct flights from Moscow to Tel Aviv and then we'll both be wiser?' I challenged. Gromyko didn't answer. Maybe it was fortunate for him, the perfect product of a blinding system, that he was spared knowledge of the chaos, the economic and political collapses, the weakening at last of the absolutism of the Communist Party in the 1990s – and the massive voluntary immigration to Israel of over 400,000 Soviet Jews. Though I am rather sorry that he didn't live to see a Soviet Ambassador present credentials to Israel's President in December 1991 – for the first time in nearly a quarter of a century.

My own conviction (it has never changed) was that we should do our best to re-establish relations with the Soviet Union – for Israel's good and that of the millions of Soviet Jewry. For all its enmity, the USSR never questioned Israel's right to exist nor pretended otherwise to the Arabs. It was not a matter, as many suggested, of Israel's having to choose between the superpowers, between one bloc or the other; nothing, no renewed links, no improvement in our relationship with the USSR could diminish or injure our existing ties, least of all with the United States. I always believed that the dialogue, never entirely broken off, should be resumed and that we should begin to listen to each other again. And when I became Prime Minister, I took steps in this direction. But even before, I campaigned for diplomatic perestroika whenever I could. In fact, my interest in this relationship predated the establishment of the state. In the days of the underground, Lehi had looked – wherever possible and usually via secret emissaries – for international connections, and links between the Soviet bloc and the Jewish state-to-be formed a central theme in the overall concept. Right after the German defeat, Lehi people met with Communist leader Georgi Dimitrov, then the senior Soviet representative in Bulgaria, asking him to transmit this hope to the Soviet Union, having already despatched spokesmen to Andrei Vishinsky, the Soviet Foreign Minister just arrived at the UN. Much later, when I was Prime Minister and Mikhail Gorbachev was President of the USSR, I met twice in Budapest, once secretly, with Karoly Grosz, leader of the Hungarian Communist Party, and talked to him about a *rapprochement*, asking that he speak to Gorbachev on our behalf – as he seemingly did.

With the French, it was more complicated. Perhaps it was just because I so admired French culture, so enjoyed France, had been so thankful for French assistance in my Eritrean exile, that it was harder in a way for me to face the unfriendliness of the French Government to Israel – ever since the Six Day War when we 'disobeyed' de Gaulle by going ahead with our pre-emptive strike – than the turning-away from us, for instance, of the Soviet Union. It was as though, consciously or otherwise, the French were drawing a parallel between Israel's struggle for a homeland and the Algerians' fight against their empire, and reaching the entirely incorrect conclusion that since the Algerians had been in the right, so the PLO must also be in the right. In general, it is stimulating, pleasurable even, to talk politics with French statesmen – regardless of differences of opinion. French intellectuals, I learned, go straight to the root of problems: subject them, as they have been trained to do, to rigorous analysis and discuss them in depth. There were perennial sources of such debate and disagreement between French colleagues and myself, one subject being the PLO; I, reflecting the stand taken by all governments of Israel thus far that this is a terrorist entity committed – despite whatever headline-making statements it may issue at seemingly appropriate times – to the obliteration of the State of Israel and thus disqualified from negotiating with us about anything; my French hosts rarely swerving from their tolerance of the PLO and resolute in their determination to view it as ('all things considered') moderate and misunderstood. I taught myself to enjoy such exchanges, if only for the pleasure of hearing the fine French in which these evaluations were couched.

Two events took place in 1981 that were immediately to affect the Middle East and in one of which France played a critical role, to that nation's discredit and, finally, I think, regret. The story of the Israeli air-force strike, on 7 June 1981, against Osirak, cannot be told, however, without first paying tribute to Menachem Begin. There can be little question that had it not been for Begin's decision to order the annihilation of that installation, the Gulf War that broke out ten years later might well have had a far grimmer outcome than it did – not only for Israel but also for the US-led coalition and its troops, let alone for Iraq itself. Despite this, the gratitude owed to Begin has never been adequately expressed, least of all by those eventually forced to wake up to the real nature of Saddam Hussein and his regime. In Israel, there had never been any doubt about this; by the late 1970s, when Saddam Hussein formally assumed the leadership that was actually his for years, he made no secret of his intention to erase Israel from the map of the world and 'to wash away the stain'.

The Iraqi reactor, south of Baghdad, had been inaugurated in 1968, upgraded in 1971 and, in the view of experts, likely to be capable of detonating an initial 'nuclear device' by 1985, able soon afterwards to produce bombs deliverable by aircraft or ground-to-ground missiles. Its construction and function were made possible by the continued 'contribution' of everything from the actual building to scientific and technological know-how – and radio-chemical facilities – by the USSR, France and Italy in exchange for highly profitable oil-based agreements, the French, in particular, having granted Iraq immense credits in return for vital nuclear 'goods' and experience.

By the summer of 1980 we were sure, despite Saddam Hussein's fiery denials and talk of 'peaceful purposes', that the Iraqi efforts to attain military nuclear capability were indeed meeting with success and that it was imperative to alert the French to the full measure of the menace facing us. Accordingly, I met with the then French Chargé d'Affaires, Jean-Pierre Chauvet, to demand that under no circumstances should military-grade fuels be placed at Iraq's disposal. Chauvet heard me out and then explained that our fears were 'entirely' unjustified. It would be sheer madness ('unthinkable'), he said, for Saddam Hussein to drop an atom bomb on Israel because by doing so he would also kill thousands of Arabs – an argument I recalled without amusement in 1991 when Iraqi Scuds fell indiscriminately on Israel's Jewish centres and on Arab-populated parts of the administered territories, to say nothing of Saudi Arabia – or, indeed, of Kuwait. At all events neither the French nor the Italian Governments shared our apprehension. The Italian Foreign Minister, Emilio Colombo, pointedly reminding me that, unlike Israel, Italy had signed the Non-Proliferation Treaty, similarly assured me that Israel had nothing to worry about, advice also dispensed by German Chancellor Helmut Schmidt. In New York, only days after the invasion of Iran by Iraq, I expressed Israel's fears to the then US Secretary of Defense, Harold Brown, and to Secretary of State Edmund Muskie, neither of whom gave me any reason to hope for effective US intervention with the reactor's sponsors. Nor did the French Foreign Minister, Jean François Poncet, whose Government, I was told, saw 'not the slightest reason' for Israel's alarm.

However, we were not entirely alone in our fear of the reactor; at the start of the Iran-Iraq war, the Iranians promptly demonstrated their own deep concern by twice firing missiles at Osirak though they only inflicted minor damage. But the attack apparently made an impression in Paris. A week later I was received at the Elysée Palace by President Valéry Giscard d'Estaing. Very pro-Arab, very nationalistic, Giscard d'Estaing was no friend of Israel. I remember once saying to him something about 'notre communauté Juive' and his abruptly stopping me. 'Votre?' he queried haughtily. 'They are French, above all.' I tried to explain that French Jews are also part of le peuple Juif, but the President was not interested in the complexities of Jewish history. He greeted me – as I had been warned he would – with considerable coolness but listened attentively to what I had to say. Always aloof, none the less in his own way he was somewhat more forthcoming than de Gaulle, Pompidou or even he himself had been in the past. 'Please believe me,' he said. 'If ever we have reason to suspect Iraq of trying to produce nuclear weapons, we will see to it that this does not happen.' When I met him again in December 1980, he reiterated the same assurance, adding that 'nothing untoward has been seen.'

Not for the first time nor the last, it was clear that it would be up to us to remove the threat since no one else was going to do it for us. But before Israel embarked on any attack against Osirak, a number of crucial questions had to be posed and answered: if mounted, how sure could we be that the attack would succeed? Was it really feasible?

And if so, how would the world respond to this unilateral act? The US? The USSR? Egypt? I myself was convinced – as I would be in years to come, under other circumstances and in connection with other issues – that no punishment meted out to Israel would be comparable to the peril awaiting us if we let world opinion overrule our sense of self-preservation. The Cabinet discussions went on for months; each time we met there were new data, new factors to be taken into consideration and new political risks to be weighed. Finally in March 1981, Begin demanded a decision: together with nine other ministers, I unhesitatingly voted in favour of his proposal.

Thinking back to the charged atmosphere of those weeks of secret emergency meetings, to the life-and-death considerations involved, to the presentation of detailed arguments both pro and con that lasted for hours at a time, above all I see Begin, driven, insistent, begging that, since in Iraq it was hoped the reactor would be operational by July, we move fast, at once. He would, I think, have resigned had the vote not gone the way he so prophetically wished, or had the date, postponed so often, not been set at last. At one stage, news of the proposed strike reached the Alignment leadership (miraculously it was not leaked to the press) and Peres wrote to Begin demanding that the operation be cancelled. Carefully avoiding specific terminology, he said: '... Israel will be like a thorn in the wilderness. ... I add my voice to those who tell you not to act, certainly not under ... the present circumstances.' The matter of timing was critical: there were good grounds for hoping that François Mitterrand, due to take office as President, would be less hostile to Israel than Giscard d'Estaing. He had long been noted for his pro-Israeli sympathies and had close ties with ranking fellow-Socialists in Israel. There would also be a new President in the United States: Ronald Reagan, an outspoken supporter of Israel, whose new Secretary of State Alexander Haig was equally well-disposed towards us. As for Sadat, whom Begin and I were to meet at Sharm el-Sheikh just three days before the bombing, though nothing was more precious to Begin than the Israel–Egypt Accord, that too was a risk that had to be taken. 'I feel certain that whatever Sadat may proclaim publicly, he will do nothing to upset our relationship drastically,' Begin said. But what overrode all else, when it finally came, was the answer of the then-commander of the Israeli air force. 'Yes, it is risky, but it can be done,' he told the Cabinet. The preparation of special Israeli air-force crews began almost immediately.

On 7 June, eight uncamouflaged Israeli air-force planes, and a smaller escorting umbrella, made their way to Baghdad. At the Prime

Minister's home, in the downstairs reception room where the Cabinet
had gathered, Begin told us that there would probably be a three-
hour wait till the job was done and the planes were safely back at
base. At 5.30 p.m. the phone rang; Begin answered it in the adjacent
study. It was the IDF Commander-in-Chief, Rafael (Raful) Eitan, later
to be my Minister of Agriculture. 'Everything is in order. They're on
their way home. Everything, that is, except the target. That's been
destroyed.' Nothing had gone wrong. The combined pride, relief and
instant rush of worry about what lay ahead now were almost
immense. We took a couple of minutes to drink '*lehayyim*' and then
began to discuss the Government's announcement.

The Arab world as such was stunned; Sadat's official condemnation
was severe. ('I told him nothing,' Begin reported. 'I couldn't burden
him with any prior knowledge.') The US government also denounced
the bombing, unconvinced of its justification, though years later,
answering a reporter's query in the summer of 1991, Secretary of
State James Baker admitted that he was 'not prepared to be critical
of the action, using 20–20 hindsight'. But in 1981, among the voices
raised in support of the resultant US sanctions against Israel, few
were louder than that of the then US Vice-President, George Bush.
As for President Reagan, he was horrified; somehow, in a lamentable
bureaucratic tangle, no one in the outgoing Administration, or in his
own, had filled him in as to the existence of the Iraqi reactor, let
alone its significance. Perhaps the most distressing was the all-out
castigation of the Government by Israel's Labour Party, which,
breaking with the long-standing Israeli tradition of solidarity in crisis,
permitted itself to be overcome by partisan chagrin and make the
outrageous charge that the operation had been mounted primarily
as a local 'election gimmick'. I must confess that even I was startled;
never an admirer of his, in those days I still found it hard to believe
that the Labour Party's head, Shimon Peres, was capable either of
such pettiness or lack of political acumen.

In the end, we weathered the storm. The US sanctions, though
applied, were revoked; the wave of foreign ill-feeling receded; even
the French statement denying France's pre-eminent role in the
construction of the reactor and scolding Israel for the strike
('unacceptable, dangerous and a violation of international law') was
less irate than I expected. And Sadat? Having studied the letter which
Begin despatched to him right after the bombing and having again
pronounced himself appalled by the use of force, he asked our
Ambassador to Cairo, Moshe Sasson, to deliver a personal message.
'Tell this to Begin,' he instructed Sasson. 'May God forgive you O

Menachem; and tell him also that I am silent.' Then he assured Sasson that he would go on working for peace with Israel and the United States. He kept his word as long as he lived.

On 6 October 1981, in New York attending the UN General Assembly, I learned, on the 6 a.m. news, of Sadat's assassination in Cairo by fundamentalist Moslems, as he reviewed a military parade marking the eighth anniversary of the Yom Kippur War. Staring at the screen, only half-listening to the commentary, I recalled Sadat, as I had seen him only months earlier when Begin and he had met (it was their last meeting) at Sharm el-Sheikh for what were called 'summit talks' – though mostly they posed for photographers and talked about the scenery and how Sharm (which Israel had taken in 1967 and renamed Ophira) bustled with activity, with hundreds of Israelis come to settle and develop it and crowds of holiday-makers drawn from all over the world to its transparent sea and yellow sands.

I also remembered how at lunch that day, Sadat had turned to Begin in a burst of apparent enthusiasm. 'When you have evacuated all of Sinai,' he had said with his usual intensity, 'nothing will change here, for sure. Everything will stay as it is now; the highway from Eilat, the Israelis, the divers, the swimmers, the tourists. Everyone will move back and forth freely. Everything as now – except for the soldiers. They will be Egyptians!' And he had laughed with pleasure, I thought, at his little joke – and at the future he foresaw. Did he mean it? At the time, I wasn't sure and, even now, so many years afterwards, I wonder if it would have been that way had he lived.

Flying back to Israel on the night of his murder, I thought also of my own last meeting with him. We had spoken together for an hour or so in what had once been a royal palace, outside Alexandria, set in a magnificent garden that stretched as far as the eye could see. Sadat seemed very relaxed, and we conversed with ease. 'You know,' he said, at one point, leaning towards me a little in his eagerness to communicate, 'we are both ancient peoples, experienced and very patient. There is nothing we cannot discuss – provided there is no more war. Everything between us will eventually be solved, even the question of Jerusalem. We will talk and talk until we agree. Do not be afraid. It will take time but it will be all right.' Begin had understood and shared that approach; we were not contestants in a race; nor, in a sense, contestants at all. Because the Peace Treaty with Egypt could not, from the Arab point of view, have been signed without reference to Israel's control of Judea and Samaria, Begin had developed the idea of autonomy, of interim arrangements, of gradual change, and Sadat had gone along with these, he too believing, as Begin did, that there was not only a tomorrow but also the day after – always, of course, given a methodology for talking today. And, anyhow, he had certainly achieved his real goal.

Because the funeral was to be held on a Saturday, the three representatives of the Jewish state – Menachem Begin, Dr Josef Burg (then Minister of the Interior and chairman of Israel's team to the autonomy negotiations) and I – flew to Cairo the day before. We landed in an almost unrecognizable city, empty and silent; only the army and police moved around in the heat while the millions who live in Cairo were kept off its streets in the name of security and order. The arrangements were perfect. The Egyptians, stricken and tense, had achieved a remarkable degree of efficiency; everything worked when and as it was supposed to, including the kosher food supplied for us at the overnight accommodations that made it possible (if not effortless) for us to attend the funeral without having to ride on the Sabbath. Early next morning we set out for the long, hot walk; three middle-aged Jews in dark suits and hats on their way to pay tribute to the slain Egyptian, who, less than a decade ago, had launched the Yom Kippur War. Who could have imagined it? When the walking and the rites were over, it was time for the condolence calls; first to the gracious Jehan Sadat, then to Sadat's Vice-President and successor, Hosni Mubarak, who had been with him on the reviewing stand but miraculously escaped unhurt. 'Peace will continue,' said Egypt's new President, but, although he treated us as brothers in bereavement, none of Sadat's persuasive fervour was in his voice; not then, not since. Nor was it irrelevant that the only heads of Moslem states to attend Sadat's funeral were Sudan's Numeiri and sheikhs from Oman. The Arab world continued its rejection of him. He had committed the worst of all crimes: peace with Israel.

Indeed, as time passed, Mubarak made clear his own attitude towards the Treaty and us. On the surface, he was punctilious, reasonable, the strong, eminently suitable heir of a legendary man. But his deepest political and emotional allegiances were not to Sadat's vision but rather to what might be considered its diametric opposite: to Pan-Arabism and the dominance of Egypt in the Arab world, seeing these (although Sadat saw otherwise) as best serving Egyptian interests. Bound to the Treaty, unable without severe consequences (and perhaps by now not really eager) to wholly free himself from it, wherever possible Mubarak has minimized its importance, barely obeying the letter and consistently ignoring the spirit, treating it as an irksome obligation, manipulating the relationship between Egypt and Israel to suit purposes never projected at Camp David and occasionally permitting himself to mount violent personal attacks on me – though always presenting himself internationally, and especially for Washington's benefit, as second to none in his concern for Egyptian–Israeli amity. This, while in Cairo the Peace Treaty is still coldly referred to as the 1979 Agreement; Israel is acknowledged, recognized, but neither truly nor warmly accepted; and the deliberate imbalance carefully maintained. The Egyptian Ambassador is fêted in Tel Aviv, but in Cairo the Embassy of Israel is still suspect, largely unvisited, and the Ambassador is isolated; and, despite our constant complaints, much of the Egyptian press entertains its readership with crudely anti-Semitic cartoons and articles. There is still no two-way tourism: the few Egyptians to apply for visas are interrogated and watched, though there is a trickle of cultural exchange; trade remains minimal – under a special arrangement we buy Egyptian oil, partly drilled from the fields we gave back. In no respect has normalization been part of Egyptian policy since 1981. Over the years, I often invited Mubarak to Jerusalem: 'Come, see for yourself, tour the country. I promise you the warmest possible welcome.' But Mubarak is no Sadat, neither anxious to star in an international drama nor about to risk death for the Treaty's sake at the hands of Moslem fundamentalists; and not even the Americans have managed, though they have tried hard, to persuade him to visit us. He has always turned down the invitation or made his response conditional on major changes in Israeli policy; and he has also as consistently refused to invite me to Cairo unless I brought some major concessions with me. 'I will not meet Mr Shamir just to drink coffee,' was the way he put it.

How sad that the autonomy that might have taken us past main hurdles into a new era, into what, by now, would have been a creative fait accompli, has remained undone, wrecked on the rocks of Egyptian disinterest.

We had promised to make a final withdrawal from Sinai by 25 April 1982 – and did. We evacuated our military bases, dismantled villages and townships, and withdrew our forces right up to the international boundary, government and people united in the hope that, for the sake of peace, the sacrifice, and the hazards, would be justified. An article ('Israel's Role in a Changing Middle East') I wrote that spring for a foreign affairs journal gives no hint of the strong emotions, mine and those of almost all other Israelis, that accompanied the pull-back and the levelling of the town of Yamit in the north-east corner of Sinai, acts that came to represent the finality of our side of the 'exchange'. 'By ... May, 1982, implementation of the territorial aspect of the Israel–Egypt Treaty will have been completed. ... The normalization of relations ... will enter a new phase,' I wrote, expressing more hope than I felt. In the suspense that preceded the withdrawal, Begin, restless and anxious, asked Reagan and Mubarak for personal guarantees, in writing, that they would continue to abide by the Camp David Accords, especially in connection with the Palestine problem (meaning continuation of the autonomy talks), and never seek any other solution. The reassurances came at once.

Dated 20 April 1982, both replies were equally emphatic and affirmative though different in tone. President Reagan wrote:

... the Camp David Accords and the Egyptian–Israeli Peace Treaty ... represent the highest standard against which other efforts to achieve peace must be measured ... it is in the United States' abiding security interests to ensure that the Treaty of Peace is rigorously applied and respected and that challenges to it from whatever quarter are met and overcome. ... You, President Mubarak, and I are in agreement that the Camp David Framework Agreement is the only agreed plan to solve [the Palestinian problem] ... the United States remains committed to ... pursue an early and successful conclusion of negotiations for full autonomy ... for the Palestinian inhabitants of the West Bank and Gaza as called for in the Camp David Framework Agreement. ... I am convinced that history will show that your sacrifices have ensured the security of the State of Israel and the Jewish people.

President Mubarak wrote:

... The Arab Republic of Egypt is determined to fulfil all its obligations under the Camp David Accords and the Peace Treaty in good faith ... This is the only course ... compatible with our interest and in fact with the interest of all peoples of the Middle East ... it is vital that we set in motion the process of solving the Palestinian question because we are determined to reach a just, comprehensive and durable settlement of the Middle East conflict in accordance with ... the Camp David Frameworks ... the only binding document between our two countries. This is our policy today and it will remain unchanged in the future.

He ended with a reference to 'the problem of the boundary line near Taba': 'Fixing a date for settling the matter will not hurt the legitimate interest of either party. It is a technical point ... I count on your wisdom and good judgment.' There was, or seemed to be, no alternative to going through with the abandonment of Yamit.

It had looked, earlier, as though most of the 2,000-odd townspeople (and roughly the same number living in the moshavim and kibbutzim of the region) would part from their homes, and from Sinai, unhappily accepting the generous financial compensation made available to them. But as the deadline loomed, rage and grief overcame many of them. Yamit's last weeks were marked by desperate bargaining for more money with which to relocate, by the formation of a 'Stop the Retreat from Sinai' movement and by the arrival of passionate young families from Judea and Samaria to swell the ranks of those determined to block the razing of everything they had built and prevent the obliteration, once again, of an Israeli presence in the Sinai they had come to love. There were hunger strikes and suicide threats, even the dread possibility of armed confrontation between militant settlers and the young soldiers of the IDF assigned to erase Yamit. But on the designated day, army sappers completed the town's demolition. The last structure to be destroyed was a memorial to Israeli troops who had taken the area in 1967. On 26 April, all of Sinai was in Egyptian hands and we had established what I believed was a most dangerous precedent: we had given up Jewish settlements and returned to the 1967 borders between Egypt and ourselves – which is where we had been when the Six Day War broke out. I was filled with regret at the end of the bright chapter of Israeli enterprise and hope in Sinai, and with foreboding.

Six weeks after the trauma of the erasing of Yamit, the war in Lebanon broke out. That I have left mention of that war to the end of these recollections of my days at the Foreign Ministry is not because this conflict has turned, with time, into an after-thought for me. The contrary is true; the years have sharpened the anger that accompanied my own involvement, such as it was, in a series of events that left behind them not only a trail of still unanswered questions but also a bitter taste. A military action that started out, as I saw it, with one clearly defined goal, it ended, when it finally did, in a way, and at a time, that no one anticipated. It cost the lives of hundreds of Israeli soldiers and it kept the IDF bogged down for more than two years in the occupation of a lawless land, devastated by a civil war in which thousands had been killed, and still at the mercy of warring and fanatic Moslem, Christian and Druze militias. Alone among our wars, the controversial Lebanon campaign was fought not only in the absence of a national consensus but also in the face of a public protest in Israel that almost in its stridency and exaggeration matched the hysterical response it evoked abroad. Nor is Lebanon at peace today – with us, though it might have been, nor with itself. Even as I write, terrorism, treachery and anarchy continue their rule there. Except for the Israelis who since 1982 live in a new tranquillity in the north of our country, and those who mourn the fallen, it is almost as though nothing had happened.

Operation Peace for Galilee, launched on 6 June 1982, was intended to last no more than forty-eight hours, to penetrate Lebanon to a maximum depth of some forty kilometres and to destroy the PLO headquarters, bases, personnel and gigantic arms stores that, for nearly a dozen years, threatened the safety, not to say the sanity, of the men, women and children of Israel's northernmost towns and settlements. Ever since the PLO, thrown out of Jordan by King Hussein in 1970, arrived in south Lebanon and took over there, disrupting and brutalizing civilian life and acting as a catalyst in a new phase of the ongoing civil war, the population of Israel across the border served as the target for terrorist assaults. These ranged from shelling and rocket attacks to the ambushing of buses, the storming of schools and apartment houses, the murder and maiming of adults and children alike. It is to the great credit, let me interject, of this sorely tried population that it did not take to its heels and flee en masse – though the extent and cruelty of PLO terror were well known, and the connection between the PLO bases in Lebanon and terrorist attacks worldwide were also no secret.

All of Israel's limited aims were achieved: the infrastructure of the PLO in Lebanon was smashed and its links to most of the international terror organizations severely, if not permanently, dislocated. But the campaign did not stop there. Having finished off the PLO in south Lebanon, the IDF pushed northwards, reaching the environs of Beirut, a city turned into an armed camp by the forces of the PLO, those of the rival Maronite (Christian) Phalange and yet others. Although at first the PLO refused to admit defeat and leave Beirut, it was logical to assume that once the Palestinians were forced out, the way would be open to creating at least some equilibrium between Lebanon's Christians and Moslems, to bringing calm to Israel's north, and perhaps even to negotiations for peace between Israel and a second Arab state.

But the IDF siege of Beirut lasted for much longer than expected. Then, one month after it was broken and the PLO finally expelled from the city, the young Israeli-backed Christian President-elect of Lebanon, Bashir Jemayel – it was hoped that he would play a pivotal role in bringing about a new relationship with Israel – was murdered, obviously by Moslem assassins, and Lebanon was once more plunged into chaos. On 16 September 1982, three days after Jemayel's assassination, the Christian Phalangists moved into the now-notorious West Beirut Sabra and Shatilla refugee camps (both sites of

Moslem terrorist bases) for mopping-up operations. Once inside, in a terrible act of revenge, the Phalangists butchered nearly 300 innocent men, women and children. By the time the IDF intervened, it was too late; Israel was blamed throughout the world for the massacre. Suddenly Lebanon's misery, ignored for so long by so many, became the focus of international outrage. In Israel there was also dissent: public agitation over the continuing war, its accompanying casualty lists and horror at the cold-blooded slaughter perpetrated in an area under IDF control, forced the Government to establish a Commission of Enquiry – even before the war ended. That Commission, headed by Supreme Court Chief Justice Yitzhak Kahan, absolved the state absolutely of any direct responsibility for the Sabra and Shatilla killings, but held it to have been indirectly responsible. The Kahan Commission heard forty-two witnesses; nine of these, including Prime Minister Menachem Begin, Defence Minister Ariel Sharon, Chief of Staff Rafael Eitan, the Chief of Military Intelligence and I, were served with formal prior warning that we were likely to be 'harmed' by the Commission's findings. I was appalled to learn that, insofar as I was concerned, the Commission had concluded that, although I had received a 'report' from Communications Minister Mordechai Zippori regarding 'the actions of the Lebanese forces' in the camps, I had taken 'no appropriate steps' to verify this or to bring it to the knowledge of the Prime Minister or the Defence Minister – thus not fulfilling my duty as Foreign Minister.

This rebuke was based, incredibly enough, on a remarkable interpretation of one short telephone conversation. On the evening of 16 September, I had heard, for the first time (at a Cabinet meeting), about the Phalangists entering the two camps; it was mentioned as routine information and not made the subject of any discussion, nor even of comment. Next day, Zippori, sitting with journalists in Tel Aviv, phoned me to say that he had 'heard' that the Phalangists were 'running wild' at Sabra and Shatilla. No details, just that. 'Why call me?' I asked, surprised. 'Because I can't reach anyone else and I think someone should know,' Zippori replied. 'Running wild' at that point described almost everything done by almost everyone in Lebanon, so it didn't occur to me that any special significance lay in what he said. Moreover, later that day, I sat with the Defence Minister, with the Chief of Military Intelligence, with the head of Israel's General Security Services – all of whom had come to my office to meet US negotiator Morris Draper; again, nothing was said about any untoward action in the camps.

It was only the next day that I learned what had taken place.

Menachem Begin, I believe, never recovered from the shock; Ariel Sharon, charged with 'disregard of obvious dangers', had to resign as Defence Minister; as for myself, I learned one more lesson about the unpredictability of events and people and have never, until now, referred publicly to the Kahan Commission report. What I may never recover from in relation to Sabra and Shatilla is the memory of the indecent haste with which Israel was condemned by the media abroad for the crime – as though, at best, we had directed it or, at worst, done the job with our own hands, as though we were in Lebanon pursuing misunderstood and noble refugees rather than the brutal gunmen of the PLO, and as though Israel's true face was revealed in our violation of peaceable Lebanon.

All of which was, of course, nonsense. But it was also injurious, malicious and (in not a few instances) anti-Semitic. A climate was created in which anything was permissible – from outright lies to elaborate carelessnesses, from staged photographs of atrocities all the way to phoney interviews – just as long as the Jewish state and the IDF were besmirched. An outstanding example was when, in August 1982, no less a personage and friend of Israel's than Ronald Reagan himself showed me the photograph of an armless baby girl wounded in an Israeli bombing of Beirut. It so moved him, he said, that he kept it on his desk. When I got back to Israel and made enquiries, I discovered that the baby had not lost her arms at all; she had suffered a fracture in one of them. I had just become the grandfather of a baby girl and knew how I would feel were she to be wounded, but the implications and emphasis of the photograph and caption that someone had taken the trouble to give to the President of the United States were poisonous. I sent the correct information to him at once, but doubted that it would be an adequate antidote.

The more distorted Israel's image became abroad, the greater the outcry within Israel against the war, its rising toll (in all close to 700 young men fell in Lebanon), and the seemingly endless and reluctant IDF occupation of somebody else's dangerous country. Other ingredients were also involved in the growing pressure to pull out at once and at almost any price. Throughout the years of Labour Party hegemony in Israel, of Labour Governments, the Opposition had refrained from publicly criticizing any military action, or, if it did so, waited until after the event, as was the case, for instance, following the Yom Kippur War. This time, however, the Labour Alignment was the Opposition and it attacked Begin's Government relentlessly. God knows, we weren't in Lebanon to annex it, to enslave its people or to become embroiled in its instabilities and internal wars. We had gone there to get rid of the terrorists. That done, we wanted guarantees that they would not be able to return; no, not guarantees but firm security arrangements. As Begin once said, 'There is no guarantee that can guarantee a guarantee.' We wanted nothing ad hoc, unofficial or likely to be temporary.

Although I had no hand or say in the conduct of that war (in which the main roles were played by the Prime Minister and the Minister of Defence) until the time came to work towards an Israel–Lebanon peace – and although I believe that, as is true for other conflicts, only historians, Israeli and perhaps others, will be competent to assess the circumstances and personalities involved – it is my duty to make certain comments. To begin with, I neither disclaim nor minimize my role in the Government decision that initiated Operation Peace for Galilee, nor, even now, have any doubt that it was a justified and urgently needed campaign though, undeniably, sub-sequent mistakes and miscalculations of a most serious nature were made and cost precious lives. Far too often the Government had no alternative other than to endorse measures already taken, without explicit approval or adequate information; on several crucial occasions, the time-lag between military action and Cabinet decision being inexcusable, especially when viewed in retrospect – though I must allow for the possibility of prior talks (at which I was not present) between Prime Minister Begin and Defence Minister Sharon.

As for Sharon ('Arik' as he is known in Israel), I didn't need the Lebanon war to form an opinion about him. I have known him and had close contact with him in his capacity as a member of the Herut Party, of the Likud that he did much to create, of Cabinets to which I also belonged and, of course, as a member of Cabinets I headed. What do I think of him? I think he is completely dedicated to Israel, a natural and fearless leader of men, hampered by a degree of inborn extremism and recklessness that has frequently severely injured him and, much more importantly, hurt the cause around which his life has been centred. He and I are too unlike, too basically different in our perceptions and behaviour to have been friends, and within the Party we found ourselves often in angry opposition: he loudly mocking me for undue caution, I making clear my distaste for his wilfulness and disregard of accuracy. None the less, when I entrusted him with overall responsibility for co-ordinating the absorption of the immigrants pouring into Israel in the early 1990s, it was because I knew that if the job could be done at all – despite the great difficulties – probably only Sharon could do it, given his intelligence, tenacity and also perhaps his desire to be remembered not only for a bitterly controversial military career but also for his role in the continuing Ingathering. In this enormous effort he was once more charged with overstepping bounds, though, as in Lebanon, had events evolved differently, his 'bulldozing' and lack of restraint might well have been praised to the skies.

In Lebanon, where, in many respects, he behaved like a Viceroy, he went so far as to make a deal, on Israel's behalf, with Bashir Jemayal's brother Amin, who took his place as President, a document that Amin even signed but which, they promised each other, would not be made public unless and until mutually agreed, the secrecy having been primarily intended to keep the United States from knowing about it for the time being – though, of course, official negotiations were being conducted at the same time by the Foreign Ministry, with the help of Reagan's Special Ambassador Philip Habib, backed by US Secretary of State Shultz and US Defense Secretary Casper Weinberger. Predictably, Sharon leaked the story of his 'break-through'; Habib was furious, Amin almost had a heart attack, and the quarrels going on all the time between Sharon and the Americans increased in frequency and depth. But they ended as soon as Sharon left the arena.

By May 1983, I thought that the twelve-page agreement which we had laboriously managed to negotiate with the Lebanese Government – helped by the Americans, and navigating carefully around the Syrian presence (strong in Lebanon ever since the middle 1970s) – would be adequate, would permit our soldiers to come home and would bring peace to Galilee. But it was not to be. No one in Lebanon, including President-elect Bashir Jemayel and later his brother, Amin, had been strong enough, brave enough or wise enough to make peace with us. To do so meant being able to resist the dictates and will of a formidable array of Arab states (first and foremost Syria) for whom any form of normalization of relations with Israel was and is anathema. For this, the Lebanese were too exhausted, too lacking in physical and moral fibre.

But we, on the other hand, were not going to let the chance of peace slip through our fingers just because we were getting tired or even because our casualty figures were still increasing agonizingly, though the 'formal' fighting was over. No one was safe in Lebanon in those dreadful times; snipers, mines and terrorist traps were everywhere, and thus violent death. For weeks beginning 1 January 1983, Israel's negotiating team, headed by David Kimche, met in my office at sunrise before setting out for the day's almost invariably discouraging talks with the Lebanese – the sessions held alternately in one of the Israeli towns the PLO had battered for so many years (Kiryat Shmoneh or Nahariya), or in the Lebanese townlet of Khalde. Day after day, the Lebanese bargained over each proposed detail of the terms of an IDF withdrawal, alarmed, they claimed, that Israel would encroach on Lebanon's sovereignty, though, in reality, there was no such thing any more. It had long ceased to exist. I was guided by the same thought that was to direct most of my actions and attitudes in the years ahead. Big countries, I told myself, can afford to make mistakes; small ones cannot. We are after the only prize, peace, that can justify any war; we must not lose our nerve – or rush. And I did my best to go on believing that it was possible to negotiate with a President who barely presided over a state that barely functioned.

In Washington, I reiterated what we believed to be the essential mechanics of withdrawal: joint patrols, observation posts, regular contacts between Lebanese commanders and commanders of the Israeli zone. 'We must arrive at co-operation: bona fide, close and based on mutual confidence,' I repeated over and over again at the various US forums I addressed on the subject of Lebanon.

The Americans, even-handedly, had decided to let Israel and Lebanon take their respective cases directly to President Reagan, to Shultz and to other US policy-makers. Since the Lebanese refused any direct contact with us, we went on virtually identical but always separate routes, whether it was to the State Department or to major American TV talk shows. Wherever they went, the Lebanese described their internal situation as 'wonderful, really', with no hint of the true havoc or weakness that existed – and to my astonishment, the Americans accepted this odd version of the state of affairs. At a lengthy March 1983 State Department session on Lebanon – in the presence of a US representation headed by Secretaries Shultz and Weinberger and including a host of US generals – which faced a handful of Israelis (the head of the IDF Military Intelligence among them), I was torn between the feeling that we were in some kind of witness box and amazement at the way each general solemnly reported on yet another aspect of a 'Lebanon' I couldn't recognize. At issue was the ability of the Lebanese army to keep peace – and the PLO at bay – in Lebanon. To the best of our knowledge, there was no properly functioning army at all and yet here we were listening to descriptions of the 'normal training procedures' this army was providing for its recruits, the conclusion being that we could leave Lebanon with impunity. It was an experience so bizarre that I can recall what went on in that rectangular situation room ten years ago with absolute clarity. On the other hand, it was typical of Shultz's thoroughness, of his desire always to examine in depth all aspects of a problem, and I was quite certain that he didn't, for a moment, feel that he was placing us on trial.

Anyhow, the Lebanese methodically turned down each of our suggestions for a free flow of goods and people across the borders, completely rejecting our demand that the IDF and the Lebanese army co-ordinate security arrangements for the next few years.

There was much urgent going back-and-forth. Shultz indefatigably shuttled between Jerusalem, Beirut and, not least, Damascus. I returned with the new Defence Minister, Moshe Arens, to Washington for more and even longer talks. Whenever we thought we were making some headway at last with the Lebanese, reaching some kind of understanding, it turned out not to be so. Nor was it always clear, though it was vital to try to guess correctly, from what direction the ill winds blew. From Syria? From the Soviet Union? Would they make it impossible for Amin Jemayel to stay the course? All the time I was also worried about something else: Begin's health. He didn't look or sound well; Mrs Begin had died in November 1982 when he was in the United States and his grief, combined with the war, seemed to have extinguished some light inside him, and I was very uneasy about him.

Lebanon seethed with its multiple rivalries: Moslem Shiites and Sunnites, Maronites, the Druze and remnants of the PLO; Syria redeployed its troops there; the Soviet Union warned against 'further Israeli offensives'. None the less, we persisted. Working around the clock at the Foreign Ministry, we racked our collective brains for new inducements to lure the Lebanese in the direction of peace, but what we presented in the middle of May was hardly a peace treaty. A kind of political agreement, in itself it was perhaps no mean achievement, but neither was it a reason for jubilation nor even of relief. It confirmed that the 'state of war' between Israel and Lebanon no longer existed, that all Israeli forces would shortly be withdrawn, and that the 'territory of each Party would not be used as a base for hostile or terrorist activity against the other Party'. Certainly had it been ratified, it might have formed the basis for the start of a new relationship. But it wasn't – and didn't.

At first accepted by the Lebanese, the agreement was soon permitted to lapse, then was nullified; the Syrians had leaned very hard on Jemayel and he had (possibly not unhappily) given way – though we were repeatedly told by Ambassador Habib that the Syrians had agreed to all the US proposals. None the less, there were 'benefits' in terms of our ties with the US; both Reagan and Shultz demonstrated their satisfaction with the agreement, believing – with typical American optimism – that it would prove to the more moderate Arab states, and to various European governments, that Israel was, and had always been, eager for peace, and thereafter and for a long time we were in the Administration's good books. In the event, the IDF stayed on in Lebanon, withdrawing in phases until the early spring of 1985, when it withdrew unconditionally to a six-mile-wide security zone in the south – at last abandoning the rest of Lebanon to its continuing unenviable fate.

8

PRIME MINISTER

ON 28 AUGUST 1983, at a Cabinet meeting, Begin resigned. He said, 'I cannot go on,' and left the room. It was a terrible moment. We sat there, around the table, unable to say anything to each other or even, for a few seconds, to look at each other. I remember my own feelings distinctly: the shock, the sharp sense of something irreversible and crucial having happened, the feeling that nothing would ever be the same again and, combined with these, the knowledge that, of course, for weeks we had all watched Begin – increasingly gaunt and withdrawn, almost listless – slowly move away from us, from the people, the issues, the challenges he had faced with such power and dynamism, and had been unwilling to accept what now was revealed as inevitable and final. He no longer talked with the same energy, the same richness of expression, the same flow of ideas, this man so fluent that the remarkable and powerful speeches for which he was famous were never delivered from a text. He spoke with only a few notes on a piece of paper in front of him, reminders of the facts, images, comparisons and conclusions that he so brilliantly presented, everything resting on his phenomenal memory. The longer and the harder I try to understand what actually led Begin to resign in that way and at that time, the less I think it was due to any immediate political circumstances or developments and the surer I am that it was a sort of judgment he passed on himself when he simply had no reserves left with which to go on leading the nation. He had always depended on his own great strength, on his ability to make decisions and to abide by the results, on his inner resources, never turning to anyone else for assistance, no matter how competent and loyal his would-be helpers were. And when he felt he had used up that which had nourished his creativity and zeal, he reached the despair implicit in those tragic words of resignation.

We did everything possible to persuade him to change his mind –

to no avail. He listened to every one: to the pleas of intimates, to small distraught groups of long-time disciples, to delegations of petitioners representing a vast and stricken following. He was patient, polite, regretted the extreme distress he was causing, argued with no one but explained nothing. All he had to say, or would say, was that he could not go on. In retrospect, knowing what I now know, I understand him better than I did then. Now I understand how he no longer felt strong enough to ward off the attacks against him, to ignore the lies, to shake off the slanders as he had done for so many years. Maybe one day he just decided that there was nothing he could do, that no efforts of his would change anything and that even when everything that could be said against him had been said, the ugliness and the defamation would continue. And if so, better perhaps to protect himself with a shield of indifference and leave it all – however much this was at odds with his self-confidence, his belief in his own truth and his immense sense of being responsible to his people, the masses whose love and respect he so fully returned. I only hope that he found some modicum of peace and quiet in that other existence to which he retired but, since he left no word behind him, we will never know.

As for the orphaned Likud, the demands of the present were urgent, though the mood was despairing. Without Begin, how could there possibly be continuity? How could the Party be expected to survive? The trouble was not only the void of Begin's absence, it was also that he had never concerned himself with a future leadership. He had never wanted to know or even think about what would happen if, and when, he himself was not at the helm. He had never groomed or boosted anyone, not even among the people closest to him. On several occasions I had hinted (because he would certainly not have accepted any outright suggestion) that we should be on the look-out for possible successors, for fresh cadres that could take 'our' place one day and that, when we found them, we should make it our business to give them visibility. 'Let people see and hear them,' I said. But he had never shown the slightest interest. Gradually we reconciled ourselves to reality; a new leadership had to be put together even before any of us had time either to recover properly from the trauma of Begin's departure or to reorganize after so many years of his absolute authority. Even now, nearly a decade later, the Likud still has no real rules or regulations, no binding code as to how elections are to be run or how decisions are to be taken. Everything is still highly debatable, and is being debated.

When the time came for someone to be chosen to take Begin's

place, my name came up. The people who proposed me were those who, several years earlier, had recommended that I be appointed Foreign Minister. I myself said nothing. I have never 'run' for office and couldn't imagine marketing my virtues or attributes, though this time I was more and better prepared for what might await me, had much more self-assurance, and was at least able to listen to other people sing my praises, though I winced at the exaggerations.

There were two likely Likud candidates to take over. I was one; the other was the then Deputy Prime Minister and Minister of Housing, David Levy (eventually to become my Foreign Minister), an energetic, ambitious man, senior to me in the movement, with a large following but also many detractors who belittled him for his vanity, considered him a lightweight, deplored his 'lack of sophistication' and made tasteless jokes about him. In fact, he was a true product of the times, a 'new' Israeli, the Moroccan-born child of the great North African immigration of the 1950s, a man fully entitled to represent the so-called 'oriental', i.e. Sephardic, Jews, himself living in a development town and the head of a big family. Also he was only forty-seven and determined, as he had been from boyhood, to get to the top and sure that he would do so. I, on the other hand, was far from being an obvious choice. I was sixty-eight, had spent much of my life in covert activities, wasn't well-known, had no grass-roots following and no special aspirations. It had certainly never occurred to me that I might be Prime Minister or should seek that lofty office. I wasn't even a member of the close circle of Begin's 'Fighting Family'.

It wasn't the last time David Levy was to enter the ring against me; he sought the Prime Ministership again in 1992 and after those elections hoped to lead the Likud. I liked him but didn't think he could or should lead the movement. Also he was much handicapped, in my view, by his followers, who, whenever he failed, at once raised the flag of 'ethnic' protest, claiming the 'oriental' Jews were being discriminated against in a party controlled by 'Ashkenazi' Jews (of European origin). But though this cry may have had some validity where other political parties were concerned, in the case of the Likud, or before it of Herut (over half of whose members were 'oriental' Jews), or even before that of the Irgun and Lehi, the charge was absurd. The contrary was true. There has never been the slightest 'tokenism' within the Zionist right wing. Even its most hysterical opponents have never made that accusation, nor had Levy ever made it himself.

I didn't for a moment believe the Party was done for or that it had no future without Begin. The Likud had a clear-cut ideology, strong principles and a platform that had been put to the test, and I was sure that our voters, understanding the critical basic issues separating the Likud from the Alignment, would vote for us again.

I feel it necessary at this juncture to write a few lines regarding Likud ideology, and when I write about the Likud, I include of course the Herut Party at its heart. From the time that Begin decided on signing a peace treaty with Egypt, on the Camp David Accords and on the Israeli withdrawal from Sinai, certain shifts had to take place in Likud thinking. Back in pre-state days, in the 1930s and 1940s, the nationalist movement had a clear unalterable position regarding the Land of Israel: no part of it was to be relinquished by the Jews to anyone under any circumstances. But the Camp David Accords of the 1970s raised significant ideological questions for many, if not most, Likud followers: Begin had given up Israeli control of Sinai for the sake of peace with Egypt. True, Sinai was not part of the Land of Israel, but Jewish history recorded no precedent for the enforced evacuation by the Israeli Government itself of settlers from Jewish settlements established, with government aid and encouragement, in Sinai. Nor was there any precedent for Begin's commitment to conduct negotiations regarding autonomy for Arabs in Judea, Samaria and the Gaza district. These developments created a new situation: since then the Likud has not absolutely a priori rejected all Arab demands for Israeli withdrawal from territories, within the Land of Israel, held by Israel since 1967. As long as Begin determined matters virtually single-handedly, everyone looked to him for guidance. Now that too changed. But the basic decision that Israel should not pay for peace with parts of its land remained as it had always been, an article of collective faith.

For myself, I was sure that Israel needed a government that could, at one and the same time, maintain an unending vigilance against all potential underminers of Israel's sovereignty – and seize every possible opportunity to fulfil the Zionist mission as we interpreted it. So though I had little appetite (to understate) for campaigning and the in-fighting this always involved, when pressed to run, I agreed – without joy, not without trepidation, but fairly certain, if nothing else, that I could at least be useful in this bleak period, useful to Israel and to the Likud.

For the first time in thirty years, the Party really chose a leader not by what amounted to acclamation. That is, there had been secret balloting in Begin's day (he insisted upon it) but it was taken for granted, correctly, that ninety-nine per cent of the votes cast were for him. On 1 September 1983, by a vote of 436 to 302, the central committee elected me as its candidate to succeed Menachem Begin – no, not to succeed but to follow him. Late that night Shulamit and I returned to Jerusalem from the Likud headquarters in Tel Aviv, already accompanied by an additional bodyguard. We sat in the back of the car without talking, each of us thinking about the future and what it would hold, knowing that we were heading for uncharted but certainly deep waters. How would it be? Would I be out of my depth? It was one thing to serve as Foreign Minister, another to head a government; one thing to serve under Begin, another to lead a party that felt itself to be fatherless. I would not have accepted the nomination had I not felt competent to contribute to Israel in this capacity, but did I really know – for all my experience – what being a Prime Minister entailed? No, not yet. But I knew something else. As had been true at other junctures of my life, including in the underground, I felt that I had had no alternative other than to do what I was doing. I didn't, even to myself, think in terms of 'destiny', but maybe that is what being impelled to answer the call of duty really is.

Thus I became Israel's seventh Prime Minister. On the whole, the local public reaction to this was, as one might have expected, a measure of relief that at least the processes of governance and of the search for peace would not be delayed or hindered. As one Israeli journalist wrote about me, expressing I think what most people felt, correctly or otherwise: 'What he appears to be is really what he is; there will be no surprises.' Abroad, the only response I recall was that of the London *Times*, which at once published a 1948 document from the British Public Record Office in which I was described as 'a fanatical terrorist', a campaign, by the way, that was to continue till after the elections when the same newspaper concluded that 'for Israel ... to choose to be led by a man with such a record ... may seem rather remarkable and indeed rather sad'.

In the meantime, I had less than a year (it took till the middle of October to form a new government) to try to fill the vacuum created by Begin's leaving, to continue and improve our relationship with the United States and finally to work towards getting the IDF out of Lebanon entirely, under the best possible conditions and with the least possible risk to Israel.

By 10 October 1983, I had formed a sixty-four member coalition comprising much the same components and people as before, could announce the formation of a government and ask the Knesset to approve the guidelines of its policy. I had broached the idea to the Alignment (its coalition numbered fifty-six) of considering a government of national unity. It was not only my natural urge for unity at a time of difficulties or that the Likud generally, and I specifically, were ever unaware of, or pushed aside, the differences between the Alignment and the Likud. How could we have done that? These were deep and of long standing. But the salient question was, how else could we deal seriously and rapidly with major mounting economic and political problems? I thought unity was the obvious answer. But Mr Peres turned me down, partly because the situation did not, in his view, call for such dire measures; partly because territorial compromise was, always has been and still is a central Alignment plank and the Likud, he knew, was not going to agree either to a stoppage of new settlement activity in Judea and Samaria or to the 'return' of any part of the Land. We also disagreed over other issues: the conditions under which the IDF should leave Lebanon; whether Security Council Resolution 242 which talks of withdrawal from 'occupied territories' should also be a basis for talks with Jordan, as Labour wanted, or that these should be held only within the framework of the Camp David Accords, as the Likud insisted; whether the out-going Government's decisions on autonomy should be reconsidered, etc.

I was sorry about the negative response to a government of national unity but was not deterred from going ahead with setting up a narrow Likud government, which I now presented. Before I did so, I looked up for a moment at the Knesset Visitors' Gallery. Shulamit smiled at me, happily, I thought. So did the 'children' – themselves both already parents, both professionally successful, both serving the country – Yair then a high-ranking air-force officer, Gilada in the Ministry of Defence. I was very proud of them and hoped and assumed that this was a proud day for them as well.

Then I turned to the matters at hand, first to the reasons that led me to seek a government of national unity:

Such a government would contain that process of polarization [among our people] which has reached excessive proportions and threatens our unity; it would contribute to clearing the air, restore the norms of democratic and civilized debate among the various schools of thought; enhance the deterrent image of Israel in the eyes of our enemies who have begun to believe that Israel is weakening due to sharp differences of opinion, and raise our political prestige in the eyes of friends and enemies alike. As a result of this effort, we had the rare opportunity for serious, deep and open-hearted dialogue between representatives of the Labour Party and of the Likud on issues which today occupy a central place on our national agenda. ... I am still convinced that it would have been possible to form a unity government, provided neither side sought to impose its views on the other. ... At the same time I am convinced that the dialogue was not in vain. ... It is my intention ... if an opportunity arises to resume this attempt, even at the risk of failing again.

Next I turned to economics, to the grave problems of an inflation that had reached an annual rate of 400 per cent, to the need for restraining private consumption, cuts in government spending and a reduction in the balance-of-payments deficit; warned that Israel's standard of living would have to stop rising until we achieved a balance and recovery of the economy, and I pledged that we would continue the previous Government's social welfare programmes directed at disadvantaged neighbourhoods and at a reduction of the social gap. There was nothing in these statements, nor in those on national security or the peace process, that could not have been undersigned by the Opposition, including my assessment that there had been a revolutionary change in Israel's position in the entire region – '... [we have] become part of it not only on the map but in ... day-to-day developments' – or my appeal to the people and governments of the Middle East to come to 'the tables of negotiation and peace' and to the Soviet authorities to throw open 'the gates of emigration to the Jews of the USSR'. But in closing, I came, at last, to that credo which was unacceptable to the Alignment and signified Likud policy:

Paths must be opened and cleared for Jewish settlement throughout the Land of Israel. The previous Governments led by Menachem Begin have great achievements to their credit in this area; Jewish settlement has planted its stakes and kindled lights in many new places, in Galilee and Samaria, in Judea and the Golan. This sacred work must not stop; it cannot stop; it is the heart of our existence and life. ... We often frighten ourselves; superlatives of blackness are frequent in our political lexicon. Let us see matters in the proper perspective. ... We are a small nation that must stretch its capability to meet the tests and challenges it has set for itself. But that is how it has always been, ever since we became a nation, and with the strength of belief and historic inevitability we have succeeded, and overcome. If we believe this, we will succeed, since the story of the State of Israel from its establishment to this day has proved to be the story of an unparalleled success.

On the floor, friends and colleagues rushed to shake hands, to wish me well, to say 'well done'. I didn't know whether it was really well done or not, but I knew I had done my best.

In November, an invitation came from Washington, but it was as if to another Washington. The contrast between this visit and my last one was so sharp I could hardly believe that the cast of characters and scenery were the same. But, of course, in the interim much had altered: we had tried very hard to arrive at peace with the Lebanese; the IDF was no longer in Beirut and was well on its way out of Lebanon; Sharon had been replaced as Minister of Defence by Moshe Arens, who had served as Israel's respected Ambassador to Washington and was much liked not only in Congress but also at the Pentagon, and, most importantly, by Shultz, to whom his intelligence, directness and restraint appealed as much as they did to me. Also the US Administration had undergone a change of attitude regarding the Lebanese situation and was in itself in the course of realizing the extent of the unreliability, confusion and instability that had come to typify that unfortunate country. Probably among the other factors contributing to the new climate were the heavy casualties suffered in the bombing of the US Embassy in Beirut and of the US Marine barracks by Syrian-supported terrorists, the Syrian refusal to leave Lebanon, the US disappointment at Saudi indifference to what was happening in Lebanon, and Jordan's refusal to enter the peace process. The US Administration was arriving, it seemed, at the conclusion that, not for the first or the last time, it had somewhat misread the admittedly hard-to-read Middle East.

But, above all, both Ronald Reagan and George Shultz wished Israel well. They had reproved us severely; there were subjects on which we did not agree and, what's more, were not likely to agree; but the President of the United States and his Secretary of State had Israel's interests at heart and, whenever they found it possible to do so, they demonstrated this. My November 1983 visit was one such occasion, and by the time it ended there was no question but that Israel was again perceived as the only country in the Middle East upon which the United States could unhesitatingly and permanently rely, an appreciation that, within only a few years, experience would prove to be entirely justified, if only reluctantly acknowledged and no longer an operative White House premise.

The altered mood was apparent from the start of the two days and nothing clouded it. I was royally treated: brought by helicopter to the White House, provided with a Presidential plane for the return trip to New York, hosted at a dinner held in our honour by Vice-President and Mrs Bush. But however heart-warming the reception, the real fruits of the visit were to be revealed in the words of the President in his 'departure statement'. This is the last and, in a certain sense, the most important of the 'stations' of such a visit.

After the background work, the welcome, the hospitality, the toasts, the 'photo opportunity' and, above all, the talks themselves, this is what the President of the United States chooses to make public about the visit and its outcome. Each word, each nuance, is very carefully weighed and, though I already had some idea of the direction President Reagan's statement would take, I was profoundly reassured by its content and tone. It was, for a long time, to serve as the basis for Israel's all-important relationship with the United States. Herewith are some of its key phrases:

We have held two days of intensive talks with Prime Minister Shamir and his colleagues covering a broad range of subjects, including political-military co-operation, Lebanon, Israel's economic situation and the pursuit of the Middle East peace process. These discussions, as could be expected between close friends and allies, have been very productive. We reconfirmed the long-standing bonds of friendship and co-operation between our two countries, and expressed our determination to strengthen and develop them in the cause of our mutual interests. I am pleased to announce that we have agreed to establish a joint political–military group to examine ways in which we can enhance US–Israeli co-operation. This group will give priority attention to the threat to our mutual interests posed by increased Soviet involvement in the Middle East. Among the specific areas to be considered are combined planning, joint exercises and requirements for pre-positioning of US equipment in Israel.
    We have agreed to take other concrete steps aimed at bolstering Israel's economy and security ... these include ... asking Congress for improved terms for our security assistance to Israel ... [and] offering to negotiate a Free Trade Area with Israel. ... We reaffirmed our commonly held goals of a sovereign, independent Lebanon free of all foreign forces, and security of Israel's northern border ... [and] we, of course, discussed the broader goal of peace between Israel and its Arab neighbours. The Egyptian–Israeli peace treaty remains the cornerstone of the peace process. ... Our two days together have revealed substantial areas of agreement, and resulted in a number of specific, concrete steps we will take to strengthen our ties. We have also discussed some issues on which we do not see eye-to-eye. But disagreements between good friends do not alter the unique and sturdy foundation of our relationship. I know Prime Minister Shamir shares with me the renewed conviction that the friendship between the US and Israel will endure and prosper.

The President's statement had stressed positive policy, good intent, warm encouragement and genuine assistance. Unequivocally it had expressed US readiness to help Israel increase its strength in the security and economic spheres – notwithstanding those areas in which we had agreed, as it were, to disagree. The United States had been lending us money, mostly in the form of military assistance, on which we had to pay interest, thus making our national debt per person one of the heaviest in the world. Now it was decided that what used to be given as a loan would be a grant-in-aid, as a result of the new US understanding that if you really wanted to help an ally that could not fend for itself (to give one example of our fiscal burden, relocating from Sinai cost Israel $3 billion in loans and foreign interest), staggeringly large loans, though generous, were not perhaps the way to do it. Additionally, agreements were reached on the conversion of US aid funds into Israeli shekels for use in Israel in the total amount of $250 million, and regarding the US commitment to purchase products from Israeli industry for the US military and to sell port and airport services to these forces. 'Did you at least leave Reagan his ranch?' a reporter asked me the next day at the National Press Club.

In general, I believed that decisions having to do with the economy should not reflect my personal priorities. If, as Prime Minister, then or afterwards, I was totally opposed, for instance, to the idea that the Israel–Arab problem could be solved via an international conference, then that was that; in such matters I felt that I knew best, that I was right, that my obligations to the country and to its future lay in a given direction and nothing could or did ever budge me from this position. But about economics, I knew I did not know best and had no profound inner convictions. What I wanted, and mostly got, were feasible decisions reached by the system, i.e. the Government, through the good offices of the Finance Minister and the Bank of Israel. The one possible exception was when, days after I became Prime Minister, the then Finance Minister, later our Ambassador to the UN, Yoram Aridor, floated the idea of making the US dollar a basis for the shekel – which I at once felt would severely restrict Israel's sovereign policy-making power and, accordingly and angrily, forbade any further discussion of it

No part of that US visit had been less than memorable or without consequence. But in later years one aspect was to stand out for me: from 1977 to 1984, the seven years that had passed of Likud government, 230 settlements had been established, seventy-nine in the 'territories', i.e. Judea and Samaria, the Jordan Valley, on the Golan Heights and in the Gaza region (in addition to those in the Galilee, the Negev, the north and centre of the country). A new map of the Land of Israel had already been created, and though disapprovingly mentioned in various US Administration statements, those settlements were never placed in the forefront of US Middle

Eastern policy, never in those days described as or considered to be illegal or awarded the intense and negative attention they received first from President Carter, afterwards from President Bush. Fortunately, President Reagan was free from any such fixations, and his 'departure statement' had made this clear.

One facet of Israel to which the President – and the vast majority of Americans (including, in those days, the US media) – reacted with support and admiration was our determination not to give way to the Arab terror which waxed and waned but was always with us. The so-called *intifada*, the Arab disturbances in Judea, Samaria and mostly Gaza of the late 1980s and early 1990s, was still far off, but, in fact, there was no time when Israel's vigilance could be relaxed. This, of course, was quite apart from the around-the-corner Iran–Iraq war, which, by its very ferocity, made the Israel–Arab conflict pale and, by this time, had been going on for nearly four years with no end in sight, and no international figure, or element, willing or prepared to stop it – an object lesson in itself for us.

The Arab anti-Jewish terrorism, responsible in 1984 for almost daily attacks of increasing brutality – ranging from bombs in schools and buses to the killing of two students strolling near a monastery – was not only a source of bereavement, maiming and fear. It was to lead also to problems some of which were, and remain, unique to Israel even though not unfamiliar elsewhere. As had happened before, when I was a young man, we again faced situations in which, paradoxically, to avoid conflicts with external factors, we had to become involved in conflict within our own ranks. There are never exact parallels – history never precisely repeats itself – but I had confronted much the same moral dilemmas before and opted for much the same solutions. One core question that arose, inevitably, had to do with the nature and degree of the protection offered by the IDF to the settlers of Judea and Samaria living in those areas in which most of the terror originated. These were Jews in the settlements mainly established by the Gush Emunim ('Bloc of the Faithful') movement, which had been founded in 1974 by Israeli citizens who believed, as I do, that Judea and Samaria are an integral part of the Land of Israel, neither 'captured' in 1967 nor 'returnable' to anyone.

They are men and women of courage, integrity and determination who practise what they preach; who went, despite the difficulties and danger, to make their homes in Judea and Samaria; and who honestly and doggedly believe that Jews and Arabs can and must learn to live together – under Israeli sovereignty. They are also deeply believing Jews: this, to them, is literally the Holy Land and it is God's will for them to settle where they do. I have always admired them and am convinced that one day they will be as honoured in this country as are its original founding fathers and that, like those predecessors, they too are creating the historical facts for which future generations of Israelis will bless them. I visited them whenever I could, attended their modest ground-breaking ceremonies, made known to them that they had my total backing, and developed a liking for the leader of their Hebron community, Rabbi Moshe Levinger, with whom I talked from time to time, and considered him a man who, for the most part, understood the relationship between the establishment of settlements and Israel's political situation – although this proved not always to be the case.

As Arab terror escalated and tension grew between the settlers and the Arab population, some of the members of Gush Emunim, apprehensive, harassed, angry and mourning, decided that the army was not going about its duty properly, that the Arabs must be reminded that, in this country, Jewish blood had a high price, and went into avenging action themselves. Towards the end of April – what a crowded tragic April it was to be – the head of the General Security Services (GSS) told me that an attempt to plant explosives on several Arab buses had been uncovered and thwarted. The perpetrators were arrested and, following their interrogation, others suspected of attack on Arab residents of Judea and Samaria were also jailed. The GSS, moving quickly and effectively, had averted a catastrophe that might have severely damaged Israel, our political struggle, our standing and security, and made a mockery of our talk of peaceful co-existence. In the course of the interrogations it became clear that only a very small group of settlers were involved, the decisive majority having dissociated themselves completely from these acts, something of which I had been sure from the start.

Eventually, twenty-five settlers from Judea and Samaria, two from the Golan Heights and two officers of the Judea–Samaria Civil Administration were arrested, indicted for belonging to an 'organization whose ... aim was violence ... liable to cause death or injury to others', charged with stealing arms and explosives from the army and conspiring to 'inflict revenge on the Arab population and intimidate it', and imprisoned. The media rushed to interview me, hoping that I would agree to draw some comparison, or at least launch into a discussion of a comparison, between the activities of what it labelled as the Jewish underground and Lehi. I found the suggestion as grotesque as it was insulting to the memory of an underground that had fought so nobly to establish the Jewish state. Now that state existed. It was almost inconceivable and very painful to me that, after thirty-six years of independence, there could be Jews in our midst who dared to deny its authority and refused to acknowledge the fundamental principle that the Government, and only the Government, was responsible for Israel's security – and that of its citizens.

There wasn't the slightest question in my mind that these people must be brought to trial and made to bear the consequences of their action, even if there might be grounds for their pleas of self-defence. The psychological pressures put on me, understandably enough, were immense: demonstrators calling for release of the jailed settlers paced back and forth all day for weeks outside my residence, praying, shouting reminders to me of my intellectual and emotional identification with Gush Emunim, warning me not to betray them, their ideals or the Land of Israel, and reminding me of my own past. I knew some of the accused, but there was no getting around the fact, however much it hurt, that crimes had been committed, that they had to be paid for and that they must never be allowed to recur. Still there was one thing I could do; I could and did publicly stress the purity of the movement as such, quoting Psalms ('Touch not my anointed and do my prophets no harm') and making it clear that I regarded the guilty settlers as 'deviants', not as spokesmen for the majority upon whom no aspersions should be cast.

In the atmosphere that existed, another influential group, of a markedly different hue, had come into existence. In 1977, 300 army reserve officers had signed an appeal to Begin asking that Judea, Samaria and Gaza be returned for the sake of 'Peace Now' rather than adhering to the wholeness of the Land of Israel, although unfortunately in real life no such alternative existed. It was a slogan that, like most slogans, contained a shining if misleading promise: if Israelis only wanted it enough – despite the cabal of warmongers that was the Government, and if the territories were only given back – then peace would at once descend on this troubled land. The implication, of course, was that only these high-minded champions of peace really thirsted for it or knew – though they couldn't define it – the path which we should take in search of it.

In many ways, Peace Now, born out of genuine pain and anxiety, had turned by 1984 into a typically fashionable rather self-righteous protest movement, seen by its followers and even by the general public (on whom its impact was minor) as the diametric opposite of Gush Emunim. Not overtly political, it was none the less distinctly leftist, basked in the support of the Labour Alignment, especially the kibbutz movement which supplied many of its members, and found favour, automatically, in Israel's academic and literary circles in which loathing of the Likud was both traditional and endemic. Because these circles were closely connected to their counterparts abroad, Peace Now had also developed an overseas network of sorts, and its anti-Government message, however confused, was well received wherever anti-Israel groups congregated. I used to watch some of the demonstrators and ask myself how these attractive young people could possibly believe that the Government did not want peace as much as they did. What price, in actuality, would they be willing to pay for a purchased and, therefore, dubious peace? Many demonstrators were of army age and seemingly not bothered by the fact that no such movement had arisen in any Arab country, that no Arab soldier stood, even in civilian clothes, as they did, freely, opposite television cameras, holding up placards that called upon their Prime Minister immediately, and at almost any cost, to end the hostilities.

It wasn't the first time that a group of this kind, made up of intellectuals and proposing appeasement of the Arabs, had come into being in this country. Brit Shalom ('Covenant of Peace'), founded in 1925, and Ihud ('Union'), founded in 1942, both advocated a bi-national state in which Jews and Arabs would enjoy equal rights with no distinction between majority and minority. It failed to survive for various reasons, the principal one typically being a total lack of response from the Arab side. Of course, then there was no state. I couldn't help wondering once or twice what Brit Shalom's small elite membership would have thought of Peace Now and of the comfort and strength our enemies were deriving from observing these Israelis demonstrate against their elected government.

One other movement so far on the extreme right that ultimately it found no place in Israel was the infamous Arab-hating Kach ('Thus'), headed by Rabbi Meir Kahane, whose membership was very small but whose repellent message, especially in these times, didn't always fall on deaf ears and who had to be, and was, carefully watched. I had met Rabbi Kahane back in the 1970s in Tel Aviv. I knew only a little about him: in the United States in the 1960s, he had founded and led the Jewish Defence League, which undertook to protect Jews from anti-Semitic thugs in urban neighbourhoods and was made up largely of tough Orthodox young men; he had been very active in demonstrations on behalf of Soviet Jewry; he was the subject of much talk; but what could be wrong, I thought, with a man whose mission in life was to defend Jews? When he moved to Israel, he was very anxious to meet Begin. 'You see him,' Begin said to me. 'Talk to him and tell me what you think of him.' So I invited Kahane to my home and we spent about half an hour together. It took a lot less time for me to realize that he was 'not well'. We spoke about Soviet Jewry and he talked like a wild man. I told Begin next day that I was sure Kahane was unbalanced and that they ought not to meet, which Begin accepted. When he settled in Israel, he launched his violent anti-Arab campaigns.

Gradually he and Kach became more visible and, in 1984, stood for election to the Knesset. During the campaign, when billboards were covered with political posters, Kach's yellow placards showing a clenched fist and the words 'Never Again' were the most conspicuous, especially in disadvantaged neighbourhoods where rabble-rousing answered the inner needs of people filled with anger against Fate, or the Government, but mostly against the terrorists. In the elections, Kach won only 25,000 votes, but they gave Kahane a seat in the Knesset. It was only a year or two later that legislation was finally passed banning political parties from participating in Knesset elections if found to be undemocratic, racist or negating the existence of Israel as the state of the Jewish people. Ruled illegal, Kach essentially ceased to exist and Kahane himself met with violent death in the United States. It saddened me that, for many, this evil man came to represent religious militancy as such rather than derangement and the exploitation of furies evoked, among other things, by the persisting terror.

In that same April of 1984 something happened that was to develop in the course of a couple of years into a drama reaching, as nothing before or since has done as far as I know, into the heart of Israel's security services, upon which so much of the safety of our population depends. It was to uncover the story of the downfall of a formerly praiseworthy man, to illuminate a horrifying conspiracy, to throw the darkest of suspicions upon me personally, and to remind those concerned of the intricacy of the moral dilemmas that, in a country like Israel, unavoidably accompany the battle against terrorism. One day, I am sure this drama, its details unfolded, will be the subject of a book, if not of several. In the meantime, it must at least be recorded here.

The story began on an April evening when Bus Number 300, an ordinary Israeli bus on its ordinary southward trip from Tel Aviv to Ashkelon, was hijacked by Arab terrorists who managed to get it to a field in the Gaza Strip, where it was at last stopped by having its tyres shot and then, just before dawn, stormed by a military unit. All that was known up to then was that there were four armed Arab hijackers, that a couple of passengers (it was they who informed the police of the hijacking) had been allowed to leave the bus and that the other passengers escaped from it during the storming – except for a nineteen-year-old girl soldier who was killed and seven people who were wounded. All night, prior to the storming, negotiations had gone on with the terrorists (who demanded the freeing of a large number of Arab security prisoners in return for the passengers) in the presence of the Defence Minister, Moshe Arens, the Chief of Staff, the head of the police and senior GSS personnel. Also present were the press, which hadn't been made to keep its distance, and a small but growing crowd of bystanders.

When it was over, an IDF communiqué reported that the four terrorists were dead; two killed during the storming, two others having died of injuries. But press photographs showed, and bystanders had seen for themselves, two of the hijackers being removed from the scene 'under their own power' by security personnel. Something was clearly wrong. Suddenly there was an uproar of a characteristically Israeli kind: just how had all four terrorists died? Had two in fact been killed after they were captured? Was a cover-up now in force? Investigations were set in motion within the IDF, the police, the State Attorney's Office and, of course, the GSS to ascertain what had taken place in the half-dark, the tension and confusion. Finally, it was established that while two hijackers had indeed died in the course of the storming, the two others had been killed shortly afterwards. How could this have happened? Who had given the order – that question which both plagues, and defines, democracy? The IDF proved that it had turned the terrorists over to the GSS and had had no further contact with them. So who had? In time, suspicions began to focus on the GSS, headed then by Avraham (Avrum) Shalom, a man I had met when I worked in the Mossad and whom I liked and respected. I had never heard anyone speak of him with less than regard and for many he served as a model of courage, initiative and dedication to the people and missions for which he was responsible. No one is perfect, of course, but Shalom had seemed to come close to being so in terms of his work. Thus it never occurred to me to doubt him when he told me that the two terrorists in question had, in fact, been fatally injured during the storming and subsequently died.

I accepted this and was glad that the incident had been properly checked out. But the investigations were far from over. The State Attorney arrived at the conclusion that members of the GSS, acting on the orders of their Chief, had not only killed the hijackers but had deliberately lied about their deaths and, by implication, had incriminated others including, incredibly enough, a brigadier-general, Yitzhak Mordechai, who had been at the site of the storming. When this monstrous charge didn't hold water – it amounted to an accusation of murder – Shalom began to lose his nerve, probably for the first time in his life. Yes, he finally admitted, the GSS had been responsible for the deaths but it had acted according to orders. Whose orders? The Defence Minister's, said Shalom. Arens, furious, instantly denied the ridiculous accusation. Well, it wasn't really Arens, Shalom said. When the investigation continued, he told his colleagues that he had had the backing of the Prime Minister both for murdering the two captured terrorists and for his attempt to deceive his investigators. I was stunned when I learned about this later on – not so much by his audacity as by his attempted betrayal of me, for which I could only account by assuming that fear of the consequences of his initial lie had, in some dreadful way, trapped him.

Months later, the Alignment called for a judicial Commission of Enquiry, something which would have lent major political dimensions to the entire unsavoury affair and, more than that, would inevitably have hurt the GSS badly. I decided to suffer the poisonous political atmosphere in silence and to rely on the police and the Ministry of Justice to get to the truth, which they did with the help of four top GSS members, who, knowing the facts, found them intolerable and decided to co-operate in nailing the lies and disclosing the conspiracy. At this point, Shalom became even more reckless in his accusations: I had first 'instructed him to kill the Arabs and then abandoned him', he claimed. In the end, he was found to be guilty and I, of course, was vindicated. He never came to see me, to explain or to apologize for the lies and the damage he had tried to do me. We never met again.

It all took months, filled with rumours including allegations of my responsibility. I said nothing to anyone; my great concern was to safeguard the morale and good name of the GSS, then so much involved in fighting terrorism. For the same reasons, afterwards I suggested to Mr Peres, by then Prime Minister, that the President pardon Shalom and that he be permitted to resign his post. Other GSS personnel connected with the incident were also pardoned and the file closed. The story ended, but its bitter lessons were not forgotten; justice, at least largely, had been seen to be done; and it had been made unarguable that Israel's security could not and would not be built on lies. Avrum Shalom's crime had been twofold: the forbidden order to kill captives that he had given; and the lies he had told not to the enemy but within the 'family' itself. I want also to put on record, even in this very fragmentary account, that in the whole saga of abduction, death, intrigue, concealment and defamation – in which I was meant, at a given point, to play a leading role as victim – the one encouraging aspect was the intelligence, skill and determination to get to the truth of two young lawyers, Likud Members of the Knesset, who greatly aided me: Dan Meridor and Ehud Olmert.

By the time the summer came round I felt and, I think, was more or less at home in what only a few months before had been an entirely new role. My initiation hadn't been easy but I had survived it and, which mattered more, so had the Likud despite all earlier forebodings. I had learned about vulnerabilities, mine and those of others, and about the limitations of my position: that I could interfere and operate levers and have access but didn't own the state, couldn't influence everyone and had no protection from misrepresentation, let alone misquotation. On the other hand, everything I had experienced in adult life until then was coming to my aid now; ingrained habits, physical and emotional, bred of the underground and the Mossad and reinforced by my basic nature, had combined to make it possible for me to husband my resources.

What I needed and wanted to do I found myself able to do: I wanted to live as normal a life as conditions permitted, not to reside in a permanent state of emergency, but to concentrate my attention on those developments which I considered to be of national significance, and avoid being distracted by issues which, though they might be given periodic prominence by the media in Israel or elsewhere or by the Opposition, weren't likely – as I saw it – to affect Israel's future or survival. Neither then, nor later, did I go around explaining any of this. The people who worked with me understood my priorities and I didn't care much about the opinions of anyone else, or whether I was perceived by critics as 'detached' or 'blinkered' – the two adjectives most frequently applied to me even then by non-admirers. In private life, I also lived by rules I had learned long ago under different circumstances. I ate little, didn't smoke, hardly drank though I had once appreciated a brandy, went on long walks whenever conditions permitted and, thanks to Shulamit's forbearance, came home daily for a lunch and nap, returning to the office till evening. There was always reading to do at night – files, intelligence reports, position papers – but also there were the constant ceremonies, dedications, official dinners, speeches, not all necessarily spiritually stimulating but all obligatory.

The one prerogative I took for myself, turned into part of my routine and refused to give up, was the not-to-be-invaded privacy of my Sabbath. This was the one day I spent with the family, with my grandchildren, talking not on the phone for a change but face-to-face with Yair, sitting around the table with Gilada and her husband Natan, and Yair and Ella, my daughter-in-law, over some favourite Bulgarian dish prepared by Shulamit – and, as a rule, talking about 'the situation', whatever it happened to be. About Shabbat, I admit to intransigence; nothing short of national emergencies, the hot line, my military secretary's voice, could induce me to sacrifice those few hours of real privacy, and I believe they were restorative. Daytime callers, whoever they were, were directed to phone again after dark. We have always been a very private family, celebrating birthdays and holidays by ourselves. Even the Passover Seder for years was limited to the four of us and always held in our own home. That changed, of course, when grandchildren, in-laws and bodyguards had to be added and our number rose to thirty or more, but we have remained a tightly knit family, jealous of its privacy. In any case, the regimen, the self-discipline, a bit like a soldier's or that of an athlete in training, worked to my advantage. Even when I was particularly worried or in a very bad mood, it was never to a degree I couldn't control – which was just as well since, suddenly, elections loomed.

Normally Israelis go to the polls once every four years and the next elections should have been held in November 1985. Instead, they were advanced by sixteen months when Tami ('The Movement for Tradition in Israel'), a three-man 'ethnic' coalition faction, defected from the Government – in the wake of protests regarding economic issues – and joined the not-in-the-least surprised Alignment in proposing dissolution of the tenth Knesset, an exercise that perfectly illustrated coalition mathematics. Elections for the eleventh Knesset were then set for 23 July 1984.

Once more within the Likud there were two contenders; this time, the other one being Ariel Sharon, who challenged me for the Prime Ministership – and lost. So I was the Likud's nominee again, while in the Alignment, still in disarray from 1977, its leadership acrimoniously divided between Yitzhak Rabin and Shimon Peres, Peres topped the list. The election campaign, complete with high-powered public relations gimmicks and a US-style televised debate between Peres and myself (in which I spoke, as I was to do until election day, of 'national unity'), was, on the whole, fairly tranquil. There was a feeling in the air that the Likud would win though not sensationally, and that the Alignment would go on doing badly. People scanned the polls, watched with decreasing interest the paid political ads, heard messages of a flurry of little parties ('The Tenants Protection League' or 'The Movement for Abolishing Income Tax'), knowing that these would vanish for ever in a week or two, but listened also to the Likud whose message I helped to deliver all over the country, growing daily hoarser.

The final score was not what the general public or the pundits expected: the Likud had forty-one seats (seven less than in 1981) out of the total of 120 and the Alignment forty-four (as opposed to forty-seven in 1981). No less than twenty-six parties had participated though 'only' fifteen got into the Knesset; the line-up, however bewildering, displayed the remarkable, if exaggerated, variety and dynamism of Israeli politics. Of the five religious parties, a relative newcomer, the Orthodox Shas, which spoke in the name of the Sephardic Jews and was one of several that, like Tami, combined ethnicity with religion, had won an astonishing four seats.

Then, as now, I was unenthusiastic about so-called ethnicity. I thought it ran counter to the basic spirit of the Ingathering of Exiles and the making of a new breed of Jews, the Israelis, sharing a single faith and formed from a multiplicity of cultures into one nation. I could see little virtue in the existence of political parties whose first, often only, criterion for membership was whether one was a Moroccan or a Yemenite Jew. Not that I didn't understand the response which these parties and their, in the main, charismatic leaders evoked in people who felt marginal or downtrodden or discriminated against; but, in the final analysis, I felt that they were not only anachronistic but also essentially divisive.

What resulted from the 1984 elections was so close a vote that it was, in fact, a tie. Since neither of the two major blocs, neither the Likud nor the Alignment, could form a government with a clear Knesset majority, what was necessary was for one, or the other, to head a coalition formed with smaller parties as, unfortunately, has been standard Israeli procedure since the state was established. Coalitions – the making of them, the wooing of their would-be components (i.e. the small parties), the persuasion, promises and political pay-offs involved – have been the bane, however unavoidable, of all Israeli Prime Ministers from Ben-Gurion on, including Golda Meir, Menachem Begin and myself. No one party has ever enjoyed an absolute Parliamentary majority; no Israeli Prime Minister has ever been able to form a cabinet without being dependent on parties other than his own. Holding the balance of power in this way makes it possible for very small groups, sometimes even a group represented by only one Member of the Knesset, to wield considerable influence, not perhaps enough to topple a government, but enough to cripple it badly – to say nothing of the price that has to be paid by the Prime Minister-designate, often in the form of a ministerial post, so he can, at last, form a coalition, present it to the President and ask the Knesset to approve it. The haggling that precedes these deals, however essential they have been, flatters neither party and leaves everyone, including a disgusted public, swearing that Israel's long-overdue electoral reform must at once get under way so that we are released from the cumbersome and backward system of proportional representation, and select one of many possible alternative systems that have long been under discussion.

As for the continued presence in this country of religious parties, desirable or otherwise, well, they have been there from the start, inherited from the World Zionist Organization in which the first of them, predecessor of today's National Religious Party, was founded right after the turn of the century. There is nothing new about the idea that the Torah should be the spiritual heart of Judaism. However the subject is of extreme complexity, depth and importance. It, in fact, concerns the very nature of this state, because it poses those two most difficult of questions: who is a Jew and what is the place of Judaism in the Jewish state of the twenty-first century? It is not for me even to attempt a reply in these pages, perhaps not at all. All I know is that I myself, not an observant Jew, dearly cherish much of the Jewish ethos, the basic philosophy of Judaism and the national culture. As to the question: how shall we live in a state in which significant facets of daily life are still not free from directives arrived at centuries ago in response to totally other needs? I can only agree with those who demand that ancient prohibitions be modernized and made relevant to this day, age and land, though I have no idea either how or when this will be done.

Until the revitalizing change comes, as it must, goodwill and mutual understanding are sorely needed. These would, I am convinced, be summoned up in greater quantities but for the fact that in Israel the effective spokesmen of Orthodox Judaism – its intolerant, inflexible minority apart – are so deeply involved in political bargaining, so concerned with possible gains and the maintenance of their frameworks (however worthy), that insufficient time, thought and fervour remain to consider a future finally free of the threat of destructive national dissent, of a '*KulturKampf*'. And Israel's secular majority, on the other hand, must continue to be represented as, on the whole, it has been, by those who are genuinely well-intentioned, truly honour their own past, and do not automatically and shrilly deny the religious parties their right to battle for their own vision of a Jewish state, however burdensome the process of compromise about which, although I already knew a lot, I was to learn a lot more.

Anyway, 1984, while it proved no exception to the coalition rule, produced what I think was an entirely novel variation of it. The Alignment had not succeeded in enlisting the support of the religious parties for a narrow coalition government, and the more left-wing groups, Labour's natural allies, had not mustered enough Knesset seats to provide the Alignment with a working majority. So though the Alignment had ruthlessly attacked the idea of national unity, it really had no choice but to accept our offer. From the beginning, I had been sure that our assessment of the national will approximated reality. People were tired of the endless arguments between the parties; the debate over the Lebanese war had exhausted everybody; Israelis wanted a bit of stability, a little quiet and some unity in the political leadership now that the elections were over, and the Alignment finally read the message of the polls in much the same way as we did.

The other big factor in the decision to join forces was, of course, that we, too, could not pull together as strong a Knesset support as we felt the situation required. There were the religious parties with their natural affinity for the traditionalist Likud (which under Begin had become more so) but which would back whichever bloc pledged more aid for their widespread educational and settlement networks; and Tehiyya, a small party to the right of the Likud, founded in 1981, which in 1984 added two seats to an original three. It rejected all territorial concessions and included in its leadership the noted physicist, Professor Yuval Ne'eman, the former Chief of Staff, Rafael Eitan, and Geulah Cohen, once the voice of Lehi's clandestine radio station, whose fame stemmed mainly from her dramatic, very voluble heckling in the Knesset, the peak of which came when President Carter appeared there at the time of Camp David. I am never charmed by rudeness, nor have I ever approved of her extremism, but she is a strong woman who has fought intensely for her intense beliefs. Tehiyya, of which Geulah was one of the founders, was a breakaway from the Likud but, the spectrum and issues being what they were, was also its likely partner.

There were also other possibilities for forming a narrow Likud government, but I was sure, in my own mind, that national unity was what the hour called for and what the economy, the troops still in Lebanon and everyone really needed. What happened was not merely the formation of an 'ordinary' national unity government, but the rotation of power between the two blocs, alternating over a period of fifty months, each governing the country for innings of twenty-five months; Peres and I to share the Prime Ministership – the Odd Couple, as someone not inaccurately termed us!

It took many meetings between Peres and myself, and meetings between the people he and I delegated to represent us, to reach agreement on this most unusual but theoretically quite feasible plan. All around us were mutterings of displeasure. Alignment forces had been unrestrained during the election in their charges that the Likud was responsible for the 'economic' deterioration and the 'entanglement' in Lebanon, and its partners to the left of it threatened to quit if it joined up with the Likud. Also there was far from unanimity inside the Likud; the so-called camps that clustered around various Likud personalities were not at all eager to surrender those anticipated influential government posts which, in any such arrangement, must inevitably pass to erstwhile rivals. I always objected to the existence of these cliques, but since they were based on rivalry over potential portfolios, not on matters of principle, I could and did live with them for the sake of cohesion. Hindsight, as ever, presents the possibility that this was a great mistake.

I also didn't relish being without an opposition; a good opposition, I believe, is a prerequisite for good government. Without it, one is no longer in a self-correcting situation, has less protection against the wastage of energy in factional disputes, and things tend, in my experience, to be looked at more for their own sake, less in order to score points. I thought when we were in opposition we had substantially strengthened Israel's democracy and, later, when the Alignment broke up the National Unity Government and became the opposition again, I much regretted its weakness, indecisiveness and ineffectuality in this role – and regarded these as our loss.

Later, I tried to convey to the Likud's central committee the extent of my belief in the need for national unity, even in this unconventional, not to say daring, form:

Creating this kind of government has not been simple nor will it be simple to ensure that it survives. Achieving co-operation and co-existence between such ancient rivals may be an impossible mission, but if we acknowledge the real needs of the hour, of history – and it is this acknowledgment that has now been made by both sides – we will find the strength and initiative with which to overcome the obstacles and, together, pilot the state to safe shores. This is the first time that Israel embarks on such an experiment. Let us hope that it will succeed despite the complexities, and that maintaining balance and equality between the parties concerned will lead not to their neutralizing one another, but rather to the doubling of their respective effectiveness and capability.

And I advised the Party itself to follow suit, to turn the often tenuous partnership between its factions into the real working unit that I hoped would characterize the entire Government.

On all levels it was, of course, much easier said than done. Apart from the obvious difficulties that presented themselves with each team knowing that the man at its head would be Prime Minister for only a limited period of time, what had to provide the adhesive for the fifty-month duration of the Government were, first of all, agreement, broadly speaking, on many, if not most, matters and, secondly, a shared lack of an acceptable alternative. What I had not taken into consideration was how much Peres hated the ideology I represented, a hatred he inherited from Ben-Gurion (one of whose bright young men and devoted disciples he had been) and which served to 'justify' his subsequent behaviour. I suppose, if I am frank about this, that had he been able to conceal his feelings, things might have been slightly different, certainly simpler, but not very much so. Peres's desire to govern, to rule at almost any cost, his driving ambition, his permanent (as they turned out to be) difficulties within his own Party despite his important ministerial posts, were so self-destructive that, in the past certainly, he was always in the end the loser. Not that he lacks sympathizers or admirers; his rapport with Israel's intelligentsia and with many prominent Western European intellectuals is considerable; he is persuasive, articulate and efficient, but impossible to work with and (I write this on the basis of experience) not to be totally relied upon – though others may fare better in this respect than I did.

In the course of those fifty months, however, whether it was when he or I was Prime Minister or Deputy Prime Minister and Minister of Foreign Affairs, it became steadily harder for me to find any saving grace in him. The grand coalition meant nothing to him, nor did the Government's image. We had totally different attitudes towards the actual structure of the Government. I too, obviously, would have preferred a government controlled by my own Party, but I thought that there were intrinsic merits to the system we'd arrived at. I thought it proved Israel's political maturity and the ability of its political establishment to overcome very significant differences of opinion in a creative way, and that, in many places, this would increase the state's prestige – as I am sure it did. Peres, on the other hand, seemed to regard it only as an evil decree against which he had to fight in any and every way possible. This being the case, the areas in which we were ideologically apart rose to the fore instead of being set aside for the duration, as I had envisioned and hoped they would be.

There was also something else. Everything, all the inherent incompatibilities, was made more serious by the spreading infection of leaks that throughout afflicted, even handicapped, the National Unity Government, sometimes even endangering the state's reputation, and for which, in my view, Peres was to blame. How and why should any foreign government do business with another government that suffered so badly from this disease that the agenda of confidential sessions could, quite possibly, if not probably, be featured in the next day's headlines? The answer to this non-rhetorical question is that if one is sufficiently set on trouble-making, on appearing in the press oneself, on attracting attention, then worrying about the Government's good name isn't likely to be a deterrent, and Peres was indeed not deterred. I understand that one cannot keep everything from everyone for ever, but certain things must be kept secret for a certain time – a rule of thumb that he all too often deliberately chose to ignore, to the Government's detriment and to my fury. But though I knew that Peres was not liked in the Alignment, least of all by his long-time nemesis and rival, Yitzhak Rabin, I still thought that we could operate together for Israel's greater good. So we sat down to talk terms: the rotation was to involve only Peres and myself in the way I have just described; he was to be Prime Minister for the first twenty-five months, I for the second; each 'side' would get ten ministerial portfolios (later a ten-member inner Cabinet was created, also adhering to strict parity), and it was agreed that Rabin would be Defence Minister for the entire fifty months.

I have often wondered whether the National Unity Government might not have operated better had it been Rabin (who, as I write, again serves as Israel's Prime Minister) rather than Peres who shared the Prime Ministership with me, though one never knows; maybe not. Rabin and I got along more easily but, in any case, Rabin, slow-speaking, analytical, far more adept than Peres at hiding his real feelings, perhaps less sensitive and unquestionably less devious, was an asset. His military experience and reputation (he had been Chief-of-Staff during the Six Day War and, in my view, was the best Israel ever had) effectively combined with his experience at the highest levels of government, as Ambassador to the United States and then as Prime Minister (the first born in Israel) following the Yom Kippur

War. Ideologically, he was just as committed to territorial compromise as Peres. But Peres was more inclined than Rabin to hold talks with non-Israeli elements without letting his partners (i.e. us) know, and far more extreme in his opposition (it too amounted to hatred) of the settlements established beyond the so-called Green Line of our pre-1967 borders. For reasons I never understood, they literally enraged him.

There were other differences: Peres, for instance, made a point of cultivating Europe, felt at home there, thought we should do much more in Europe in the direction of what are currently called confidence-building measures, and that Europe, in general, should be a major orientation for Israel. Rabin was much more at home, in all respects, in and with the United States, knew America better and worked, as Defence Minister, very closely with Americans, both in the Pentagon and in the State Department.

On the surface, on paper as it were, we made not a bad team, provided one didn't look too closely. The new Government's Basic Guidelines, signed in September 1984, also bespoke relative harmony and indicated that there was reason for measured optimism, if not more. The Government promised to continue the peace process within the framework agreed upon at Camp David; to resume negotiations on providing 'full autonomy' to the Arab residents of Judea, Samaria and the Gaza district; to call on Jordan to begin negotiations 'in order to turn over a new leaf' in the region; to oppose the establishment of an additional (additional to Jordan, that is) Palestinian state in the Gaza district and in the area between Israel and Jordan; not to negotiate with the PLO and to strengthen Israel's ties with Egypt. In addition were the two clauses that permitted the Likud to enter into this arrangement with the Alignment, which stipulated that 'during the Unity Government's term of office, there will be no change of sovereignty over Judea, Samaria and Gaza except with the consent of the Alignment and the Likud'; and that 'the maintenance and development of the settlements established by the Government will be ensured, their development to be decided by the Government'.

The Likud wasn't especially happy about this nor were many members of the Alignment, but it was the best the negotiators could produce. Anyhow, happiness was not a declared objective of what was known ever after in Israel simply as the 'Rotatzia', and on behalf of which I now became Israel's Foreign Minister again (presumably until late in 1986), though I had, in fact, retained that Ministry for myself during my first eleven months as Prime Minister and, therefore, was now starting my fifth year in that job.

9

FRIENDS – AND FOES

FROM THE INCEPTION of the National Unity Government, Peres had been not only unwilling but unable to reconcile himself to the results of the elections. It says something about him, I think, that when, in October 1986, he resigned as Prime Minister, as called for in the 1984 guidelines, he was congratulated for doing so because it was considered far from impossible that at the last minute he would renege. But my becoming Prime Minister made matters worse; he was now unstoppable in his determination to have his own way. Not long ago, looking through old files, I came across a copy of a note I sent to Peres back in 1984, after he and I (in the United States at the same time) found ourselves together at Shultz's home. Peres talked and talked. I didn't want to interrupt him but next morning I wrote him a few words:

I must tell you that I took exception to some of the opinions and evaluations you voiced yesterday, particularly those concerning Syria ... Taba [see page 170] and raising what you called the 'quality of life' [of the residents – meaning the Arabs] in the territories. It seems to me that our positions on sensitive topics like these should be gone into at home and within the proper frameworks.

Only a few words but though they were scribbled at the very start of the 'partnership', they could have been written at almost any point regarding almost any issue between 1984 and 1990 when the National Unity Government finally ended.

In my speech to the Knesset on 20 October 1986 presenting my Government at the start of the Rotation's second half, I opened by speaking about national unity. It was not, I said, 'just a matter of Parliamentary convenience'. Those who had conceived the idea of the Unity Government 'hoped by its formation ... that it would project a message of unity and true co-operation ... [and] this government which I head will indeed make the unity of the nation its chief concern'. I also addressed myself both to the Arabs of Israel ('We will continue to act to ensure ... their rights and the advancement of their living conditions, and appeal to public figures and educators in the Arab sector to exert their influence to deepen the affinity ... of Israeli Arabs towards the state') and to the Arab residents of Judea, Samaria and the Gaza district ('It is our aspiration that they will be able to run their affairs by themselves but the necessary condition for this is absolute severance from the terrorist organizations'). And I stressed that the Government would 'continue to create conditions enabling Israel and Jordan to live in peace alongside each other. But we will not attain this without free direct discussion. No international forum can serve as a substitute for direct negotiations.'

However, one major bone of contention between the Likud and the Alignment, or, more specifically, between Peres and myself, was to be Peres's obsessive campaigning on behalf of an international conference (originally envisaged only as a 'forum') intended by him to be part of a 'grand strategy of peace' and to solve for ever the differences of opinion between Israel and the Arabs. Tirelessly, he promoted this idea wherever and with whomever he could – King Hussein, President Mubarak, Morocco's King Hassan II, President Mitterrand, Mrs Thatcher, to name just a few of those whom he managed to persuade, to one degree or another, of the cardinal importance of such a conference in total defiance of my extreme opposition to a concept I believed imperilled Israel – most of the time operating behind my back and always disregarding the resultant damage to the coalition. What's more, he pursued this project with the same disregard of propriety whether he was Foreign Minister at the time or Prime Minister. All that seemed to matter to him was that he should get his own way.

The international conference that Peres so indefatigably advocated was no Madrid Conference with its opening confrontation between Israel and the Arabs and at which the Soviet presence was purely formal and the United States functioned as co-host and trouble-shooter, making sure that there would be the subsequent direct bi-national and multinational encounters upon which we insisted and which indeed ensued. Not at all. Peres (basing himself on an idea made public in 1975 by Leonid Brezhnev, then leader of the Soviet Government and Communist Party) was proposing a conference to be sponsored by the five permanent members of the UN Security Council, the twenty-one Arab UN-member states – and Israel. To me, it was clear from the start that, given this list of participants (the majority were on record as supporting the PLO, which would therefore probably also participate, one way or another), the abandonment of the Camp David Accords and the relinquishing, for the first time since 1948, of Israel's demand for direct negotiations with the Arabs, a conference of this kind boded ill for us. I thought that we would all too soon find ourselves more and more isolated, under the kind of intensive international pressure that we might be unable to withstand, and forced to yield to Arab demands (backed by almost everyone else) that would return Israel to the untenable territorial situation in which we had lived prior to 1967.

The Likud, of course, had always perceived the Camp David Accords as binding, their indisputable legality and importance serving Israel as a shield against pressures inimical to the national interest and certain to bring about the long-awaited direct talks – free of outside intervention or coercion – that sooner or later would lead to peace. Signed by the United States, Egypt and Israel, we regarded them, despite everything done to dilute them, as central to the hope of a durable and just peace. The Labour Alignment and Peres, on the other hand, were willing to forgo the Camp David Accords in order to arrive faster at what, in their view, would be peace with the Arabs – even though, as the Likud and I saw it, without the Accords and under the circumstances Israel's very existence would be endangered. Moreover, it should be remembered that the Camp David Accords laid the basis for negotiations aimed at 'permanent settlement' of the conflict. In these negotiations, following the five-year interim period (the autonomy), Israel was not to be bound by any preconditions – a stipulation of considerable significance. At the time of Camp David, Begin had declared that in these final negotiations Israel would insist upon the right to Israeli sovereignty over Judea, Samaria and the Gaza district and upon its implementation. This declaration, of course, only committed Likud-led governments. The Alignment's position in favour of the projected international conference was indicative of a basic readiness, in principle, to accept Israel's withdrawal from Judea, Samaria, Gaza and even the Golan Heights in return for a peace treaty.

But 'peace' secured in this way, under duress, would only bring even greater demands in its wake until everything the Arabs wanted would, at last, be theirs, even Jerusalem. Later events were to prove the Likud right, that by not giving way, by persevering, it was possible, thanks to the Camp David Accords, to enter into direct negotiations with the Arabs, unhampered by any preconditions, without imperilling Israel and even, as happened between 1990 and

1992, to break out of the diplomatic isolation that had been imposed on us for years. Today there are very few countries in the world, other than the Arab states and some of their Moslem friends, that do not have full diplomatic relations with Israel.

Of course the conference held considerable personal as well as political attraction for certain other leaders. King Hussein, for instance, though weaker than Sadat, suddenly had a Sadat-like mantle held out to him. I believe he wanted to negotiate with us but had been waiting for the right formula, and the right sponsors. Peres met with him in London, in April 1987, by implication offering him the role of a major Arab peacemaker and a method of talking to Israel that was relatively risk-free because it would be under US and USSR patronage, so the rejectionist Arab front and the PLO, from which Hussein had suffered so much, would be less likely to accuse him of betraying the sacred anti-Israel cause. The King even signed an agreement with Peres.

Something of Peres's modus operandi can be learned from his hope that, if no one else, at least George Shultz would be able to persuade me to accept this so-called London agreement, and from his instant despatch one of the two Director-Generals of the Foreign Ministry to Helsinki to 'intercept' Shultz, who was on his way to Moscow to arrange for the Reagan-Gorbachev summit. In Israel Peres read the agreement with Hussein to me but refused to leave me a copy of it, though by then I was Prime Minister. For that I had to wait several days until the then US Ambassador to Israel, Thomas Pickering, arrived to present me with the text of the agreement. Thus it looked as though it were an American initiative, which would have exonerated Hussein in Arab eyes of the sin of talking to us and cleared Peres himself of the charge of deception. Needless to say, neither aim was accomplished.

Like every other Israeli Prime Minister, I too had a message for Hussein. Speaking in January 1987 at the Dead Sea to members of the National Democratic Institute of International Affairs, an audience that included former US Vice-President Walter Mondale, I addressed myself to the King 'on the other side of the sea' and suggested that we meet face to face, anywhere he chose, to discuss peace between our countries:

Obviously no one can force an independent government to do anything contrary to its perception of its own interests [I said], but we submit that there is no substitute for direct negotiations and that, at some point in the future, Jordan will come to realize that this path will, in the long run, ensure the best rewards. No international conference can produce the solution to our problems. Israel remains committed to the principle of the Camp David Accords bearing the signatures of Egypt, Israel and the United States. True, and regrettably, there has been no progress in the last few years, but we must not despair. Much can be done. Nor should we waver in our quest for this goal or permit it to be jeopardized in favour of illusory short-range and temporary gains. We must not confront the major and explosive issues such as territory and sovereignty at the very start of the process.

But nothing distracted Peres from his rounds, from meetings always described as 'summits' – the Alexandria 'Summit' with President Mubarak; the Atlas Mountain Summit with King Hassan II – and from diligently retracing his European routes. But eventually, in the absence of the unambiguous US support he required and with the end of the Rotation, the conference idea faded. In October 1987, when Shultz was in Israel (for the award to him by the Weizmann Institute of Science of an honorary degree), the Secretary opted for neutrality in the Israeli domestic dispute:

It is more than ever true that Israel cannot afford to make even one serious mistake in the calculus of strength and diplomacy. But it is also more than ever true that serious opportunities for peace must be explored with energy, unity and resolve. For failure to do so may turn out to be that one serious mistake.

I suppose both Peres and I read into those words what each of us wanted to.

Another less critical area of prolonged conflict between Peres and myself (and limited to the context of Israeli–Egyptian tensions) was Taba. I wonder how many people outside Israel today even remember the name of this 1.2 square kilometre of seashore, just south of Eilat, the site of an Israeli-built luxury hotel and holiday village, and one of a dozen or so disputed points on the Egyptian–Israeli border after our evacuation of the Sinai Peninsula in 1982. But for seven years, Taba was a symbol of Egyptian rejectionism in a bitter argument finally settled in Egypt's favour by arbitrators of an international tribunal as, all along, I had feared and warned might be the case.

According to the Camp David Accords, disputes 'arising out of the application or interpretation of the Treaty and that cannot be solved by negotiation, shall be resolved by conciliation or submitted to arbitration'. I was in favour of conciliation for various reasons: arbitration, it seemed to me, at its best was bound to contain elements of confrontation that we should try to avoid; and, unlike conciliation, it would be binding; altogether a less appropriate and riskier problem-solving mechanism for nations so recently committed to the creation of a new and friendly relationship. After all, arbitrators form a kind of court, with each side trying to demolish the arguments of the other, to present evidence to its own advantage and so forth. At first, the Egyptians agreed; both Premier Hassan Ali and State Minister Boutros Ghali. But President Mubarak also sensed that through arbitration Israel might lose Taba and he personally and adamantly insisted on it. The United States, for some reason, involved itself in the argument, supporting the revised Egyptian stand, perhaps because the Americans felt that if we agreed to Egyptian demands, the Egyptians might be friendlier – though history has proved many times over the error, and cost, of this approach.

The Egyptians began to press; the Egyptian media started to teach the Egyptians where and what Taba was; and President Mubarak, possibly for domestic reasons, began to push harder for a decision. In Israel, the National Unity Government was formed; Peres became Prime Minister and decided to support the Egyptian demand for arbitration for Taba. Why? There were many possible reasons: the same mistaken belief that giving in to Egyptian demands would lead to closer ties; to make more likely a Mubarak visit to Jerusalem under Alignment auspices; to make more likely also a state visit by Peres to Cairo; to guarantee the rapid return to Israel of the Egyptian Ambassador who had been recalled when the Lebanon war broke out. Whatever the reasons, Peres characteristically dealt with my opposition to arbitration by sending his own emissary off to Cairo to assure the Egyptians that he would co-ordinate positions with them. So, as happened repeatedly, the Prime Minister's Office and the Foreign Ministry were in very public disagreement. Under any circumstances, this was deplorable and, in what purported to be a government of national unity, it was also exceedingly confusing.

At a certain point, Peres went so far as to threaten to pull out of the Government, something which might very well have meant elections again. Taba, I decided, though important in itself and precedent-setting, wasn't worth a major political crisis with all that it would have entailed. The vote in 1984 had been so close that it was possible that the Likud might lose, which would be far more serious for Israel's future than the loss of Taba. So finally I gave up. I had hoped for years that we could arrive at some settlement on Taba with the Egyptians; divide the tiny territory; make Taba extra-territorial; perhaps a jointly run tourist project, a symbol of peace. But there was no one to talk to. 'Each grain of Taba sand', to quote the Egyptians, had become precious to them; the fact that the whole of Sinai other than this one pinpoint on the map had been returned made no difference.

The haggling dragged on for a total of seven years, up until the very last moment in March 1989, a moment described by the chief Egyptian negotiator as 'happy for Egypt', the Israeli flag having been pulled down the night before when it was already dark and hardly anyone was around to see. It wasn't a happy moment for me; I remained unhappily convinced that if we had held out united we could have kept Taba – without forfeiting anything – and I thought it was ironic that I, and those who like myself resist handing over bits of land to Israel's enemies, should be castigated for 'fanaticism' while no one at all protested or even paid any attention (except the Likud) when the Egyptians, risking peace itself, clutched at Taba solely for reasons of national prestige. Of course nothing changed after Taba; it was as though nothing had happened. Israel was as far as ever from a normal relationship with Egypt and there still seemed no way of improving the situation. The one-way tourism, the absence of cultural exchanges, the minimal trade relations, the often totally unbridled attacks made against Israel, and me, in the Egyptian press – along with blatantly anti-Semitic caricatures – the virtual quarantine imposed on Israel's Ambassador, all went on, Taba or not. When we complained of the frequent savagery directed towards Israel in their newspapers, the Egyptians spoke to us about the glories of a free press; when in October 1985 seven Israelis, including four children, vacationing on the Sinai coast were killed for no known reason by an Egyptian security guard, eye-witnesses reported that they had bled to death because at the site, no one, including medical personnel, had been allowed to see them, a fact regarding which the Egyptian Government demonstrated less concern than might have been expected. Even today, though Sadat's pledge of 'No More War' has been honoured, Israel is still very far from being permitted to enjoy anything resembling a normal relationship with its Egyptian neighbour.

It is not my purpose to say much more regarding Peres's strange interpretation of unity, but I do want to point out that he also set a bad example for others, including Ezer Weizman whose direct, then illicit dealings with the PLO I followed in the evidence presented to me as Prime Minister, with no small anger. I understood perfectly well that Weizman himself believed that since he was in favour of ties between the PLO and Israel, he was, accordingly, entitled to go ahead with this relationship as he saw fit. This was, of course, nonsense. In the second National Unity Government, which was to come into being in November 1988 and last till March 1990, free of the limitations of the Rotation, and of which I was Prime Minister, he served as Science Minister and was fully aware that government policy was to have nothing to do with the PLO. I felt about him as I had felt about Peres: putting up with this behaviour was part of the price paid for national unity and, for a long time, I thought it was worth paying, even if it took its toll of me. As for Israel, I was sure it could survive these misdemeanours.

In the end, Weizman outdid his model, went too far and made contact with a spokesman of Yasser Arafat's, who saw to it that the media knew of the meeting. I asked Peres and Rabin to speak to Weizman, to let him know that I would have to take action. They both declined the invitation so, at a Cabinet meeting, I simply announced that I was firing Weizman and explained why. At that point people intervened to ward off a government crisis, which, by then, I wouldn't particularly have minded. Rabin suggested that Weizman be removed from the inner Cabinet but remain a minister, for the sake of appearances, to which I agreed. There were other consequences, but what stayed with me was astonishment that among the people who yearn for such contacts are some who would much rather talk about the Arab−Israel problem with Arabs, even with sworn enemies, or to foreigners, than with Likud ministers, and who trust the PLO more than me.

A very partial anatomy of diplomacy in action at this level is perhaps not uninteresting. In October 1987, when Shultz was on his way to Moscow, knowing that the Middle East would be discussed at the forthcoming Reagan−Gorbachev meeting, he visited Israel. There were all kinds of speculation in Israel as to what would happen, what means he would use to try to get me to change my mind about the international conference so that the United States, in turn, could reach agreement with the USSR and so forth. However, I was sure that he was not coming to pressure me (not a wholly unknown occurrence in the long history of US−Israel relations) and wasn't alarmed. I couldn't imagine that Shultz would, in any way, exploit the friction between the Foreign Minister and his Party and me and mine, something which would have been against his deepest convictions. I also knew that he was not likely to be in a great hurry about the international conference nor particularly anxious to give so crucial a decision-making position in the Middle East to the Soviet Union.

Anyhow, he arrived, spent Saturday and Sunday here, flew to Saudi Arabia and back and, on Sunday evening, Mrs Shultz and he had dinner alone with Shulamit and me at our home and, of course, talked about the 'situation'. Shultz suggested an idea with which, he said, President Reagan was familiar: Reagan and Gorbachev would ceremonially and jointly invite the heads of the Middle Eastern countries involved to join the superpowers (how long ago it already seems that one used that plural) in seeking a solution to the Israel–Arab problem. The United States would take the lead, providing it was clear to all concerned that the invitation would lead to direct Israel–Jordan talks, thus concluding its international aspect. If King Hussein wasn't interested in the suggestion of 'co-sponsorship', well then, the appeal wouldn't be made. He also proposed that some ceremonial 'gimmick' perhaps be found to indicate UN interest in this dramatic move.

'If I even get a flickering green light from Israel,' Shultz said, 'I'll make the suggestion to King Hussein at once. If he agrees, I'll talk to the Russians.' It wasn't clear whose idea it had been, but the copyright was certainly American. The White House? The State Department? Shultz indicated that it had been contributed to by the President himself. Later, I learned that the seed had been planted by Mrs Thatcher, to whom Reagan always lent an extremely attentive ear and who was rather given to Peres's influence. I told Shultz that, yes, I thought it should be followed up and in our next two meetings we talked about the idea in greater detail.

On the Monday, Assistant Secretary of State Richard Murphy arrived from London to tell me that Hussein had turned down the idea on the grounds that, had I been willing to accept any Israeli withdrawal, I would have gone along with the concept of an international conference in the first place, which was true. From Washington, Shultz informed me that both Reagan and he had greatly appreciated my 'flexibility'. As for Hussein's negative reply, it served to reinforce my belief that the Arabs were interested only in our withdrawal from territory, not in peace as such – which the US Administration was now finding out for itself.

The presenting and rejecting of peace plans went on throughout the duration of my Prime Ministership; not a year passed without some official proposal being made by the United States, or Israel, or even Mubarak, each one bringing in its wake new internal crises, expectations and disappointments – though I had become more or less immune to the latter. There were few if any new elements, just old proposals recycled, changed a bit, always centring on Israel's withdrawal from territory; Israel always turning down preconditions; the Arab states and the PLO always insisting on what, however it was phrased, amounted to peace in exchange for territory; recognition in exchange for territory; never 'just' peace.

In March 1988, I was invited to meet again with President Reagan. I was scheduled to stay in Washington for a few days and talk also to Shultz, of course, and to the Secretary of the Treasury, James Baker, who struck me, at our first meeting, as a ser ous man, worthy of being approached cautiously. In Jerusalem, worried colleagues fretted and commiserated with me; the trip, they said, was poorly timed, bound to be difficult and doomed to fail. Early in December 1987, the Arab uprising in the territories, the *intifada*, had broken out; inevitably it would cast a heavy shadow over my meetings in the United States. As always, Israel was being harshly blamed, both for the uprisings and for trying to put them down. My presence would only make matters worse. Also, in February, Shultz had come back to Israel with a slightly different version of the international conference plan which he told me 'everyone' liked but which was still not safe or different enough for me to accept. But instinct assured me that it was possible to turn Shultz down without creating a rift with the United States (such was the extent of my confidence in its essential and lasting goodwill), and though I must admit I didn't prepare for the journey in very high spirits, I made up my mind to go, regardless of what awaited me.

Just before I left Jerusalem, however, I was surprised by a large, spontaneous demonstration of support cheering me on my way. It seemed like a good omen and one that I knew would be rapidly relayed to Washington. The scene was to repeat itself at Kennedy airport: a sea of posters that said 'Hold on' and 'We're with you'; hundreds of faces that smiled encouragingly; a forest of hands that waved a welcome. The same note was struck again in Washington at the United Jewish Appeal Young Leadership Conference, where thousands received me with an ovation, clapping and stamping, their emotion unconcealed. It was not entirely for me, nor even entirely for Israel; my visit became an opportunity for these American Jews to protest the unfairness of the US media towards Israel, to comment on the open promotion of the Palestinians who had become its darlings, and to make a statement about the extent to which, in certain circles, virulent anti-Zionism was becoming fashionable. Once these young people understood that I couldn't be forced into acquiescing in any potential weakening of Israel, that nothing could induce me to lend a hand to any attempt in this direction, they backed me with relief, with no reservations and with no small measure, I think, of affection. That reception was something else unplanned that did not go unnoticed in Washington, where even Shultz had hinted to me once or twice that my stand lacked massive US Jewish backing; he was now learning otherwise.

In Washington, for three tough intensive days (Kissinger told me afterwards that they represented a 'heroic' achievement) I talked, listened and argued. There was no apparent pressure. Only, as usual, the presentation of highly contrasting interpretations, mostly of Camp David; attempts at persuasion and predictions; would-be soothing explanations that the conference, if called, would be neither 'authoritative' nor 'plenipotentiary'. But there was Presidential intervention. When I was alone with him briefly, President Reagan was, as always, friendly, well-informed and candid. He told me he thought that the international conference idea should be encouraged, that Israel's anxiety was not justified and that the United States would never let us down. I replied that I believed that the projected conference would be diametrically opposed to direct negotiations and that the participation in Israel's fate of the USSR, China and the Europeans was more than likely to 'complicate' severely real negotiations. The President, wanting to reassure me, repeated that he was proud of the relationship between Israel and the United States, and hoped and expected that it would endure. Little had been said but his goodwill was almost tangible. Afterwards came the 'usual' meeting: the President, ten members of his Administration and ten of 'us'. The conversation became more specific. Among the subjects were Shultz's suggestion regarding the 'co-sponsorship'; the PLO and its unsuccessful attempts to drive what Reagan called a wedge between the US and Israel; the *intifada*, in connection with which I told the President that although the Middle East was used to the slaughter of crowds, we would not be provoked into killing hundreds in order to keep the peace; and, finally, Soviet Jewry and my chance for me to thank the President for his great personal help. 'I always talk to Gorbachev about the condition of the Jews,' he said. 'I don't think he likes it much.'

Breakfasting in his home with Shultz next day, I had the feeling that, for once, we had failed in some important way to clarify things to each other. 'I'm talking about Israel's survival,' I told him, over Mrs Shultz's pancakes. 'With all my friendship and deep respect for you, you must understand that I cannot agree to what I believe may be in store for us as a result of such a conference. Please go slowly. I know how much you do not want to injure us.' He didn't reply. He just nodded, glumly. One might say we parted then though we were to meet again several times. He kept on hoping against hope that we could arrive at some better, more official modus vivendi with King Hussein – not necessarily at first anything to do with territory, but some sort of regular meetings on economic, political or security matters of common interest. Not long ago when I was in Los Angeles I phoned Shultz in Stanford and he came at once to meet me. We hugged each other, so glad that we were able to talk. He said that he would always do what he could to help Israel, but he wasn't in touch with the new Administration and he was worried about the *intifada*. He thought that it was serious that we hadn't been able to put it down; it would give the impression that the Palestinians were stronger than either the Israelis or the Americans had known. That was why, he explained, he had so much wanted the interim period cut and a permanent settlement reached as soon as reasonable (i.e. three years) after the autonomy was launched. When I think of Shultz, as I do right now, it is not only in terms of his generous efforts on behalf of peace, but also of the senior US statesman who, visiting Moscow as he did in 1987, chose to attend a Seder on the first night of Passover with refuseniks because that was how he felt about their struggle for freedom – and about the land they sought to reach.

The point of the interim period was that it would make possible a learning experience for us and for those who would manage the autonomy, and give everyone a chance to put co-existence to work, to find out how best to deal with the myriad practical, emotional and political problems that would inevitably arise. I had asked Begin where the idea came from. He said, 'When I sat with Sadat, he insisted that peace couldn't be made without an agreement on the sovereignty of "the West Bank and Gaza". So how could we overcome this dilemma peacefully?' They had arrived at the concept of a five-year transition period; Begin had wanted ten years, knowing that it would make things easier if a whole decade of new habits and know-how could be assured for the creation of a better climate for negotiations. But that wasn't acceptable to Sadat, so they had agreed on the five-year period which Shultz, impatient for peace, had longed to shorten.

Shultz also knew that I didn't believe Hussein was interested in the autonomy. The King's main concerns, I was convinced, were to keep Jordan from turning into that independent Palestinian state that it, in fact, almost is – an impressive majority of its population being Palestinian; and to ensure survival of the royal Hashemite (originally Bedouin) house his grandfather had founded and he has headed virtually all his life. Later that year, in the summer of 1988, Hussein indeed declared Jordan's disengagement from Judea and Samaria, announcing that he was doing this in order to assist the Palestine cause, but actually trying to keep the *intifada* from spilling over into Jordan and thus, among other dangers to him, agitating and perhaps strengthening Jordan's large Palestinian population. He had already lived through Palestinian uprisings and was not about to endure another 'Black September'.

The social highlight of that Washington visit was Vice-President George Bush's dinner in my honour. I remember the hundreds of guests, many of them Jews, the gift the Vice-President gave me of Truman's Proclamation in which he recognized the State of Israel in 1948, and that he and I talked for a while about the American elections and his candidacy for the Presidency, but he made no particular impression on me other than that he was a pleasant, knowledgeable host which, from my brief earlier exposure to him, I took for granted he would be. Much as I would like to claim credit for having foreseen the role he was to play in Israel's life, and mine, I cannot do so.

In his 'departure statement', bidding me goodbye, President Reagan again reinforced Shultz's faith in the international conference. 'Let us be clear about several things,' he said. 'The United States will not slice this initiative apart and will not abandon it. ... Those who will say "No" to the United States – and the Prime Minister has not used this word –', he added, 'need not answer to us. They will need to answer to themselves and to their people as to why they turned down a realistic and sensible plan to achieve negotiations.' It was true that I hadn't said 'No' aloud, but I was fully prepared to answer to myself – and to 'my people' – if needs be; though I knew that the President, in fact, was referring to King Hussein and the PLO. He ended his statement with the hope that Israel would have a happy fortieth anniversary, marking 'the beginning of ... peace and accommodation in the Middle East'. He himself had done what he could towards achievement of this goal, but in eight months time he would no longer be President of the United States and a lot would change.

By the time I was about to return to Jerusalem, and after it had been subjected to nearly four months of televised reports from the territories that managed unfailingly to project an image of Israeli 'storm troopers' mercilessly chasing terrified Arab women and children, the American Jewish establishment finally awoke from its bad dream. I was glad I was there when this happened, able to answer questions, to tell the truth, symbolize the connection between them and us, and remind them that we were one people, and a singularly moral and caring people at that. Something started penetrating through the fog; a certain clarity at last pierced it. Thousands upon thousands of American Jews suddenly realized that in their acceptance of the distortions, they had risked loosening the historic ties on which their identification with Israel has been based ever since the Return began. I was glad also, chiefly for their sake, that a *New York Times* lead editorial came out that week in support of some of my objections to the US proposal and to my 'exposure of the Shultz Plan's short-comings'. 'Mr Shultz', wrote the *Times*, 'is wrong to insist that it be accepted in its present form.' It also supported my demand for a five-year interim period before settling on the final status, as stipulated in the Camp David Accords, rather than the three years that Shultz suggested. 'Mr Shamir is right ... since all is at risk.'

There is, of course, always the discordant minority. In this particular context, and on this particular visit, it was typified by the unsolicited statement presented by seven prominent Jewish intellectuals (including Isaiah Berlin, Isaac Stern and Saul Bellow) from Great Britain and the United States calling upon me to accept the 'admirable' Shultz Plan, which they had decided was compatible with the security of the State of Israel. Adding nothing to the situation except inexpert opinion, it was in sharp contrast to the feelings of the Jewish crowds that surrounded and heartened me wherever I went.

In Israel, the *intifada*, born in the squalor of the refugee camps of Judea, Samaria and the Gaza district, raged on. At one level there was the actual physical uprising, the hurled rocks that killed, the petrol bombs that burned, the iron pipes and steel chains that maimed – though the death and wounding of Israeli soldiers was rarely if ever seen on television screens anywhere. Nor did various other aspects of the riots interest the global media: the hundreds of Arabs gruesomely murdered by other Arabs for having co-operated with Israel was only one example of the PLO-affiliated and Islamic fundamentalist terror so viciously turned inwards as well as against us; the Arab schoolchildren forced by masked Arab youngsters to participate in rioting; the habitual use of ambulances and hospitals as refuge for rioters. There is not much point in making lists like these in our callous day and age. But within the law, those measures that could be applied by the IDF to put out the flames were of necessity – legal, political and human – highly limited, subject to constant scrutiny and strictly controlled. When excesses occurred – and how could they not occur given the intolerable provocation – they were few and severely punished. It may surprise some readers that one of the main reasons that the *intifada* lasted as long as it did – and the violence still flares sporadically – was that the rioters were only too familiar with the restraints we imposed upon ourselves, endlessly debated and even quarrelled over, and counted with justification on Israel's collective morality and restraint.

In addition to pain, grief and fear, dire economic consequences were also forced on the Arab refugees by the Arab instigators and organizers of the *intifada*, including the PLO – which we are expected to deal with concerning our future. By crippling normal activity, calling prolonged strikes and bringing down upon the population equally long IDF curfews, even when there were lulls in the violence, the life of the Palestinians, perforce living under Israeli military rule, was not to be envied. But we didn't need Amnesty International to teach us pity or respect for human rights. If, and when, in the course of the *intifada* these rights were threatened, there were enough Israelis on the look-out for abuses, and it was as infuriating as it was ridiculous that Israel's charge sheet should be the most detailed of any Middle Eastern country. Even for those whose admiration for the Jewish state is minimal, the repeated accusations of Israeli brutality must have been somewhat suspect, if not seen as downright discriminatory. It is true that democracies ought not to be judged by the standards of non-democratic regimes, but I believe that, in the rush to portray the riots as a confrontation between the Israeli Goliath and the Palestinian David – the roles, now that we are not in mortal peril, apparently reversed – the media missed the essential meaning of the uprising. It was not a demonstration; not a spontaneous venting of frustration; not civil disobedience. It was a form of warfare against Israel and against the Arabs who want to live in peace with us. Ultimately, it was a continuation of the war against Israel's existence, its immediate purpose to push us back to the 1967 lines and to establish another Palestinian state in the areas we leave. So there could be no question, however tempting the prospect, of unilaterally leaving Gaza, as some Americans suggested, 'to stew in its own juice'.

I won't pretend that my rare visits to the territories at that time – protective convoys, hovering helicopters, troops standing guard wherever I looked, journalists who moved wherever I did – were the way to see life as it really was under those conditions of deprivation, unspeakable crowding and abject poverty in which the refugees lived. But even what I saw for myself reinforced my conviction that, of all the sins committed by the Arab states against Israel, none has been more severe than that committed by these wealthiest of the world's

Visiting the Pope at the Vatican, 1983.

With President Ronald Reagan and US Ambassador to the UN, Jeane Kirkpatrick, 1984.

With a group of immigrants from Kurdistan, 1984.

With German Chancellor, Dr Helmut Kohl, 1985.

National Unity, 1986.

In Washington with two of my closest advisers, Yossi Ben-Aharon (left) and Elyakim Rubinstein, 1988.

With President George Bush in the Oval Office, 1989.

With Prime Minister Margaret Thatcher and Denis Thatcher at 10 Downing Street.

With President François Mitterrand, Elysée Palace, 1990.

The Bakers join us for dinner at the Prime Minister's residence in Jerusalem, 1991.

The Gulf War, January 1991: visiting a house destroyed by a Scud missile. Tel Aviv's Mayor, Shlomo Lahat, is on the right.

With Ronny Milo, David Levy and Ehud Olmert, 1990.

Speaking at the Madrid Conference, October 1991.

Visiting the West Bank settlement of Beit El, 1992.

On a state visit to Bulgaria, Shulamit's country of origin, 1992.

In Rujenoy, 1992.

With my grandchildren.

nations against their own people. Not only did the Arab states refuse to accept and absorb the Arabs who fled Palestine in 1948, but they kept them in the camps for forty-five years solely for the anti-Israel propaganda benefits to be derived from the sight of people living out marginal lives on inadequate charity, living weapons aimed by their own co-religionists at the hated Jewish state. These are men, women and children, thousands of children, who could have been rescued from their dreadful lives a hundred times over by the investment of a fraction of the Arab oil revenues and helped by the Arab rulers to relocate somewhere in the Arab world. Israel cannot solve their basic problem but, God knows, there are those who can and should; time and time again we have offered to assist, in every way, in projects of rehabilitation, but there has been no response from any quarter although Israel consistently tried to improve living conditions in the camps, drew up plans and took steps to improve the refugees' conditions by giving them proper housing and services.

Residential projects were built, housing some 10,000 families who chose to leave the camps, each of which got a plot of land, and more than seventy per cent of whom built their homes near the camps: provided with electricity, water, sanitation and roads, each neighbourhood was also equipped with schools, clinics and mosques. The policy was never written off the books though the *intifada* rendered it theoretical. A little-noticed UN Resolution on the Gaza Strip, adopted most recently in 1987, stated that 'the General Assembly ... reiterates its demand that Israel desist from the removal and resettlement of Palestine refugees in the Gaza Strip'. That year, the vote on this Resolution was 150 for, and two (Israel and the United States) against. A similar annual Resolution on Judea and Samaria, also readopted in 1987, stated that the Assembly, still alarmed by plans to resettle Arab refugees and to destroy the camps, called once more upon Israel to refrain from any action leading to 'the removal and resettlement of Palestine refugees' in Judea and Samaria. On this one, the vote was 145 for, and two (Israel and the United States) against. How could it be that so many of those preaching the need to erase the horror of the camps should repeatedly lend a hand to UN Resolutions that, if implemented, would perpetuate the bitter and growing problem?

There was no response, not even when in 1989 in Israel's peace initiative, we called among other things 'for a multinational effort, under the leadership of the US, and with substantial Israeli participation, finally to solve the Arab refugee problem, perpetuated by Arab governments while Israel absorbed hundreds of thousands of Jewish refugees from Arab countries', stressing that 'all these refugees should have decent housing and live in dignity, a process which does not have to await a political solution or to substitute for it'.

The *intifada* changed nothing in our basic situation. It served instead to underscore the existential nature of the conflict. When it spread, as it did in varying degrees, across the Green Line – in an effort to destroy the oneness of Jerusalem, as it has almost done – it proved to me once more that the conflict was not over territory but over Israel's right to exist. It had to be put down within the known limitations, but no one in Israel was more aware of the moral and physical dilemmas involved than the young soldier patrolling the alleys of camps, interrogating frightened inhabitants, subduing rioters, helping to haul thousands off to detention, shooting only when he had to, and facing trial himself if he erred and shot too soon. But he also knew that in this draining way he was protecting his country no less than on a border facing rockets and tanks. When I toured the *intifada* front and looked at these Israeli boys, I needed no one to tell me how hard it was for them. I could see it in their eyes.

At the end of 1988, Israel went to the polls again. The National Unity Government had certainly not been an unqualified success; differences of opinion over the peace process, differences of style, above all differences of ideology had not prevailed totally, but both Peres and I devoutly hoped that the voters would enable us to run our own governments, with our own coalition, and only one person in charge. Reviewing the troops, as it were (though considering my involvement with the peace process this is perhaps not a suitable word), I thought I could count on three elements which, combined, would give the Likud a victory. One was the Party's militant stand regarding Judea, Samaria and Gaza – a matter of primary concern also to that sizeable section of the public which is opposed to 'peace for territory', even though otherwise not likely to vote for us for a variety of reasons and which had no fewer than twenty-six other parties to choose from. The second was my own reputation as a tough, committed negotiator; and the third was the electoral attraction of the 'Princes', whom I mentioned before and who included Dan Meridor (to become Minister of Justice), Ehud Olmert (to become Minister of Health), Ronni Milo (among other positions of importance, to be Minister of Police), Moshe Katsav (later Minister of Transport), Binyamin (Bibi) Netanyahu (our Ambassador to the UN and Israel's much-praised spokesman at Madrid) and Begin's only son, Ze'ev Binyamin Begin.

I had encouraged and groomed almost all of them, hoping that when I retired my successor might confidently be chosen from their ranks and that the 'succession', therefore, would be easier in many ways than it had been in 1983. That particular wish was not to be granted me, but what I did know in the autumn of 1988 was that the Alignment could not produce anything resembling the 'blue-blooded' and experienced cadre of 'Shamir's Princes'. Of course there was, as there must always be, another side to the coin: the Likud's older stars, their light now dimmer but their abilities and ambitions still intact, who were in perpetual competition for power, both power in the present and, even more fiercely, in the future. Any one of these was capable, inadvertently or on purpose, of unravelling the fabric of Party unity I had so carefully tried to weave, so I made my way through the composition of the Likud list very warily, keeping contentious lions at bay, reining in vigorous cubs, hoarding my own strength, and certain that whatever happened I would incur enmity in one quarter or another But I was used to that, by this time, and the Party meant more to me than did its individual personalities – and the Land more than the Party.

The election results revealed that the Likud had won forty Knesset seats; the Alignment, thirty-nine; the four religious parties, with a total of eighteen seats (six more than before), triumphantly wielding the balance of power; and three small right-wing parties that accounted for another seven seats. One of these, Moledet ('Motherland'), urged putting an end to the uprising and, indeed, to the Israel–Arab conflict by moving ('transferring' was the operative word) the Arabs of Judea, Samaria and Gaza to neighbouring countries; another, Tsomet (an acronym forming the Hebrew word for 'crossroads'), primarily advocated the use of tougher methods to suppress the *intifada*. The 'transfer' proposal was not something that needed to be taken seriously, and I had no argument in principle with Tsomet. By 1992, the third, Tehiyya, was to join the heap of small parties the Israeli public in its wisdom regularly examines for a while and then rejects.

However I did the arithmetic, the inescapable fact remained that the Likud and the Alignment were again tied. If there was not to be another two-headed government – and I would, under no circumstances, agree again to any form of rotation – then it was up to me to initiate the necessary courtship with the Orthodox parties so that together with them and with Moledet and Tsomet, the Likud could form a strong government. More than ever before, I had a sense of urgency about this. Not only Israel had gone to the polls that month; in the United States there were far-reaching changes. Who knew, who could foretell the pattern of the future? How could I, out of dislike for bargaining, out of squeamishness, make it possible for the Alignment – prepared as it was to turn its back on the Camp David Accords, help bring into being a Palestinian state, give away parts of the Land of Israel and resultantly gamble with Israel's survival – to speak and act alone on Israel's behalf? It was out of the question. I had no choice in my own eyes, in terms of my conscience and my love and fear for Zion, other than to attempt and succeed in forming a government in which the Likud's voice would not only be heard but would dominate, and ours would be the awesome responsibility of navigation.

That month I found myself, in a melancholy pose, on the cover of *Time* magazine under the headline 'Israel Divided' (referring to the election results). I didn't feel that either the photograph or the headline accurately reflected the reality, but undeniably I was not in the least looking forward to the wooing or even the winning on which I now embarked – though not alone, for when they were not talking to me, the Orthodox leaders were busy meeting Peres and hearing his offers.

The election results being what they were, it was unavoidable that the Likud and the Alignment should compete furiously for the support of the religious and ultra-Orthodox parties, using whatever means they could, each side desperately trying to outbid the other with constantly escalating bids for political spoils. One main difficulty was the insistence of the ultra-Orthodox that the Law of the Return of 1950, which proclaims that 'every Jew has the right to come to this country as a settler', thus acquiring immediate citizenship, be amended insofar as converts to Jewry were concerned. For the purposes of this law, they demanded that only those converted by ordained Orthodox rabbis be allowed to qualify. To say that I didn't in the least want to yield to this demand would be a gross under-statement. I was reasonably sure that the incorporation of this amendment into Israeli law would create not merely a storm of protest abroad, or serious differences of opinion within world Jewry, but might very well lead to a major rift, quite possibly one of historic proportions. As to the response that would come from the Jews of the United States, with their deeply ingrained opposition to Orthodoxy, I had no doubts at all about that. All I could, and did, do was try to dodge the issue. But that didn't work for very long and, in the meantime, the bidding was daily becoming more heated.

One day there was no time left. The Alignment, we learned, had agreed (subject to certain conditions) to accept the terms of the ultra-Orthodox parties, of course including the 'Who is a Jew?' amendment. I had to move at once and did. I could see no real option: either Israel was to be led, in these fateful times, by the Alignment with all that this implied, or, with heavy hearts and many misgivings, not to say anxieties, the Likud would have to give in to the Orthodox ultimatum so that we could go on trying, as we understood it, to safeguard the Land of Israel. I had anticipated trouble, dispute, anger, even grave consequences, but not, I must confess, the profound sense of outrage with which world Jewry, in particular the American Jewish establishment, reacted to the news that the Likud agreed to the amendment. Was there now to be a difference between converts to Judaism to whom the Law of the Return did apply and those to whom it would not apply — for instance non-Jews converted by Reform or Conservative rabbis? In Israel, ninety-nine per cent of all marriages, divorces and burials are, for better or worse, under the jurisdiction of a strictly Orthodox rabbinate, but was it conceivable that converts elsewhere, converted by non-Orthodox rabbis, be delegitimized in this way?

The storm that broke about my head was of nightmare dimensions. There wasn't a day that delegations of Jews didn't arrive from somewhere, not only from the United States, to try to persuade us not to surrender to the Orthodox ultimatum, each delegation presenting its own case, making its own black predictions, threatening, warning and berating in its own way. I couldn't refuse to see them but, to tell the truth, there was little I could say to calm or reassure them, because there were hours in those days when I, too, felt that no less than the unity of the Jewish people, a unity that had withstood so much, was now in danger of collapse, of crumbling in the face of this unparalleled buffeting from within. Nothing was worth that risk. I had taken my full share of chances in life, personally and politically, but this was one chance I dared not take. As I listened, day after day, to these tragic pleas, heard Jews tell me that passage of the amendment would produce a trauma 'with damaging consequences for Israel in ways we cannot imagine' and speak to me about 'irreversible alienation', I felt that I could not possibly do other than respond to their entreaty and join with Peres in another government of national unity, rejecting totally the attempt of the ultra-Orthodox to amend the Law of the Return.

Only the extent and depth of that reaction could have persuaded me to break my word, to go back on an agreement I had made and re-enter, albeit with significant differences, into shared responsibility

with the Alignment, despite my inner conviction that this coalition −
brought into being so reluctantly by its main components − was
doomed to be short-lived. But things happen; circumstances are not
always within one's control; mistakes are made. I had always believed
that nothing human was either all white or all black. Now I had to
compromise and put my trust in an arrangement that, at its very
best, I knew could only be grey, and I wasn't even sure of that. It
didn't take long, however, before I realized that my decision had been
a correct one. I had not only prevented something destructive from
occurring, but I had also removed it altogether (or at least for a long
time) from the national agenda while, on the other hand, the ultra-
Orthodox soon resumed their co-operation with me as though nothing
had happened.

The Alignment, anxious not to lose everything, accepted my terms:
no rotation; I would be Prime Minister throughout the Government's
lifetime and Peres would go to the Finance Ministry (though he
continued from there all too often to act as a surrogate to the
new Foreign Minister, Moshe Arens). Rabin would remain Defence
Minister, and David Levy (after much wrangling within the Likud)
was appointed Deputy Prime Minister and Minister of Housing, Ariel
Sharon going to Industry and Trade. It took fifty-two days of marathon
talks to form the Government, each bloc being allotted nine portfolios
and eleven ministers. Finally it was agreed that should either Party
decide to leave the Unity Government, neither would try to set up a
narrowly based government in its place, but instead would call for
new elections; also that eight new settlements would be founded,
additional ones requiring the approval of the Finance Minister −
which seems to me a somewhat self-defeating clause. As for the ultra-
Orthodox parties, they never forgave me or forgot the breach of
promise, and I can't say I blamed them. I could only plead that they
had gone too far, though I should have stopped them in their
tracks. As it was, the new Government's guidelines included a
clause specifying that the status quo in matters of religion would be
preserved, which it has been. Incidentally, once the storm died down,
the amendment was never heard of again, which shows that world
Jewry, Israel included, can manage to survive without it.

Sometimes I was seized for a moment or two by nostalgia for long-
past days when my life was certainly in greater peril than it ever was
in the 1980s or afterwards, but when I could at least indulge in the
luxury of concentrating on, and often solving, one problem at a time.
The issues now preoccupying me, though they were all part of the
same central battle, were scattered over a variety of combat zones in

none of which we could afford to be defeated. My mind wasn't given over only to the unavoidable, and possibly even crucial, struggle that might await me in Washington or to the dangerous antics of the PLO, which, from Algeria, had just proclaimed an independent Palestinian state, and with which the departing US Administration, in a complicated way hoping to help Israel, had decided to launch a dialogue, or even to the internal rivalries that simmered on and on within my own Party. There was still also the EEC, which had, as I have written, threatened for years to drive me to the brink of that despair of which Genscher had once spoken.

The Common Market, in which we had a free-trading area and which was a main customer for our industrial goods, was a tremendous challenge for one of the state's most spectacular achievements: the abundance of vegetables, fruit and flowers that had made Israel a household word even in places where people would be hard put to identify the Dead Sea Scrolls, the IDF, the location of Tel Aviv or the name of Israel's Prime Minister. By the time I had become Foreign Minister, technological advances had been made in every phase of our agricultural activity, but we also faced increasing competition and, when Spain joined the EEC, the subject of our almost identical exports had to be reviewed if Israel was not to be commercially obliterated. In other words, we had to change the terms of our agreement with the Market, something which involved years of negotiation. Finally, an agreement was carved out and ratified by the European Parliament. At the beginning of 1988, the Socialist parties in that Parliament, reading their newspapers and watching TV, arbitrarily decided not to ratify the already signed agreement as a punishment for 'Israeli repression' during the *intifada*. Nor did the EC make the slightest attempt to hide its chronic anti-Israel bias. The European Parliament was ferocious in its condemnation of the temporary closing down by the IDF of Palestinian universities known to be hotbeds of Arab terrorist incitement and activity; and permitted itself to call on the EC Commission to freeze co-operative scientific and educational projects involving Israel until those universities were reopened.

All things considered – the past, the millennia-long Jewish contribution to, and impact on, European civilization, and the immensity of Europe's moral debt to the Jews, to say nothing of Europe's own history – the scolding and the sanctions were cynical in themselves and unashamedly opportunistic. Their origins, after all, lay almost solely in the dependence of the European nations on Arab oil wells rather than on genuine indignation or solid fact. I thought that the

European Parliament's behaviour amounted to blackmail, said so, and envied Prime Ministers who could conduct national business overseas without daily having to defend their countries' right to exist. I never shirked the rebuttals and explanations, but it was a relief of a sort in London that Mrs Thatcher, quite as formidable a lady as I had been led to expect, turned out to be much more concerned with telling me how she felt about the international conference and the *intifada* than with hearing my views about either. Domineering and self-important are the words that spring to my mind about her, but they are not the only ones. She was also consistent, never catered to public opinion and never, as far as I knew, betrayed her own principles – all of which were qualities I admired, though I wouldn't have especially wanted to be a member of her Government. Later I met her successor, Prime Minister John Major, and liked him at once, chiefly because he listened to the replies given to the questions he asked and his questions seemed to stem from a sincere desire to know more. President François Mitterrand too was always more interested in delivering himself of pronouncements than in getting information, and merely told me that since the conference was still-born, he would 'wash his hands' of the conflict and was glad that 'it is not I who will have to hurt Israel'. I was never sure what he meant.

Italy's Foreign Minister Giulio Andreotti, on the other hand, was one of the European statesmen whose company I most enjoyed, though he was quite frank, even when he visited Israel in 1988, about being a PLO admirer. But he was neither uncaring about Israel nor hostile to me and we got along very well. Andreotti had been in politics since his twenties in every conceivable capacity including, of course, as Premier. He had an extraordinary fund of knowledge about almost everything, told stories wonderfully and did his best to help Israel whenever he could, as when he was Chairman of the EC Council of Ministers, and I always looked forward to spending time with him. I'd been invited to Italy before the *intifada* broke out and afterwards decided to go in any case, despite the fact that the Government was pro-PLO, because, otherwise, cowardice might be added to the long list of my sins. But when I got there everything went as it should: I was met with military honours – and one of the tightest security operations ever seen in Italy for a visiting dignitary – laid a wreath on the tomb of the Unknown Soldier, and though the press, referring to me as '*Il Duro*', described me 'as the man who always says "no"', it was not abusive and the reception given for me by our Ambassador was crowded with Italian VIPs.

The only thing that went wrong, it appeared, was that I hadn't asked to see the Pope again, something which perturbed the Vatican. No, I assured a press conference in Rome, there had truly been no special reason. I simply had nothing new to say to the Pope (who was openly critical of Israel and still withheld Vatican recognition from us) and didn't want to waste his time or mine. The press was not satisfied: there must have been some other hidden motive; no Prime Minister visits Rome without asking for an audience with the Pope, and therefore I must be concealing something. It was one more very small lesson for me in the ways of the world.

As Prime Minister I journeyed also to countries that had no axe to grind and no prejudices against Israel. One such trip was to four West African countries. I don't think I have ever generated such adulation, even among the most fervent Likud adherents, as I did when Shulamit and I stepped off the Israel Air Force 707 that brought us to Togo in the summer of 1987, all the way from the shouts of 'Bienvenue Shamir' and 'Shalom' that greeted us through to the brightly dressed young people who sang and danced for us (including the Israeli 'Hora') at Lomé airport, and the tens of thousands who waved to us, among them Togolese Moslems from the north. I cannot remember ever receiving a warmer or more colourful welcome; or a better press than Togo's official daily with its many pages devoted to the visit and lead article entitled, 'Who is Shamir?', an odd foretaste of a not too differently worded question on a totally different subject that was soon to arise in Israel.

As elsewhere in West Africa – in Cameroon with President Paul Biya, in Liberia with President Samuel Doe, and in the Ivory Coast with President Felix Houphouet-Boigny – so in Togo, with President Gnassingbe Eyadema, a wise man of rich experience, I listened to national leaders speak with huge emotion of the invaluable advice and practical medical, agricultural and educational assistance Israel had rendered their people in the 1960s and early 1970s before these nations had severed relations with us following the Yom Kippur War – again, as though we had been the aggressors. Even in Africa, I wasn't totally released from having to hear about the international conference, but it was always explained that if nothing were said on the subject the Arabs would be 'annoyed' and I thought that, at least, an honest excuse.

More importantly everywhere, people who had trained in Israel or in their own country by Israelis, pushed their way through crowds to greet me in fluent Hebrew, to tell me their names, to shout requests that I give regards to former instructors and friends. I got used to hearing that ringing 'Shalom' in the most unexpected places and remember to this day the pleasure of being welcomed to Yaounde, the capital of Cameroon, by a smart guard of honour which, down to the last detail, duplicated a crack IDF unit: uniforms, purple berets, paratrooper boots and rifles, proudly representing yet another area of Israeli training. Or the satisfaction I felt sitting in Houphouet-Boigny's splendid Israeli-built palace while he spoke of the new bonds being forged between Israel and his country. Before 1973 he had been one of Israel's greatest, most grateful supporters and a personal friend of various Israeli leaders, including Golda Meir. Then it had all been swept away under Arab pressure. Now Houphouet-Boigny talked of the slow but sure return of Israel to Africa and of the deep friendship that had endured the break. It was not so all over the continent, but I left West Africa knowing that one day the past would be totally erased – as, indeed, it has been.

I must also mention the special 'call' I paid at night to one extraordinary man, the President of Kenya, Daniel arap Moi, with whom – though on that occasion he preferred the discretion of a non-public meeting – I have always enjoyed a close relationship. Whenever we turned to him for co-operation, it was most generously given, whether what was under discussion directly concerned Kenya or not, and regardless of possible complications and perils. I personally will be grateful to him for ever for the role he played in helping us bring our Ethiopian brethren to Israel. I am only sorry that he has yet to visit us despite his repeated promises to me that one day he would come as a Christian pilgrim. Since I know him to be a man who keeps promises, I am sure that eventually he will keep this one.

One more word about Africa: when all is said and done, it is hard to find a final explanation for the human misery that afflicts so much of the continent. However lavish the hospitality, however warm the reception, however fascinating the ceremonies, I don't think that I was ever unaware (on this journey or others), for more than a very few minutes at a time, of the poverty, sickness, hunger and thirst or profound backwardness of whole nations trapped by a terrible combination of nature's ceaseless harshness, their own great vulnerabilities, and the basic indifference and entirely inadequate help of the world's wealthy nations. I talked with the Africans I met about Africa's plight. I thought that they might shed more light on its causes and on the possible cures than the various experts whose explanations 'in depth' never satisfied me, but even the continent's leaders had nothing illuminating to say. I felt that I had visited lands stricken by tragedy almost as though an evil spell had been cast upon them and I could only hope that at some point, somehow, in the not too distant future, before it was too late, they would find a way, with suitable assistance, to revitalize and save themselves.

There were other worlds, less exotic, less foreign to me, of which I also came to learn more. To travel in Latin America, and by now I had visited most of that sub-continent, was a special joy, for with its many outgoing and supportive Jewish communities I could speak, at least in part, in Yiddish, the language we had in common, which I so love for its richness and intimacy though there is almost no one left now with whom I can still use it. Despite brave efforts being made to preserve it as a living tongue, it has essentially disappeared with the slain Jewish populations of Europe. But it lives on here and there in Latin America and it was in Yiddish that, in Argentina, I tried to comfort the hundreds of Jewish families looking to Israel for hope in their agony over the allegedly 1,000 'desaparecidos' of that community. 'Even if you yourselves do not realize the dream of aliyah,' I told them, 'know that Israel will protect you.' I couldn't do much, but at least I raised the matter with Argentina's then President, Renaldo Bignone, so that he too should feel the indivisibility of the Jewish people. The first Argentinian President to visit Israel was Carlos Menem, who came in 1991 and won a special place in Israeli hearts by the praise he showered on the state, the concern and solidarity he expressed during the Gulf War, and his outspoken desire to further the peace process. Young, vigorous, attractive, I thought that he might indeed, to use his own words, manage to 'change the course of history in Argentina' and perhaps, as he also hoped, help to change it elsewhere. Of Arab origin, he is certainly an ideal candidate to make the attempt.

There were other charged meetings abroad with Jews. In Romania, a day or two before the Jewish New Year, speaking in Yiddish to a packed audience in Bucharest's Great Synagogue, I was moved to tears as I wished the community 'a good year, a year of joy and a year of peace!' Perhaps my eyes filled because suddenly memories of my Eastern European childhood flooded me or perhaps because the people I addressed, sitting in front of me in silence, their eyes riveted on me, represented the fewer than 20,000 Jews that were left of a thriving community of over 700,000, all the rest having perished in the Holocaust, or settled in Israel after the war, or having slowly died off. I had seen President Nikolai Ceauçescu the day before. With no small agility he had agreed that the attainment of peace was 'conditional on direct talks', but he also told me that he favoured the international conference with PLO participation. More usefully, he promised to do 'everything possible' to keep his country free of anti-Semitism. Romania was the only Eastern European country to remain friendly to Israel after the Six Day War and the first to permit limited emigration to Israel. Ceauçescu had even tried to serve as a conduit between Golda Meir and Sadat back in 1972. Both Begin and Sadat had visited him, Sadat himself later saying that Ceauçescu had told him that Begin should be trusted. He wanted and achieved good relations with us, and better ones with the Arabs. Leaving Bucharest then, I remember wondering what would await that remnant of Romanian Jewry if anything happened to him, but I must admit that I wouldn't have believed it had I been told that he would die, as he did, at the hands of a Romanian firing squad, damned by his nation as a monster.

I cannot write even these few lines about Romania without a word or two about a most unusual man without whom the life of Jews living under the Communist regime of that country would indeed have been bitter and whose chances of immigration to Israel probably nil. I write of Chief Rabbi Moshe Rosen, as brilliant a diplomat as any I have ever met and as brave, in his own way, as any Israeli soldier, who took it upon himself to keep alive the embers of Jewish life, even of Zionist activity, in Romania – and to preserve, despite the Iron Curtain, the contact between that Jewry and Israel. All this, of course, made him suspect in many eyes. He was accused of opportunism, of overly close co-operation with the Government and – which later became very serious – with Ceauçescu himself. I, however, felt sure that had there been more Jewish leaders in Eastern Europe of Rabbi Rosen's calibre, both in the USSR and in the satellite countries, the position of the Jews would have been very different, and I continued to uphold what by now was his remarkable international reputation.

The credit for one of my pleasanter memories of travel around this time goes to Shulamit. In the summer of 1991, I was invited to Bulgaria largely because of her remarkable popularity in that country. 'If she ran for President, she would surely get in,' the then President told me. Half a century had passed since, as a girl, she had left Bulgaria (the Nazis were not yet there) for Palestine, alone, an 'illegal' immigrant, the knapsack on her back her only luggage, but her ties to Bulgaria, her fluent Bulgarian and her feelings about the country had never altered. Also, since Bulgaria had been one of the very few nations in Europe to prevent the Nazis from destroying the Jewish community and, in 1948, had given those members of the community who wanted to leave for Israel the right to do so (most Bulgarian Jews availed themselves of the privilege, making important contributions to, and being quickly absorbed into, Israeli society), Shulamit's recollections of growing up there were free of any bitterness. She had visited twice before our trip together, the first time after Bulgarian Foreign Minister Peter Mladenov (later to be President) suggested to me at a 1988 UN General Assembly in New York that she return 'for another look'. That had been a semi-official visit with the door to full relations, closed since 1967, at last ajar, and Shulamit becoming, to her amazement, a media star ('More people recognize me on the streets of Sofia than in Jerusalem'), constantly interviewed on television and by the press. On that visit, she had said publicly, not really intending to be taken seriously, 'Next time, I hope to return with my husband.' And when an official Bulgarian invitation to a state visit duly followed, that is exactly what she did.

The journey to Bulgaria, which, in the meantime, had renewed diplomatic relations with Israel, gave me a chance not only to admire a beautiful country and the special open-heartedness of its hospitality, but also to tell the Bulgarian Government and people that, 'while the Jews do not forget the evil that is done to us, we also for ever recall acts of understanding, humanity and assistance'. For me that journey, of course, was unlike any other. I knew that for Shulamit it was a dream come true to be back in Bulgaria: the Jewish state a reality, its flags fluttering throughout the city, its anthem everywhere in the air, herself its representative – and Israel's Prime Minister, her husband, with her.

If I write a bit disjointedly about these travels, it is because my primary purpose in mentioning them is to try to present some picture of the scope and range of Israel's need to create and maintain friends. All Presidents and Prime Ministers, and possibly more Cabinet Ministers than necessary, take to the air these days, but not all are as beset by external and internal crises as are Israel's leaders and certainly few have the overseas 'constituencies' to which Israel's Prime Ministers both want to, and must, report. I refer, of course, to the Jewish communities, which, with us, make up the Jewish world, for as Israel's Prime Minister, I was often also an emissary, or at least a representative, of that world, not only of the Jewish state.

One conversation that brought this home to me forcibly took place in Japan during the 1980s. Overwhelmed by even the little I had glimpsed of Japanese efficiency, the prevailing work ethic, the discipline and the sheer energy with which the Japanese run their collective life, I was rather taken aback to find Japanese leaders envious of Israel.

'Your people', a ranking minister said to me (and there were others

who echoed his sentiments), 'are so fortunate with your unlimited
access and boundless influence everywhere. You are all-powerful. See
how you hold the United States in the palms of your hands.' Never
mind how strongly I protested that, unfortunately, this was not
precisely the case, my hosts smiled, nodded and clearly disbelieved
me. I'm sure none of them had read, or perhaps even heard of, the
infamous *Protocols of the Elders of Zion*, which, with its allegations of
world-controlling secret Jewish cabals, turns up whenever propagandists agitate against Jews – whether in Russia during the 1917
revolutions, in Nazi Germany or in various Arab states. Certainly
they did not wish to offend me; on the contrary, they were com-
plimenting me on the omnipotence and distinction of world Jewry
and on my having the honour to be one of its spokesmen. But talking
to people about important things in a language that is neither your
mother tongue nor theirs, or through interpreters, inevitably assists
misunderstanding and I decided, under the circumstances, not even
to try to disillusion them. Israel's relations with Japan, established in
the early 1950s, have never been broken and are good. But it is only
recently that we have appeared, so to speak, on Japan's commercial
agenda, despite the Arab boycott, and that Japanese political and
industrial leaders have visited Israel. For myself, I have long believed
that our links to the Far East – Japan, China, Thailand, the Phi-
lippines – will one day be as close as, if not closer than they are with
Europe.

Anyhow, 'all-powerful' hardly described how I felt in the weeks
following the formation of the new 1988 Cabinet, though that in
itself was a respite from the manoevring and manipulations that had
gone on for so long. The main challenge facing the National Unity
Government was the preparation of an Israeli peace initiative. As my
American friends said, there was now a new game in Washington:
a new board and very different players from those to whom I was
accustomed. No meeting had been scheduled yet with President Bush
or Secretary of State Baker, but I had already been at work for weeks
on a series of proposals backed by both the Likud and the Alignment
that seemed likely to break the stalemate and keep the peace process
alive – and moving in a direction of which both the United States
and Israel could approve. The four salient points of that initiative
were: 1. that Israel wished to embark at once on peace talks,
continuing the political process via direct negotiations based on the
principles laid down in the Camp David Accords; 2. that for this
purpose Israel – refusing to conduct any negotiations with the PLO –
now proposed that free, democratic elections be held among the

Palestinian Arabs of Judea, Samaria and the Gaza district in order to produce an authentic Palestinian representation with which Israel could indeed negotiate – provided, of course, that all violence in the territories ended and that there would be no PLO-intimidation of voters; 3. that following such elections, Israel would discuss with this representation, together with Egypt and Jordan, establishment of a self-governing administration (i.e. autonomy) in the context of an interim arrangement allowing the Palestinians to run their own affairs; and 4. that after a testing period, negotiations would be held between these parties to decide upon the permanent status of the territories. Also, the initiative called upon the Arab states to end all belligerency (including boycott and political war) and closed with Israel's urgent appeal regarding the plight of the Arab refugees and the need for collective action to be taken to solve it.

Other points in the proposal included Israel's recognition of the risks involved to itself in the search for peace, our view of the danger inherent to us in the establishment of an additional state west of the River Jordan, the importance of the involvement of the Kingdom of Jordan in the peace process (the one departure from the Camp David Accords, which refer only to the United States, Israel and Egypt) and, again, the central role in the conflict of the Arab threat to Israel and the refusal of Arab countries, with the exception of Egypt, to recognize Israel's existence. But its core was contained in the four main points; these were what I took with me at the beginning of April for my first meeting with George Bush in his capacity as President of the United States.

10

WAR – AND PEACE?

In January 1989, I called what was known as the Prime Minister's Conference on Jewish Solidarity to be held in March in Jerusalem. I felt that the time had come to give expression to the unity of the Jewish people and to dispel any idea that this people was divided, or that the bonds between the Diaspora and Israel had weakened or been loosened in the wake of the *intifada* or the 'Who is a Jew?' issue. I wanted the world to know that the Jewish people were one. Unity had always been paramount in my thinking. Now it was becoming a major element in my peace strategy, and when it was decided to organize this Conference, I also incorporated the theme of the Government's unity by appointing two co-ordinators: Ehud Olmert, a Minister representing the Likud, and Alignment Minister Mordechai Gur. The response to invitations despatched at unusually short notice to exceedingly busy people all around the world was more than even I had expected: 1,600 Jewish leaders representing communities in forty-two countries came together to demonstrate solidarity with Israel, with the Government's search for peace and with its guidelines. Not everyone was necessarily in accord with everything, but they believed me when I said that we were not staging anything, not attempting 'to stifle criticism or to silence voices of dissent', nor asking for endorsement of any partisan viewpoint. What we hoped to receive from them was their unmistakable and greater commitment to the Jewish state so that, at this moment in our history, we would not be perceived as isolated, alone or as easy targets, but as backed by the resilient, inextinguishable and united people to which we belonged. As I told them:

It was not a single event that prompted us to convene this extraordinary Conference. It is rather a trend, an evolution carrying with it formidable problems, risks and opportunities. In parts of the world there is confusion and sometimes even alienation from us, a lack of understanding for our position and our policy, and we also see a campaign to blacken Israel's name in order to create political circumstances that will endanger our interests and jeopardize our security. We have reason, too, to believe that we shall face difficult struggles in the political arena of the kind that could affect our political and military situation and well-being. We have, therefore, asked you to come to Jerusalem so that my colleagues in the Government and I should have the opportunity of sharing thoughts with you, presenting dilemmas, and listening to your reactions and advice.

Castigating those 'who took it upon themselves to conduct policy for us, to meet our enemies and speak to them in our name, and to offer initiative and political programmes of their own that affect our lives and the future of our people', I appealed to the Conference participants, and through them to the millions of Jews on whose behalf they had assembled to 'help us represent the State of Israel and its national consensus and to remind the leaders and the media in the countries where you live of our roots, struggle and aspirations'.

I spoke to them about my forthcoming trip to Washington, sharing with the vast assembly the spirit if not the letter of what I would say there: our opposition to a Palestinian Arab state west of the River Jordan; our refusal to deal with the PLO; our commitment to interim arrangements and, once these were successfully tested, to a second stage of negotiation regarding permanent status; and (evoking thunderous applause) that Jerusalem, united, would never be divided again. If only I could have been assured of as heartfelt and as positive a response to much the same words when I uttered them two weeks later in Washington. To call the Conference a success is to trivialize its impact; it was an immensely moving, even uplifting experience which, every now and then, sometimes when I least expected, touched on the very essence of peoplehood. By its close, there was no question that the Jews of the Diaspora, as represented in Jerusalem that spring week, would strengthen Israel in its resolves and that we, for our part, would give them the strength, as I told them when we parted, to 'return home and to stand up and be counted when the needs of the Jewish people and land required it'. I had every reason to believe that this message had reached the other place in which I wanted it heard, several thousand miles to the west of Jerusalem.

I was heartened by the Conference and felt reinforced by it. On the surface, there was no special reason for alarm. Before the US elections, the Republican candidate, George Bush, had declared that 'America will continue to stand beside Israel, unwavering in our support', and referred to Israel as a 'strategic ally' whose values 'buttressed the alliance' in its 'most vulnerable area'. He had also declared his approval of direct negotiations, had pledged that, if he were elected, the United States would not impose a settlement and 'will only support a role for the PLO if it recognizes Israel's right to exist'. The new Secretary of State was also viewed as friendly, at least to the extent of not wanting Israel to revert to pre-1967 borders, opposing the creation of an independent Palestinian state and encouraging dialogue between Israel and the Palestinians.

In the weeks that had passed since the President's inauguration in January, the Administration had been quietly exploring the Middle Eastern situation, but everyone else involved was in a whirl of activity generated by the change of guard in Washington. Moshe Arens met in Cairo with Soviet Foreign Minister Eduard Shevardnadze and with President Mubarak; that round of talks in Egypt, mostly centring on the still viable, though tired, topic of an international conference, was followed by a meeting in the same capital between Shevardnadze and PLO Chairman Yasser Arafat, providing a measure of the Soviet rush to participate actively in any renewed Middle East peace process. The United States, I thought, could and would take care of its own national interests, and as far as we were concerned, the Soviet desire not to be left out was leading to normalization of relations between the USSR and Israel, with all of the many implications this held for us.

What, however, did worry me was the new US Administration's less than neutral attitude towards the PLO. Regardless of all other assessments, I was as convinced as I had ever been that the only peace the PLO could produce in terms of Israel was the peace of the cemetery. I felt it was imperative to get the peace process moving and the autonomy under way as soon as possible. For this we needed partners. I flew to Paris to ask President Mitterrand to support our peace initiative and use his considerable influence in Europe and with the Arabs to further it, so that we could finally embark on interim arrangements that would exclude the PLO. Mitterrand was cordial, interested, but unable, or unwilling, to free himself from the idea of an international conference. He listened while I suggested that if no other way could be found at this juncture to hold elections in the territories, as Israel advocated, then at least perhaps Jordan and Egypt could organize a provisional delegation to negotiate with us. But he would only talk about a conference. Then, as I was taking my leave, he looked at me rather penetratingly for a second and said, 'If I were an Israeli, I would think as you do. But I am French and I have my own interests to consider.' So that was that.

My invitation to Washington, when it came at the end of March, said much, it seemed to me, about the Administration's approach: the White House announced that President Bush would receive President Mubarak at the White House on 3 April, Prime Minister Shamir on 6 April, and King Hussein on 2 May. Everything was thoroughly planned and dovetailed: Mubarak was scheduled to leave just as I arrived. All three visits would have an identical format and all three were considered 'official working visits'. Everything, including 'an international conference, the role of the Palestinians, Israeli attitudes in general', would be discussed. The White House spokesman didn't mention any new peace initiatives, but he did stress that there would be changes 'since the US began its dialogue with the PLO', something the Reagan Administration, in its last days, had suddenly decided to promote.

President Bush was extremely courteous, if cool. He had already, I was told, expressed himself strongly on a number of vital matters – the Jewish settlements in the territories, in particular – and had even told Mubarak a day or two earlier that there must be an end to the Israeli 'occupation', though at this point he said nothing of this to me. In fact, he did whatever he could, on that first visit, to demonstrate warmth. He congratulated me on the Solidarity Conference: 'I hear you did very well with it', he said; prepared 'treats' for me, as he had done for Mubarak; and took me to 'the movies' (a film on the US space programme at the Smithsonian Institute), delighting the routine sightseers. I had been asked for a list of people I would like to be invited to a White House dinner in my honour, and had sent to Washington a number of names, including those of various Likud supporters in the United States, who, like the film-goers, were astonished and delighted by the President's invitation. He had also invited some actors, of roughly my own age, if not older, that he thought I'd be familiar with, like Bob Hope and Katharine Hepburn.

One non-political incident connected with that White House dinner also connected me, if only briefly, with Mubarak. The State Department had informed my office of all the necessary details pertaining to the visit, including that the President's dinner for me was to be 'as usual' a black-tie affair. I absolutely refused to wear a tuxedo; I had done so once, I think, in Los Angeles and had felt ridiculous. The State Department protocol people, politely informed that the Prime Minister would 'rather' wear a dark suit, replied that they were reluctantly forced to be adamant. But I too know how to be adamant, and I didn't want to wear a tuxedo. The suspense ended when, fortunately, Avi Pazner, then my media adviser, remembered having seen a press photo of Mubarak and his entourage at their

White House dinner, the Egyptians in dark business suits, while everyone else, the President and his guests, wore tuxedos. Basing ourselves on precedent and on the US penchant for even-handedness, we referred the State Department to the recent past and I proceeded to wear my dark suit. I only wished, sadly, that there were more examples of full agreement between Mubarak and me, or at least agreement on more important issues.

My talks with Secretary Baker were serious and very candid. I started out by saying that since this was our first meeting, I thought he should know that he had been described to me as an 'ever-inflexible pragmatist', and I suspected that he had been told that I was an inflexible man of ideological principle. 'Well,' I said to the Secretary, 'I think our informants were wrong in both cases. I am a man of principle but also a pragmatist when necessary. I know what political compromise means. And I am sure that you, Mr Secretary, although a pragmatist, are a man of principle and that principle guides you in your approach to foreign policy.' I then told him what I had already told so many people before and what I felt he must hear from me as soon as possible: we were as opposed as always to any dialogue with the PLO, not as a matter of doctrine but because we profoundly believed that it would lead to a Palestinian state, an option which we would fight with all our strength as bearing within it no less than the seeds of Israel's destruction. I reminded the Secretary too that we were now celebrating the tenth anniversary of the Camp David Accords, which in no way at all, in my view, had lost their relevance, logic or validity, despite the battering they had received over the past decade.

Secretary Baker's own attitude to the Accords was somewhat other than mine. He talked about 'not digging one's heels in', about lost chances and the need to 'recapture the high ground'. We should, he said, start to think in fresh ways: first negotiate with the Palestinians, then arrive at terms of non-belligerency with the Arab states. He asked how I saw the future. Confederacy? Sovereignty? 'Can you at least say that a final settlement may embrace a variety of possibilities?' 'Well,' I answered, 'I'd say there will be Israel's demand for sovereignty and the Arabs will make their own demands, and that there is no getting away from direct negotiations.'

Although I knew a priori that the Administration would accept the peace proposals I had brought with me, as indeed it did, I explained that I would not go into detail until I was sure of US support and that I hoped that if there were differences of opinion between us we would, as friends, keep them to ourselves. Later, making the inevitable comparisons, I thought that, in general terms, Shultz had been interested in the historical, philosophical aspects of Israel while Baker was interested mostly, if not only, in what happened today, not what happened yesterday and perhaps even not what might happen tomorrow.

Some of the headlines of Friday, 7 April 1989, are before me now, for example 'Bush backs PM on elections'. The President's 'departure statement' was very carefully composed: 'The United States believes that elections in the territories can be designed to contribute to a political process of dialogue and negotiation. We urge Israel and the Palestinians to arrive at a mutually acceptable formula for elections.' With regard to the final status, the President, though he did not say that Israel should talk directly to the PLO, clearly did not rule this out. 'I am encouraged', he declared, 'by the Prime Minister's assurance that all options are open for negotiation.' I, however, was less encouraged and, at the press briefing immediately following, hastened to reject any step that might result in a Palestinian state, such as dealing with the PLO. To the press on that pleasant April afternoon, listening to two not particularly exciting official statements, it may have appeared that the relationship between the Government of Israel and the US Administration was essentially what it had always been. But I feared it was not so. Still, time would tell. For the present, the Administration agreed that our peace initiative opened up pathways, if not highways, to peace.

By the middle of May, that initiative had also been accepted by the Israeli Cabinet with twenty ministers voting for it, six against, among them Likud Ministers Sharon, Moda'i and Levy. As it stood, many of its details hammered out by leaders of both the Likud and the Alignment, it was ready to be discussed in depth in Washington, with the European Community, with various European leaders and with influential moderate Palestinians as well as our own Defence and Interior Ministries, which were to begin formulating the complicated procedures actually involved in such elections. We had, in fact, breathed life back into the peace process though the patient was still far from robust. Nor was the prognosis improved when, a few days after the Government's endorsement, Mr Baker decided to make public his own — more likely the President's — estimation of its prospects: without Israel's prior agreement to the principle of peace-for-territories, there could be no real peace process and thus there would not be peace. Speaking, and the choice was obviously deliberate, to the AIPAC (the American Israel Public Affairs Committee) in Washington, the Secretary touched on different familiar aspects of the problem: Israel's caution ('caution must never become paralysis'); the US's continuing lack of support for annexation or permanent Israeli control of Judea, Samaria and Gaza or for an independent Palestinian state; the Israeli proposal ('a very positive start'); the recognition that negotiations would be 'not easy' for many Israelis and that an end must come to 'the illusion of control over all of Palestine' for the Palestinians; and so on. So far, none of it was new.

Then he dropped his bombshell. 'For Israel,' he said, 'now is the time to lay aside, once and for all, the unrealistic vision of a Greater Israel.' Apart from what Secretary Shultz had once called 'Prime-Minister-bashing' (and certainly Baker's words were directed at me) and apart from his hostile tone, I had never before heard anyone talk of a 'Greater Israel', surely a misnomer for such a minuscule country even if its borders encompassed Judea, Samaria and the Gaza district! What people talked about was not a 'Greater Israel' but all of Israel, the whole of Israel, of which we would give away no part. I had often explained to Secretary Baker that when I spoke of the territories, I meant land that we considered and believed to be ours.

It is perhaps worth noting in this context that in the ongoing and heated controversy over settlements, certain myths began to assume the guise of facts, to be ritually quoted first by one source then by another, until they came to be regarded as incontrovertible. For instance, despite the impression given by the Bush Administration, inadvertently or otherwise, the settlements, however unfortunate in its eyes, were in no way illegal. The Jewish right to settle west of the River Jordan (that is, with the pre-1967 borders and in Judea, Samaria and the Gaza district) was made unassailable in 1922, when Jewish settlement in what is now Jordan was withheld by the Mandatory Government. That right, according to no less an expert than Dr Eugene Rostow, the US Under-Secretary of State who helped to produce UN Resolution 242, was never terminated. 'It cannot be terminated', he wrote in 1991, 'except by a recognized peace between Israel and its neighbours.' Or, as Jesse Helms, a ranking member of the US Senate Foreign Relations Committee, wrote: 'Israel has a just and valid claim [in the territories] in history, and in law.' None the less, the Administration, at all possible opportunities, indicated that these were 'foreign territory' to which Israel had no rightful claim at all. Another non-fact was the statement repeated with increasing frequency and volume by local opponents of the Likud to the effect that the settlements were costing the Israeli public 'billions' and therefore, even on 'non-political grounds', constituted an outrage. This also was not so. In 1991, a peak year for building across the

Green Line, the Government's total expenditure on settlements was less that one per cent of its budget: roads, infrastructure, housing subsidies for new economic enterprises all included. I would have given a lot for the figure to be much higher, but deplored the concealment of the truth in order to incite public opinion against the settlement programme and the settlers.

If Mr Baker thought for one moment that those Israelis who were determined not to trade their land for peace, dubious or otherwise, would be influenced by his advice or agree that their vision was 'unrealistic', he had badly misread them and present-day Israel with all its dilemmas, nuances and contradictions. With those few dismissive words he had reinforced Israel's extremists, weakened the National Unity Government and given the Arab leaders, but mostly the Palestinians, to understand that it was well worth their while to meet us halfway in the matter of the elections because the United States would see to it that even for that there would be a handsome reward in the form of territory. Most of all, for me personally, his phraseology confirmed that my feelings of disquiet after our initial meeting had some basis. For the next few years we were to meet and talk often, but I never completely got over that first insight I had into the Administration perception of our dream of a safe, strong, intact Israel. Much the same kind of shock must have activated the ninety-four (out of 100) senators whose response to Baker's unfortunate if revealing words was to sign a letter to him, asking that the Administration 'publicly and strongly endorse the Israeli peace initiative'.

In general, Baker was given to expressing himself in vivid ways to which I was unaccustomed. Angry because he had read that I termed the proposal for a dialogue with the Palestinians 'no longer relevant', he informed the House Foreign Affairs Committee that, 'with such an approach there would never be a dialogue on peace'. If Israeli officials were not going to adopt a 'positive attitude', the Secretary had said, 'I can only say "Take this number: 202–456–1414. When you're serious about peace, call us."' The number, of course, was the White House switchboard.

By September, three documents co-existed: Israel's initiative, a ten-point Egyptian plan and a five-point plan entered, as it were, by the United States. The Israeli initiative was much as it had originally been, though by now it had acquired a preamble that reviewed the basic premises and was organized into two distinct stages: the interim period and the permanent settlement. The substance of the elections was all there but not yet the entire battery of details, which later were to receive such intense attention and be subjected to such argument.

In June, Egypt's Minister of State, Boutros Ghali, came to Jerusalem for two days, 'to see what Egypt can do,' he said. 'We need a new momentum' – the words so often on Sadat's lips. He brought with him a verbal message of friendship from President Mubarak. I was anxious, I explained to Ghali, for Egypt's co-operation. We didn't need a 'broker', but I knew the extent of Egyptian influence in PLO circles, in the Arab League and, despite Egypt's economic dependence on the United States, in Washington. I knew that Ghali, an erudite, talented man and an expert in saying little, recalling much and keeping his own counsel, would accurately convey my return message to Mubarak – as well as my complaints about the overall and unsatisfying state of our relations with Egypt.

It didn't take long for Mubarak's 'conditions' for holding elections in the territories to arrive. Various Alignment Cabinet members, including Defence Minister Rabin, greeted the Egyptian text with considerable praise on the grounds that it did not call for the PLO to play a role at this stage, nor for the creation of a Palestinian state, nor even mention a return to the 1967 borders. But I read those ten points differently. The Egyptian President's proposals stressed the need for 'all citizens of Judea, Samaria and Gaza to participate in the elections and have the right to stand as candidates, including those under administrative detention,' which – upon careful reading – meant bringing the PLO into the peace process, and, of course, the Likud was bound by its own platform (to say nothing of the National Unity Government's guidelines) to find his Point Ten ('Prevention of settlement in the "occupied territories"') an unacceptable pre-condition, as was the inclusion of the Arab residents of East Jerusalem in the elections. That more than anything else indicated to me that Mubarak was not serious, for he certainly knew perfectly well that for me there is only one Jerusalem; it is at the heart of Judaism, it is Israel's capital, it has a Jewish majority and there is no dividing it ever again in that way or any other.

In October, President Mubarak visited President Bush in Washington again. Having turned down another invitation from me to come to Jerusalem ('there must be something to come for,' he said), he met with Moshe Arens in New York. That particular meeting resulted in an unscheduled conversation between the President of Egypt and myself. It was the eve of Rosh Hashanah, the Jewish New Year, and Arens and Mubarak were sitting in a New York hotel room. When Mubarak replied to Arens's question, 'Of course I'll talk to Shamir,' Arens seized the moment. 'Let's call now,' he said. In Jerusalem, my phone rang. 'President Mubarak would like to talk to you,' Arens said. Mubarak was all cordiality: 'A happy New Year to you and the people of Israel. Let's meet in the New Year.' 'Good,' I answered. 'We must prepare a meeting. Talk to Arens about it. Whatever you both decide will be fine with me.' Mubarak turned to another topic. 'Tell me,' he asked, 'how do you [I understood he meant Jews in general] celebrate your New Year?' 'Well,' I said, 'we pray and we have festive family meals.' 'What do you eat at those meals?' he asked with what sounded like genuine curiosity. I couldn't think of a single specific item. 'Good food,' I answered lamely. Mubarak laughed. 'Well,' he said, 'you are a rich people. You eat well. Have a happy New Year!' I would have flown to New York the next evening if I had thought that a meeting would be fruitful, but he never abandoned his position that discussion between us had to end with some concrete action on Israel's part by way of payment. I regarded that as both arrogant and hazardous, so we didn't meet.

The next document to descend upon us was more important: Secretary Baker's five points. Before I describe the developments to which these led, I want to make a general statement regarding both the relationship between the Bush Administration and Israel and between the Bush Administration and myself. It was, at this stage, to put it simply, that I felt I could no longer fend off or deny the realization that what President Bush wanted – and what Secretary Baker was determined to secure for him – was no less than Israel's total withdrawal from Judea, Samaria and the Gaza district and, if possible, the handing over of these territories to the Arabs or whatever Arab combination could be put together most effectively and palatably. What stopped this from happening was, first of all, the National Unity Government, and secondly, later, the Likud Government. I am not at all sure, incidentally, that if the Labour Alignment had been in power then and headed, say by Mr Peres, the President would have had cause for such frustration since he might have found Peres a lot easier to deal with.

Having written this, I must also clarify that at no time did the US Government cease to concern itself with peace in the Middle East, nor at any time did I have reason to suspect that the Administration was opposed to the Jewish state. President Reagan's peace initiative had also been predicated on Israel's withdrawal from the territories. But no President of the United States had ever so quickly, or so implacably, disapproved of Jewish settlement beyond the Green Line. It was this fundamental difference in our attitudes and approaches towards Israel's future that was to make for our eventually strained relationship rather than any much-publicized 'lack of chemistry', at least for me.

Secretary Baker's points, aimed at achieving Palestinian–Israeli dialogue on our 1989 initiative, the changes Moshe Arens requested and the Secretary's responses, were as follows:

1. 'Egypt and Israel have been "working hard" on the peace process and it is now agreed that an Israeli delegation conduct a dialogue with a Palestinian delegation in Cairo.' We asked that the wording be changed to 'Palestinian Arab residents of Judea, Samaria and Gaza'; that the venue not be Cairo; and that there be no possibility of Arabs from East Jerusalem or outside the territories being included. To all these requests, Baker said, 'No'.

2. 'The US understands that Egypt cannot serve as a substitute for the Palestinians and will consult with Palestinians on all aspects of this dialogue, as well as with Israel and the US.' That was all right with everyone. However, 3. read: 'The US understands that Israel will attend the dialogue only after a satisfactory list of Palestinians has been worked out and also will consult with the US and Egypt.' We asked that the wording be changed to 'has been worked out by Egypt, the US and Israel', so that it would be clear that we were actively involved in approving the list. Baker said 'No', but suggested taking the second part of the sentence out altogether.

4. referred to the US 'understanding' that Israel would participate in the dialogue on the basis of its peace initiative, stating also that the Palestinians would come prepared to discuss 'issues that relate to their opinion on how to make elections and negotiations succeed'. Arens requested that the word 'negotiations' be omitted, since a Likud decision had ruled against any such negotiations until 'all violence in the territories cease', which thus far it had not. Baker agreed to use the words 'process of negotiations' instead.

Lastly, to facilitate the process, the US proposed in 5. that the Foreign Ministers of the US, Israel and Egypt meet in Washington within two weeks. 'Any suggestion that Israel meet with Palestinians selected, directly or indirectly, by the PLO ... contradicts the spirit of the initiative', Arens wrote to Baker. Baker's people considered the changes we had asked for to be 'nitpicking'. They were very irritated. Israel had a 'built-in' veto and needn't press for the explicit right to turn Palestinians down; and, why couldn't the Palestinians talk about anything they wanted?

Within the Likud, Baker's five points sparked a noisy, basically purposeless 'mutiny' mounted against the 'capitulation' of the Party's so-called Shamir–Arens faction to the demands of the United States. There was a lot of shouting about, and at, me by the three 'hard-line' Ministers, Sharon, Levy and Moda'i, but to this day I am not sure why. I remember, however, thinking how astonished George Bush and James Baker would have been to have heard those loud accusations that I was 'weak-kneed'. Maybe what the 'mutineers' really wanted was control of the Likud, something quite beyond their reach in any case. Nothing came of the 'mutiny' except some supposed 'constraints' (to the initiative) which had very little, if any, ideological implications – though it was to flare up again in 1990. Unity, if not complete harmony, was eventually restored. The Likud central committee agreed to approve the amended plan, with no change, provided that it didn't stray from the Camp David Accords or the original initiative, and that it categorically stated that Arabs from East Jerusalem would not participate in the elections, that Arab violence would be eliminated before talks got under way, that new settlements would continue to be established in Judea, Samaria and Gaza, that no Palestinian state would be created in the Land of Israel and that Israel would not deal with the PLO in any way, shape or form.

But something was already taking place in Israel that for me dwarfed everything else, even the search for peace. In the wake of perestroika and glasnost, the gates of the Soviet Union had swung open. At long last hundreds of thousands of Jews were making their way to us in a flood that carried with it not only an ultimate affirmation of Zionism and a resounding message of Jewish unity, but also, for Israel, the promise of a stronger, brighter future sooner than we could otherwise have dared to expect. I felt the kind of emotion that I can only compare to that joy I had experienced when I first arrived in the country. For me, it was as though a miracle were taking place, something so long awaited and overwhelming that I was filled with gratitude for having lived to witness this great exodus – almost half a million Jews, men, women and children – planeload after planeload, arrive in the Jewish state, and that this state was there to receive them. To the extent that I have ever been proud of anything, I am proud that I had helped them to come and that, like so many others, I had laboured on their behalf.

I have already written of my deep early involvement with Soviet Jewry's struggle for freedom, an involvement that never lessened, though my life was to change a great deal with the passage of time. Not so my faith that, one day, many would join us. Now they were coming, in unimaginably vast numbers in the wake of an unimaginable cataclysm. There had been years in the 1970s and 1980s, when – under the remorseless pressure of dedicated organizations created in Europe, the Americas and Israel for this purpose, the intervention of foreign heads of state, parliaments and world-famous personalities – the Soviet Union, despite its anti-Semitism and cruelty, had grudgingly permitted a very limited emigration. Many of the Jews who left the Soviet Union in those years, on the strength of affidavits and visas from Israel, decided, in the transit centres set up for them in Austria and later elsewhere (before direct flights to Israel were initiated in 1991), to 'drop out', i.e. to opt for destinations other than Israel, for the United States, Canada and Australia. I had fought this development tooth and nail; the arguments (often used by the Jewish organizations that aided them to justify the 'dropping out') were that it didn't really matter where the Soviet Jews landed up as long as they were able to leave the USSR, that the choice should be theirs totally and that they should be absolutely free to settle where they wanted. I understood the argument but couldn't, and didn't, accept it.

Never mind that not all Soviet Jews were refuseniks for whom Israel was a spiritual home or that, in the seventy years of their isolation from the mainstream of Jewish life, most Soviet Jews had lost touch with its essence, were unfamiliar with Jewish history or that of Israel. Israel still awaited them as the homeland of the Jewish people. That was where they belonged and that is what Zionism is about. Whenever I was in the United States in those days, I met in long sessions with men like Morris Abram, then head of the influential Council for Soviet Jewry which at the time advocated support of Soviet Jewish immigration to the United States and we battled for hours. In the end Zionism won out and, despite the setbacks, failures, even errors that unavoidably accompanied Israel's response to this unprecedented challenge, I know as surely as I know anything that I was right.

In 1987, 2,000 Jews came to Israel from the USSR; in 1988, the same trickle; in 1989, the number grew to nearly 13,000, turning into a torrent of 185,000 in 1990, with another 145,000 arriving in 1991 and 76,000 more by the end of 1992. All told, by 1992 some 400,000 new immigrants had settled in Israel and, though recently the numbers have lessened, the immigration goes on. We had, of course, envisaged quite another pace, budgeted for much, much smaller numbers, had anticipated the need to absorb at most perhaps a total of 100,000 immigrants in a period of three fiscal years – and even that would not have been easy. However, within weeks of those decisions, it became evident that even more radical measures would be required if we were to feed, house, educate and, above all, employ these thousands of new citizens who knew no Hebrew, had lived only under a dictatorship, either had had no contact at all or only minimal contact with the West, and of whom a third were over sixty. Nor was this, in other ways, an 'ordinary' immigration. It was rich with talent. Most of the Soviet immigrants are experienced professionals: scientists, engineers in tens of thousands, teachers, musicians, expert technicians of all kinds, and no less than some 11,000 doctors. Their presence amongst us will unquestionably transform, brighten and strengthen Israel as it enters the twenty-first century. When I once called them 'a blessing from heaven', I meant every word. But in the meantime, this mass of humanity had to be absorbed. Given the huge numbers and the certainty that most of these newcomers would be far better off catapulted, as it were, into the daily life of Israel rather than being maintained in separate centres (though these too became filled to the brim), they were 'directly' absorbed and given what is known as an 'absorption basket' (enough money for essential expenses), free health insurance, the right to be professionally retrained, old-age pensions as though they had worked all their lives in Israel, made eligible for low-interest mortgages and, not least, intensive Hebrew courses. Other than help and counsel on the community level and the warmth and enthusiasm of local volunteers, they were on their own, unregimented for the first time in their lives, which, in itself, was no simple matter. Combining forces, the Ministries of Absorption and Housing plus the Ministry of Finance formed an 'Immigration Cabinet' under Housing Minister Ariel Sharon's chairmanship and my own active supervision. As always, world Jewry, through the Jewish Agency, fully, effectively and most generously participated in the gigantic undertaking, so far beyond Israel's capacity to handle alone.

We concentrated first on what appeared most urgent: housing. Every available rental apartment was immediately taken; thousands of mobile homes, caravans (though not popular, not always well built) were ordered; the Government distributed land in the expensive centre of the country at a fraction of its real cost and 100,000 building starts were made by both private and government contractors. There were difficulties and complaints, some justified, but no new immigrant spent a first night in a tent. Jobs were something else. From the beginning, the absence of available, even fairly appropriate, work for this enormous immigration was the thorniest problem of all, turning many expectant and eager immigrants, used to the virtually total job security of the USSR, into people living at close-to-subsistence levels who felt let-down, marginal and stigmatized as jobless in their new society, dependent on unemployment benefits and national insurance. Gradually the situation has improved; by 1992, the rate of employment of immigrants in Israel for eighteen months or more was higher than the rate of native Israelis in the workforce, but the waiting made for misery and answers couldn't be found fast.

There were a few, too few, easily 'transferable' professional categories. Language teachers could be retrained to teach French or English in Israeli schools; some musicians (they account for over half of the 11,000 immigrants formerly professionally active in the arts) could be utilized in the small orchestras springing up all over Israel – though not many; most computer engineers eventually found work. However, not all doctors and dentists can or want to be paramedics or orderlies (or prepare for re-licensing after years of practice), and there are limits to the number of those that can be employed. Is there a solution? Yes, there are two: time, and the money for economic growth, for the large-scale national projects, the infrastructures, the research and development facilities, the technology hot-houses – and the foreign investments that, together, can provide the number and calibre of jobs so sorely needed now in Israel; these, of course, plus ingenuity, determination and patience.

If, as I hope and profoundly believe will happen, yet another half million Russian Jews (their applications are currently on file in Russia) also settle in Israel in the foreseeable future, the overall estimated costs for the Ingathering would approximate a staggering $50–70 billion. The only way of raising most of these funds would be to borrow them from foreign banks. Israel is, after all, an ideal creditor with a perfect repayment record and a uniquely dramatic humanitarian cause. As was only natural, we turned to the US Government asking for guarantees for long-term commercial loans of $10 billion over a five-year period, something that in no way would burden the US taxpayer. It never occurred to me that anything could go wrong with this request, and I was horrified when the Administration, seeing in it an opportunity to influence our policy, linked the granting of the guarantees to the cessation of all settlement beyond the Green Line. In fact, I couldn't at first believe what I was being told.

But it was true. President Bush was making the granting of aid contingent upon Israel's political acquiescence, something no other President had ever done. Moreover, the President seemed to feel, and was afterwards to make public this feeling, that he was being deceived on matters having to do with the settlements. He charged me with having assured him that there would be no new Jewish settlement beyond the Green Line until negotiations ended, and then returning to Israel to celebrate the establishment of 'a new settlement' in the Gaza district. This he took as a personal affront. I explained that the establishment of the settlement (Dugit), to which he referred, had been decided upon long before we had talked, but I could sense Bush's dissatisfaction with my reply. Later, startlingly, he demanded that 'immigrants from the Soviet Union should not be settled in areas of Jerusalem formerly under Jordanian rule' – as though the heavily populated suburbs and neighbourhoods of Israel's capital, in existence ever since the city was liberated and unified in 1967, were the new settlements he abhorred. In reality, less than one per cent of the Soviet immigrants wanted to settle in Judea or Samaria. Free to live wherever they chose, it was natural that, as middle-class professionals, most of them preferred to make their homes in the centre of the country where suitable jobs were more likely to be found and cultural life was more varied – though by 1992 thousands of newcomers also settled in the cities of Israel's north and south. I cleared up that confusion but decided to set down on paper the cardinal points of Israel's policy, and in the summer of 1990, I sent a seven-page letter to the President thanking him for his efforts both to secure the free immigration of Jews from the Soviet Union and on behalf of Ethiopian Jews. Then I wrote, among other things:

In our meetings I endeavoured to explain our belief that the issue of the settlements is not an obstacle to negotiations and peace. As you know, there is a real dispute between us and the Arabs regarding the sovereignty over Judea, Samaria and Gaza. The only way to resolve this issue is through negotiation and agreement. Anyone in the Arab world who truly wants peace with us will not oppose the presence of Jews in these areas. Such Arab opposition is motivated by a desire to see there an Arab sovereignty which would bar the presence of Jews, evoking the repugnant *Judenrein* policies of the past. The Jewish state could, under no circumstances, be expected to acquiesce in such a design irrespective of the ultimate status of the territories. It is as unthinkable as it would be for Israel to ban Arabs in its borders.

On the question of settlements there may have been a misunderstanding between us in our last meeting. I said that the settlements would not be a problem because I am convinced that this is not an obstacle to peace. Apparently, you understood that to mean that I undertook to cease settlement activity. I regret that my words may have given an incorrect impression. ... Our top priority today is immigration and absorption. Let me reiterate our policy: Israel will not direct Soviet immigrants to the areas of

Judea, Samaria and Gaza, and there are no plans for housing projects for new immigrants in those areas. ...

It is my intention to renew my call to Arab leaders to open a process that would change the character of their relations with us from that of war to co-existence, reconciliation and peace negotiations. ... The Arab Governments' insistence that Israel deal with the PLO is an expression of their rejectionism. They have forged the PLO as a weapon against Israel, a means of challenging Israel's legitimacy and a spearhead of yet another attempt against our existence. The PLO cannot be a partner to the negotiations, directly or indirectly, because what the PLO seeks is our elimination. ...

I also clarified once more our stand regarding Arabs eligible for participation in the projected elections:

We will favourably consider any Palestinian Arab who resides in the areas and is not involved in terrorism. On the other hand, [it] is not directed at Palestinians from outside these areas. Any move to involve residents of Jerusalem in a dialogue will immediately bring to the fore the issue of the status of Jerusalem. This is one of the objectives of the PLO and those who support its demand to turn the city into the capital of a Palestinian state ... PLO insistence on participation of 'outside' Palestinians, whether deportees or others, serves notice of their demand for the 'right of return' – a euphemism for the undermining of our existence. Therefore we cannot entertain such a proposal.

Finally, I wrote:

We live in a volatile and unstable part of the world. Here, words often carry a dynamic of their own. ... We therefore feel that no positive result can be accomplished by public attacks on Israel or attempts to create the impression that it is Israel that opposes progress towards peace. ... Let me reiterate that nothing is more important to Israel than a durable peace; and nothing can contribute more to this purpose than our alliance with the United States.

However, my long letter was of no avail. Nor was anything I or anyone else said. The President continued to view the settlements as the crux of the conflict as though it had begun in 1967 instead of in 1948, his opposition pervading US policy, the guarantees, of course, included. In the meantime, Secretary Baker, appearing before a Congressional committee, sent Israelis (and I suspect many native English-speakers too) to their dictionaries by declaring that since money was 'fungible', loans for immigrant absorption could (and, he implied, would) release other funds permitting Israel to go on with its wicked settlement programme. It was another 'first' for the Bush Government; no Secretary of State in the past had ever spoken of fungibility on other similar occasions as when the United States gave billions in food export loan guarantees to Iraq, the probable fungibility of which was shortly and unpleasantly to be demonstrated. But even if the word was not familiar, the use it was put to in this case was, and the Arabs were entitled to feel, as they did, that this Administration was embarking on some kind of collision course with the Government of Israel I headed.

Early in March, just after the Administration had given its highly conditional approval for the loan guarantees, the National Unity Government fell, taking no one, least of all myself, by surprise. It had trembled on the verge of collapse for about fifteen months, had survived my firing of Ezer Weizman, been shaken by disputes over Mubarak's points and, in general, had reinforced rather than blurred the basic differences between the Likud and the Alignment, in particular within the inner Cabinet. Much of the trouble was due to the manipulations of Shimon Peres. What I had wanted, and was prepared to fight for ever since 1984, was a real government of national unity, which, even if its components were not always in agreement, at least agreed on major issues and could operate in an atmosphere of mutual trust. What happened instead, and I certainly should have anticipated this, was that the differences of opinion between Peres and myself on matters affecting all our lives, and those of future generations, widened until a split was unavoidable.

It came about as the result of the Alignment's determination to run its own foreign policy and maintain its own contacts with Washington, Cairo and the PLO, and was triggered by Peres's insistence on immediate acceptance of Baker's desire to include East Jerusalem Arabs and Arab deportees in the projected talks. 'Chalk it up to a Bush–Baker success,' wrote one of the newspapers, and I suppose it was that, for what it was worth. Anyhow, when Peres presented me with an ultimatum: 'Sunday is the last day for the inner Cabinet to decide,' I fired him. While it was true that a decision had to be made and that Baker was waiting to hear from us, there was no need, as I saw it, to rush. Our response to Baker's points would not only create precedents of cardinal importance when the major negotiations actually began, but also a priori they defined and legitimized postures and assumptions which, in the nature of things, we would be bound to accept as the talks developed. If more time were needed, we would take it. After all, Secretary Baker was not 'running' the peace process; he was helping the involved parties to implement it. It was we who were the only party to the talks asked to relinquish or risk anything, though Israel was not the only country concerned with the Middle East. Also we could only address the US Administration, the Arab leaders, the Palestinians in one voice, not two; not the Government's plus Mr Peres's or Mr Rabin's.

So I told the Cabinet that 'Mr Peres asked to bring about dissolution of the Unity government and undermined its existence by unjustly charging that this Government is not trying to advance the peace process – its principal task; this leaves me no choice but to terminate his service with this Government.' This information precipitated, as it had to, the collective resignation of the Alignment ministers. It took three months before a new coalition was formed. When Peres finally failed in his anxious attempt to form a government, on 11 June I presented a second narrow coalition (based on the right wing and some of the religious parties) to the Knesset and Labour returned to the opposition. It was my fourth Government.

The new Government's guidelines were obvious: no Palestinian state; no negotiations with the PLO; Jerusalem to remain united under Israel's sovereignty; new settlements to be created and existing ones broadened; and the Arab states and non-PLO Arabs to proceed on the basis of our 1989 initiative. 'At the top of its agenda', I told the Knesset, 'are immigration and its absorption.' Regarding US–Israel relations, I declared,

the relations of alliance and friendship between Israel and the US continue to be a cornerstone in Israeli foreign policy ... [though] it is no secret that there are differences between us concerning the peace process. The source of these is first and foremost the US Administration's attitude towards the PLO and dialogue with it, in our eyes a severe blow to stability and the chances for peace. We are convinced that the Administration's expectations from this dialogue have not and cannot lead to positive results. ... Experience shows that whenever the Arab countries perceive a crack in the wall of US–Israeli friendship, dreams of aggression against Israel float anew to the surface.

In the new Cabinet (I described it in my address as 'united by the concept that the Land of Israel is an idea, not merely an area'), I appointed two Deputy Prime Ministers: David Levy, who also became Foreign Minister, and Moshe Nissim, formerly a Minister of Justice who now also became Minister of Industry and Trade. Moshe Arens became Defence Minister; Yitzhak Moda'i took over the Finance Ministry; Rafael Eitan, the former IDF Commander-in-Chief and a farmer, became Minister of Agriculture; three young Ministers, Dan Meridor, Ronni Milo and Ehud Olmert, became, respectively, Minister of Justice, Minister of Police and Minister of Health. Ariel Sharon, as

I have written, was made Minister of Construction and Housing and the Tehiyya's Professor Yuval Ne'eman became Minister of Energy and Infrastructure as well as Minister of Science and Technology. It looked like and was, I thought, a good team and it went to work energetically.

Within weeks, in August 1990, the invasion of Kuwait by Iraq heralded the start of the Gulf War. By mutual agreement, the urgent question of the guarantees was put aside for a while, but the immigration didn't pause for a moment. The same charged airport scenes were re-enacted almost daily: the tears, embraces − sometimes, heartbreakingly, the reunion of a parent and a son or daughter who had not met for decades − the crowds of elated well-wishers and relatives and the weary representatives of municipalities, ministries and the Jewish Agency. Even when gas masks had to be distributed and carried by everyone, including the people just getting off planes, the immigrants didn't stop coming. Even the Scud missiles, which the winter of 1990–91 brought to Israel, didn't once empty the airport of Israel's newest citizens or of the people who came to greet them. But not only the Russians came.

A second memorable immigration in which I was much involved took place only three months after the Gulf War ended. In Operation Solomon (it lasted all of thirty-three hours) in May 1991, Israel's air force lifted over 14,000 Ethiopian Jews from Addis Ababa to Tel Aviv, thus essentially ending the 2,000-year-long exile of a Jewish community which, though isolated from the rest of the world for so long, had never surrendered its identity. Painstakingly planned, in watertight secrecy, impeccably executed despite the awesome logistics, Operation Solomon did more than deliver these Jews from Ethiopia's drought, famine and the degradation in which they lived. It snatched them from the dangers of that country's fierce civil war, then in its last violent stages, and reunited them with the thousands of Ethiopian Jews that we had brought to Israel in earlier, smaller but not much less challenging airlifts, of which the best known is Operation Moses in 1985. Behind the successful rescue efforts lay the story of fourteen years of attempts, many of which failed, of underground railroads that became unusable, of a tiny legal immigration permitted with the resumption of diplomatic ties between Israel and Ethiopia (severed by Ethiopia in 1973), and of a secret visit paid to us by Ethiopia's leader. Mengistu Haile Mariam, acting as the 'protector' of the Jews, solemnly promised me that he would let up to 1,000 Jews leave Ethiopia each month, but did not keep that promise. What he wanted from us in return was military aid. But we weren't interested and the United

States was opposed, so there was no deal and there were no Jews for a long time. In the end, thanks to other African rulers, to the diplomatic skills of our former Ambassador to Ethiopia, Uri Lubrani (one of Israel's unsung heroes), to a host of men and women of goodwill in many places who cannot yet be named, and to President George Bush, Operation Solomon was mounted.

President Bush's part in the saving of Ethiopian Jewry won him my deepest gratitude, the more so because my request for his help came at a time when he and his Administration were angered by what they believed was Israel's hampering of the peace process and the settlement question had been turned into a burning issue. None the less, when Mengistu, himself in peril, finally made a 'covering letter' from the President of the United States his condition for letting the Jews leave, that letter from President Bush was instantly, unhesitatingly forthcoming – though up to the last minute we couldn't be sure it would work. As soon as I got back from the airport – moved beyond description by the sight of those hundreds upon hundreds of people descending so quietly, so trustingly, from planes landing as though from assembly lines into a society of which they knew almost nothing, except that it contained Jerusalem and their kin – I phoned the President. He too was in a plane, en route to somewhere. I told him that I was calling for two reasons: to share with him what I had seen and to tell him that the Jewish people would never forget what he had done and how he had done it, with no tortuous analysis of the pros and cons, no 'what ifs' or 'yes, buts'. Human beings had been at risk and he had responded at once.

Beyond the standard needs of immigration, housing, employment and schools, beyond the unavoidable stresses (and distresses) of relocation, the Ethiopian Jews need also to be introduced to the achievements and discordances of modern life which they are now encountering for the first time. Few things have given me more satisfaction than the knowledge that they will adjust (for I have not the least doubt of this), make their own distinctive contribution to Israel and, early in the new century that is almost upon us, be among the 'old-timers' caught up in all aspects of the dynamism that characterizes the Jewish state, including the continuing Ingathering of which I am equally sure.

11

BAGHDAD – WASHINGTON – JERUSALEM

I CAN THINK of nothing that went more against my grain as a Jew and a Zionist, nothing more opposed to the ideology on which my life has been based, than the decision I took in the crisis preceding the Gulf War – and implemented throughout the war – to ask the people of Israel to accept the burden of restraint in the face of attack. The carrying out of that policy under the existing circumstances was one of the hardest tasks I ever imposed upon myself. I did not, of course, arrive at that decision alone, but the ultimate responsibility for it was mine, and there were times when I found its weight close to unbearable, feeling myself like a captain on a bridge in a stormy sea, with fog all around me, committed to bringing my ship intact through the straits. The risks were incalculable. There was not a day from 18 January 1991 – when the first Iraqi missiles hit Israel – until 28 February, when President Bush declared the Gulf War to be over, that Israel was not in jeopardy. Not one day on which I could be certain that our 'non-participation' in the war which was taking place, in relative terms, so near us would not in the end extract an even higher price from us than that which we were already paying. What I did know was that, virtually nightly, for almost six weeks, the entire population of Israel, sitting in sealed rooms with gas masks as ordered by the Government, patiently endured Iraqi missile attacks, never knowing until each attack was over whether poison gas or other non-conventional warheads were being used against us. The discipline and self-control for which later we were to be so lavishly praised were very hard-won indeed – and ill-rewarded. But I will come to that.

Where Israel was concerned Saddam Hussein's intentions had never been in the least ambiguous. For months before his August 1990 invasion of Kuwait, he had raged, with increasing ferocity, against Israel. In April, he had loudly proclaimed Iraq's desire to 'scorch half of Israel with chemical warfare', words that Jewish history, and Israel's seemingly endless struggle to achieve security in the face of Arab enmity, have taught Israel's not to dismiss lightly. Iraq had never reconciled itself to Israel's existence, not even signing an armistice agreement with us in 1949 after the War of Independence, and was, and remains, leader of the 'confrontationist' Arab states still dedicated, in the words of an earlier Iraqi President, 'to wiping Israel off the map' by force. Nor had the dramatic destruction of Osirak lessened Iraq's hatred for the Jewish state. Moreover, Saddam Hussein commanded the strongest of the Arab armies, was the world's largest purchaser of arms (his main suppliers being France and the USSR) and, like Syria's Assad and Libya's Gaddafi, was a dictator whose brutality was equalled only by his ambition to lead the Arab world. Then came the news. Before dawn on 2 August, my bedside phone rang: Saddam Hussein had invaded Kuwait. A new chapter in the long chronicle of Middle Eastern crises had opened; its denouement – upon which inevitably so much would depend for us – nowhere in sight.

The invasion, I knew, would not be the end. The United States would not abandon Kuwait or Saudi Arabia, with which its ties were so firm. Inevitably, Israel would be involved – if only because Saddam Hussein would seek to elevate his aggression against another Arab state by presenting himself as Zionism's arch-opponent, as the intrepid leader of a long-overdue holy war against the Jewish intruders, despite the fearful odds. I had few doubts that the Arab masses would back him, but was not at all certain how Egypt and Syria would react to the invasion. As for the PLO, its behaviour was entirely predictable, I thought. It would probably rush wildly to align itself with the Iraqi cause, as indeed it did. In between my meetings that first day, I asked myself, the Minister of Defence, the Chief of Staff and two or three of the ministers closest to me the two all-important questions: was a confrontation between Israel and Iraq unavoidable? And if so, when would it come? In the immediate future there would obviously be much to analyse and decide; in the meantime, I asked that we maintain a low profile, attracting as little attention as possible to ourselves so that we would afford no special provocation to the madman in Baghdad who was so keen to incinerate us. Also, I suggested that we keep ourselves as well and as accurately informed as conditions permitted.

Within a few days, I sent President Bush a letter to express

our solidarity with you as you lead the battle against evil forces embarked on a path of naked aggression and conquest. We are reminded of similar deeds more than half a century ago and of the dire consequences ... needless to say, we fully support your actions. We have instructed our Intelligence Services to continue the extensive exchanges with their US counterparts and pass on to you all available information. Saddam Hussein's true face has now been fully revealed, the United States has rightly noted with apprehension that Iraq may move against Israel to deflect moves against him and unite the Arab world behind him. It is no coincidence that the PLO and its leader, Arafat, have aligned themselves with Saddam and openly support his aggressions. Our military are ... ready to face the threat and challenge. We are closely monitoring the developments, including those arising from Jordan's alliance with Iraq. Defence Minister Moshe Arens has warned that the entry of Iraq's forces into Jordan would be a 'red line' from our point of view. King Hussein, against whom we have no adverse intentions, should be discouraged from serving the Iraqi dictator's aggressive actions.

I ended by assuring the President that, 'In the spirit of our alliance and friendship with the United States, we are ready for continued close consultations, at all appropriate levels, and to co-ordinate and co-operate with you as necessary.' Otherwise in those first weeks after the invasion there was no contact between us. But I understood that just as we had had to accept the fact that President Bush viewed the Arabs as the main players in the search for peace in the Middle East, so we would have to accept that he undoubtedly would view the Arab states in the same role in the search, if it became necessary, for military victory against Iraq.

But what had happened to our usefulness? We seemed not to be in the picture at all except as objects of Saddam Hussein's fury and perhaps also as its victims. When the storm passed, where would it find Israel? I could offer myself no reply to this question. But not for a second did I fool myself that Israel's situation was anything but precarious. When, in the second week of August, Saddam Hussein declared a *jihad* (a Moslem holy war) against both the United States and Israel, linked the resolution of the crisis between Iraq and most of the West to Israel's withdrawal from the territories and finally, at the end of August, stated that his forces would attack Israel, I decided that we must start taking discreet precautions. Above all, we must ascertain the exact role Israel would be assigned by the anti-Iraq military coalition being formed under President Bush's leadership. Its purpose was to protect the countries of the Persian Gulf from Saddam Hussein, most especially Saudi Arabia, whose independence President Bush had pronounced vital to US interests and which now, gratefully (not to say sensibly), managed to overcome its traditional reluctance

to permit the United States to station forces on its soil. Egypt also
actively joined the coalition for which, in its turn, the United States
gratefully later waived a $7 billion Egyptian debt. And, more sur-
prisingly, so did Syria, though its actual presence in the Gulf War
was not much more than token. However one looked at it, the
inclusion into the anti-Iraq coalition of these major Arab states was
a considerable diplomatic triumph for the President even though it
shattered the myth of unbreakable Arab unity. In October, we
began the distribution of close to five million gas masks and slowly,
very quietly, Israel moved not to a wartime footing but away from
ordinary routine into what might be called an exceedingly watchful
posture.

Israel's policy as it took form in the early autumn of 1990 rested
on five perceptions: that we were in no way a party to the crisis; that
we would do nothing to ignite a conflagration in the Gulf or to
nourish the anti-Israel propaganda then being disseminated by the
Arabs in the United States to the effect that Israel was pushing the
United States into a war with Iraq so that our battles would be fought
for us; that we would not get involved unless forced to do so but, if
forced, we would take care of our own defence; and that we would
not offer unsolicited advice. I believed strongly that it was not up to
Israel to advocate war or to promote blitzkreigs (as some of our
generals were tempted to do), and it was far better both for us and
for the United States that we stay out of the limelight and that there
be no linkage between Israel and the massive alliance President Bush
was getting together. As a result, our relationship with Washington
improved: President Bush announced that Israel was behaving 'very
well' and I went on walking what I knew was a tightrope, trying
(and, I think, succeeding) not to lose my balance and not to look too
often at the abyss below, nor try to measure its depth. No one can
live or work in a state of ceaseless worry or talk about the crisis all
the time. I did my best to distract myself for brief periods. I read,
relaxed in the evenings on the balcony, gave almost no interviews
and talked openly only with very few people. I even took a week off
from work though I stayed in Jerusalem.

One of the other things I did around that time was to see for myself
some of the thousands of flats we were putting up for the new
immigrants. I went with Ariel Sharon, who took me to Kiryat Gat,
Ashkelon and the development town of Sderot. Everywhere building
projects hummed; the bulldozers, the cranes, the sheer physical
activity were extremely impressive. I felt very encouraged and when
I met the new immigrants, as I did in all three places, and answered

their questions, it was a holiday for me from the anxiety that I was living with and was inexpressibly glad to be freed from, if only for a few hours.

Despite a UN Security Council ultimatum that he withdraw from Kuwait by 15 January or face the coalition forces, Saddam Hussein didn't move. War seemed inevitable in a world in which many orientations were in flux. Suddenly, the USSR was relatively unimportant; Jordan's King Hussein, knowing that if he opposed Iraq he might well lose his life or throne the next day, threw in his lot with Saddam Hussein, while we appeared no longer to be a 'strategic asset', our place taken by governments that, with the recent exception of Egypt, had enthusiastically joined forces for the past half century – whenever an opportunity presented itself – to eradicate us. If there was to be a war, I had to know Israel's place in a radically altered scheme of things.

In December, in Washington, I met with the President again. From the start it was clear to me that he had made up his mind that this would be a successful meeting, i.e. be free, to the extent possible, of any annoying differences of opinion on matters of substance or principle. In fact, the necessary signals to that effect were sent with great efficiency to all relevant quarters, including Congress and the major Departments. Wherever I went on that two-day visit, I listened somewhat joylessly to praise heaped on the 'low profile' we were maintaining in the escalating crisis. I found the President almost obsessively concerned about the coalition. I told him that I didn't think that there was a vast difference between the Syrian and Iraqi dictators, but the President brushed this aside. What mattered to him was that his coalition remain intact, grow in might and be ready to liberate Kuwait and destroy Saddam Hussein's war machine. Nothing was to be allowed to threaten its viability or unity. None the less, the very first thing he told me was that there would be no 'trade-off' with Iraq against any aspects of the US commitment to Israel's security, or to anything else connected with Israel. Nor, said the President emphatically, had such a trade-off been even remotely suggested. At the same time, it was evident to me that the Arab members of the coalition had conveyed to President Bush that they would not remain in the coalition if Israel joined it.

The President asked what would happen if war broke out and if Israel were to be attacked by Saddam Hussein's missiles. What would we do? I told him that we would defend ourselves and that we would consult with him. He understood that I was saying that we would not seek permission to take action and he himself repeated the word 'consult' and nodded. I also told him that we were not thinking in terms of a pre-emptive strike. We talked about an escalation of the crisis and the need, should there be war, for rapid, totally secure lines of communication. 'So we don't get in each other's way,' he said.

The President immediately instructed General Brent Scowcroft, his National Security Advisor (the only other person present – with the exception of our Ambassador, Zalman Shoval), to speak to Secretary of Defense Richard Cheney about this so that some mechanism could be set up at once, even before I left Washington. This was done, of course, and indeed, when the war began, contact was frequent and close, one result of it being the despatching to Israel of a group of high-ranking US army officers who met regularly and for hours with our military people, analysing each day's situation and in direct touch with the coalition forces. At a certain stage, a meeting took place in Washington between Israeli military leaders and those of the United States, and Moshe Arens undertook several secret missions to the States, while a US delegation headed by the US Deputy Secretary of State, Lawrence Eagleburger, came to Israel regarding joint action against the missiles. These talks were to result in the setting up of the Patriot installations – they turned out to be more effective in terms of morale than militarily – manned by American and Israeli crews in various parts of Israel, as well as to various other steps taken by the US air force during the missile attacks, including increasing co-operation between Israel's air force and the central command of Operation Desert Storm. 'I'm glad you're here,' the President said, 'and glad that our relationship has entered a new phase.'

Afterwards we were joined by senior members of the Administration and my own advisers and the discussion became more general. One topic raised was the immigration, the President asking questions particularly about the Ethiopians. Then he talked about the aid we had asked for on behalf of the newcomers. He said that the United States was interested in helping in their absorption and that the $400 million long-term loan guarantee Israel had requested would be granted but things couldn't be 'one-sided'. Israel, for its part, would have to see to it that the matter of the settlements was attended to and that they no longer remain a subject of controversy. I replied that Israel always kept its word, that we had promised not to send Russian Jews to settle in the territories and that we had also made a similar promise to the Government of the USSR. I then presented the President with a film about the absorption of immigration and with that the topic, for the time being, was closed, but President Bush had made his point.

On 17 January, at 1.30 a.m. Israel time, the US-led coalition bombed Baghdad. The White House announced that Operation Desert Storm had begun; the coalition's 400,000 multinational troops had gone to war. To save Kuwait? To teach Saddam Hussein a lesson? To create that unfortunately named 'new order' in the Middle East about which President Bush later liked to talk though it has yet to come into existence? To demonstrate the efficiency and power of the United States? Or was it to safeguard essential resources? Perhaps something of each of these considerations underlay what was undeniably to be a historic achievement, one for ever to George Bush's credit.

That night, life in Israel also changed – with the launching against us of the first eight Scud missiles, Saddam Hussein's answer to Operation Desert Storm. Schools closed; the population was asked to stay close to home; and gas masks had to be taken wherever people went. The muted preparation of the past weeks paid off; the public, as always in Israel when danger encroaches, did what it was told and waited obediently to be told more. So did the armed forces, the air force straining at the short leash it was on, waiting for the orders that were never to come. There were only, as I saw it, three possible paths for Israel to take, each with its own perils. The Israeli air force (IAF) could be directed to locate and destroy the Iraqi launchers. Or we might rely on the United States carrying out such missions with the aid of the IAF. Or – and this was the option of my choice – the IAF could act in conjunction with the US air force, each force allocated its own time and place of action.

The United States informed us that this third option was out of the question because of its unavoidable and dire political complications. Why so? The primary reason for this flatly negative response had to do with the fact that between us and that region of western Iraq from which the missiles were launched lies the Kingdom of Jordan. No action on our part, whether ground or air, could possibly preclude our entering and traversing Jordanian territory; this was something to which the Jordanians were not prepared to agree under any circumstances, as was made quite clear both to us and to the United States. Moreover, they said, they would fight in defence of Jordan's sovereignty. The Americans were convinced that an armed confrontation between Israel and Jordan – something with which we believed we could have dealt – would not merely present the coalition with problems but might even force a premature cessation of hostilities, thus irrevocably damaging coalition chances of permanently crippling Saddam Hussein. This being the case, I had to accept that Jordanian–Israeli hostilities almost surely would result in serious conflict between the United States and Israel. It is far simpler to set this equation down in writing than it was to face up to it at the time, the more so because not everyone in the Cabinet agreed with me, but I was unhappily absolutely sure that if we did not want Israel to be the cause of a possible failure of the US-led attempt to smash Saddam Hussein, we had no alternative other than to work within the framework proposed by the Administration.

What did this mean in practical terms? It meant co-operating with the United States in the areas of intelligence and consultation without any direct Israeli military intervention – always provided, of course, that our losses were not too heavy. We informed the Administration accordingly and also clarified that should the Iraqis equip their missiles with chemical warheads, we would intervene at once. For most of the war, the discussions, the debates, the arguments regarding Israel's response went on, within the Cabinet, with the US Administration, in the local media. But the Israeli public, in general – though suffering the tremendous tension and fear of the attacks, the constant presence, not to say discomfort, of gas masks, the anxiety and nightmares of small children, the broken nights and the disoriented daytime schedules (including of those people whose homes were totally wrecked in the hits) – overwhelmingly supported my decision, intuitively grasping that it was not a surrender of Israel's right to self-defence but Israel's contribution to the erasing of an evil regime. How astounded they would have been in those hellish days to learn, as we later did, that Desert Storm's commander, General Norman Schwartzkopf, dismissed those attacks as little more than lightning storms or that Defense Minister Cheney had compared them to 'mere' terrorist attacks – whatever that means. I must, however, admit that the question of public support, while it meant much to me, was at no point a factor in my decision. Had I felt that any other course of action should, or could, be taken, I would have taken it, regardless of public opinion polls.

I addressed the public as infrequently as possible, only when I had something to say that I thought needed saying. I didn't want to add my voice to the many voices of ex-Prime Ministers, assorted experts on Iraq and high-ranking IDF reserve officers appearing on the nightly talk shows. But on the fifth day of the war, I appeared on Israel Television to answer what I thought might be legitimate questions on the public's mind and to try to define the nature of the war we were fighting.

It is similar [I said] to the war waged against us by the terrorists, by people like Arafat, and therefore hard to fight. Its aim is the murder of civilians. We shall, of course, prevail. We shall not allow this war – its methods and purposes so familiar to us – to deeply disrupt our lives, destroy our economy or deflect us from our collective purpose. ... Whatever faces us, even chemical warfare, we are not faced by obliteration. So let us continue, each in his or her own way.

And I spoke also about restraint:

We have never changed our policy. We must, as we have always done, defend ourselves, but readiness does not mean impulsively, or thoughtlessly, entering into battle. Today we face a situation we have never faced before. The enemy, far away, has the means of injuring us but he is opposed by a vast army that will defeat him. ... We are not playing ping-pong; it is not a matter of 'You have hurt me so I shall hurt you.' It is a matter of our national interest.

Had I erred in my assessment of what, given the limitations, we could take upon ourselves? I think not, though there are Israelis who claim that deterrence was lost or reduced, that both Israel's self-image and its image in Arab eyes were injured, that we had been weakened by not rising to the challenge of the Scuds. But I know that our restraint was indicative of our strength; that we were able to do what was best for us and that we could not have actively joined in the military effort against Iraq without facing the Middle East, and perhaps the world, with yet another war.

The Gulf War ended on 28 February; a UN Security Council Resolution dictated, and Iraq accepted, terms that included affirmation of the twelve UN Resolutions (including trade sanctions) adopted since 2 August. The victory was hailed throughout most of the world as a spectacular coalition achievement and President Bush justly applauded as its leader, the man whose personal persistence, drive and vision had turned Saddam Hussein's 'Mother of all battles' into what was then seen to be 'The mother of all defeats' – though it turned out to be less than that. Notable exceptions to the celebrators were the Jordanians and the Palestinians – hundreds of whom, obeying terrorist orders (mainly those of the Moslem fundamentalist organization, Hammas), had climbed on to rooftops hysterically to cheer on Iraqi missiles falling on Tel Aviv. Invigorated by his success, President Bush at once turned to the challenge of 'a potentially historic peace', to that rearranged Middle East that had, for so long, beckoned to him.

Within less than two weeks of the great victory, the US Secretary of State was embarked on a swing through the area. He was to visit eight coalition member states and Israel – where he was to stay two full days. Under the circumstances, I thought this indicated a genuine interest in the country and I looked forward to his visit, knowing that it marked the start of a new round of negotiations and thus would serve both the purposes of the United States and ourselves. In two whole days, I thought, we could provide the Secretary with some picture, some real sense of how we live here and what Israel is about, to replace what I long suspected might be a kind of geopolitical abstraction with the flesh-and-blood reality, or at least part of it.

Sadly enough, Mr Baker was to experience some of the grimmest realities himself. During his visit, an Arab murdered four Jewish women, standing at a Jerusalem bus stop near a playground, and shouted that the brutal stabbings were his 'message for Baker', something that visibly affected the Secretary and gave him an immediate sense of the horror of Arab terrorism and its impact on ordinary life. This wasn't an official report despatched to him in the State Department, spelling out the aftermath of terror or Israel's responses to it or Arab complaints against us. This time he was here. I also think that he was deeply moved at Yad Vashem, not only by what he saw but also by its significance for us, another of the lessons he was learning about Israel; at our borders – the narrowness, the smallness of the country – as he saw them from the air; and at the new immigrants, Russians and Ethiopians, whom he met in the north. I don't know what he expected or whether he was surprised by anything, but he seemed to be touched by his experiences and I think that his laying a wreath on the graves of the murdered women – which he did of his own accord – was a gesture that symbolized some of his reactions.

The Secretary was insistent on our talking together privately and made it clear that he felt that much depended on me personally. He expressed the gratitude of the United States for our conduct in the war and made a point of saying that he knew that it was I who had taken the major decision. He had come to hear, he said, what we had to say, to report to the President and to decide on what would happen next. We spent a lot of time together. Baker told me what he had seen and heard in the Arab states he had just come from and that he felt that the attitudes of some of their leaders towards Israel had changed, even if only minimally, that old clichés of hatred were being discarded and that there was a real chance – which had to be taken – that better, more reasonable and healthier attitudes might now be considered. I suspected that his optimism, on the crest of victory and bred of his intense desire to bring into being the President's 'new world order', was not entirely justified but refrained from saying so. Since we seemed to be getting along well and I wanted to reduce the formality between us, I invited the Secretary and Mrs Baker to a family dinner at home, just Shulamit and myself, as we had done with the Shultzes more than once. And that evening we did talk to each other somewhat differently, less stiffly. I had a chance to explain various *sub rosa* relationships Israel had had with other countries and to 'gift' the Secretary with a shared secret or two. We even spoke about our respective children.

It was very pleasant and after dinner, when Shulamit took Mrs Baker upstairs, we sat on talking, mostly in broad generalities, though each of us managed quietly to convey an important message. I made it clear once again to the Secretary, and at some length, that the consequences of any attempt on the part of the United States to force the PLO on us might be very serious; Baker, presumably having decided to address himself only to what he considered my 'moderate' side and making no mention of 'peace for territory' or of the settlements, discussed the possibility, in the most abstract terms, of some sort of 'neighbourhood' talks, regional meetings between Israel and one or another of the Arab states – without using the word 'conference', which he rightly thought might be provocative. We made a kind of *tour d'horizon*, updating the situation in each of the neighbouring countries and, on that particular evening, I recall analysing in some depth, for the Secretary's benefit, the state of affairs in Jordan. After we said goodnight, reviewing the evening in my mind it seemed to me that it had gone well and, more importantly, augured well since in the eased atmosphere of after-dinner talk I had perhaps at last succeeded in illuminating the extent of, and reasons for, our adamant stand against the PLO.

Next day, however, when he met with a group of twelve Palestinian leaders from the territories, the Secretary none the less stressed that forgiveness for their unfortunate evaluation of Saddam Hussein's prospects was quite feasible, and that the United States would not tolerate a 'double standard', the implication being that having fought to liberate Kuwait from Iraqi occupation, the Administration would not be passive when it came to Israel's 'occupation' of Judea, Samaria and Gaza – a comparison which I found to be as repugnant as it was invalid. And, if any additional reassurances were needed to make manifest to the Arabs that the tide had turned totally in their favour, Baker provided the extra boosts. Not only did the Bush Administration not rule out future contact with the PLO (though peace, he said, could come only via dialogue co-ordinated by the United States), but he wanted the assembled Arab notables to hear from him personally that the White House would not yield to any 'domestic' pressure (the implication here being that it was not interested in the Jewish vote).

By the time Baker's forty-eight hours in Israel ended (he was to return seven more times in the course of the next seven months), I was sure that we were on the way to peace talks; that we would now be subjected to intense pressure from the White House to accept situations which might, in the view of Israel's Government, negatively affect our future; that we would reject these pressures as we had done before; but also that, however difficult the negotiations surrounding the talks, we were possibly nearer to talking peace than we had been before. The weeks that followed, until the Peace Conference opened in Madrid on 30 October 1991, were therefore filled, for my associates and for me, both with tension and, for the first time in years, with a measure of hope. Not that I thought the Arabs suddenly craved peace with us, not at all; but I did believe that, wisely from their point of view, they had arrived at the conclusion that the Bush Administration offered better conditions for negotiating than might ever exist again. As for us, as the Conference began to take shape, it became ever more evident that it represented a major political victory for Israel: after years of struggle and argument, the direct talks upon which we had insisted for so long and at such peril were now going to take place.

What's more, as planning developed and Baker's remarkable, stubborn and gifted display of shuttle diplomacy accelerated, despite various sometimes critical explosions and some not inconsiderable brinkmanship on the part of all the principals, we began to see other results of our 'intransigent' stand. One of my major objections to the now formally defunct international conference had been, it will be recalled, the participation of bodies known to be inimical to Israel. Now, in the Madrid blueprint, the United States and the USSR (having upgraded its diplomatic relations with us) were, in fact, the hosts of what was to be a one-time ceremonial procedure – lasting for three days and having no after-life – while real business was to be conducted in bilateral and multilateral talks to be initiated immediately following the opening – and which are still going on, despite entirely predictable Arab walkouts and other assorted protests. If we didn't succeed in altogether distancing the PLO from the Conference, at least we saw to it that this organization was not overtly involved though, despite the ground rules forbidding open contact with it, it pervaded the ranks of the Palestinian delegation's advisers and spokesmen and was, in fact, active. The reason, incidentally, that the huge T-shaped table (around which the delegates sat in the Hall of Columns in the Royal Palace that housed the Conference) bore no national flags was that Israel would have refused to sit anywhere near the PLO banner that the Palestinians would have flaunted. More significantly, we were able, at least officially, to preclude the presence within the Palestinian delegation of any East Jerusalem residents, since the Israeli consensus declared that all parts of Jerusalem constituted the state's capital, or residents of the Arab 'diaspora', thus limiting the Palestinians – as best we could by very close examination of their credentials – to those Arabs who were acceptable (non-PLO) representatives of the populations of Judea, Samaria and Gaza and directly involved in the projected autonomy.

Tirelessly, Mr Baker made his way between President Mubarak, Saudi Arabia's King Fahd and Jordan's King Hussein on to Kuwait, from there to Damascus, back to Jerusalem, on to Washington and back again. There were bitter, prolonged disputes at almost every point about almost everything including what the gathering itself should be called – one day, in Akaba, Baker simply termed it a peace conference, and that was that; where it should take place – almost every European capital being suggested; and whether there should be a joint Jordanian–Palestinian delegation as we wanted but to which the Palestinians raised strenuous and lengthy objections, so in the end, in Madrid, there was one delegation but two opening addresses and two of everything else. There were also furious arguments about where the bilateral talks should be located. Israel had suggested the model of the talks preceding the aborted Lebanese treaty, that is, meeting alternately in Israel and in some Arab state. The Arabs wouldn't hear of this. So the Middle East, which was what the talks were about and where we would have come to know each other better, was ruled out – for the time being. That being the case, we wanted at least to be near enough to Israel so that our people, if and when necessary, could get to Jerusalem for consultations and still be back at the talks on the same day. Rome, for instance, was quite acceptable to me but the United States wanted Washington, which was finally chosen, mostly because the Arabs hoped for the Administration's on-the-spot intervention and influence.

The sharpest disagreements, because they were the most crucial, were, of course, between the Palestinians and the Government of Israel. The Palestinians tried very hard to persuade Baker that the 'Palestine problem' had to be solved before the start of peace talks. Israel, on the otherhand, wanted, and the United States supported, a dual track: talks between Israel and the Arab states; and talks between Israel and the Palestinians. What eventually emerged contained elements of this original proposal, which, in turn, derived from the Camp David Accords that also included two stages, first autonomy and then negotiations towards a permanent solution.

At one point, towards the end of April (it was Baker's third trip), the frustrated Secretary, eager to speed things up, told me that the United States would provide the Israeli Government with 'written guarantees' to the effect that the Conference, even if it reconvened every six months to hear progress reports, would not be able to impose any settlement on Israel and that the PLO wouldn't make an appearance at some later stage. I didn't want those particular kind of US guarantees; I needed to be sure that a door could never be opened to outside pressures on the direct talks and nothing, not even Baker's persuasiveness and patience, nor his rarely visible irritation, changed my mind.

We were sitting together hammering all this out at my office when the Secretary got a phone call telling him that his ninety-six-year-old mother had died. He left at once for the States. When he came back to Israel not long afterwards, I told him that the Government had planted a ninety-six-tree grove in her memory and gave him a scroll to this effect. He was genuinely touched, but within minutes we were back to the arguments. We saw things very differently; I regarded every loophole possibly left unblocked, every possibility of irrevocable damage being done to us, every yielding for the sake of being 'nice' or 'reasonable' that might constrict or distort Israel's stand as being of the utmost importance. Anyhow, Israel wouldn't agree to preconditions of any sort or to any decisions being taken at the Conference. Everything substantive requiring dialogue had to await dialogue. I saw no point in talking about talks, and I wouldn't give in; or give up.

There were always far more questions than answers. Would Syria attend the Conference? There had been a conference, purportedly dedicated to Middle Eastern peace, in 1973 in Geneva which the Syrians did not attend, though later they dealt with us in the disengagement on the Golan Heights. Would they come to Madrid? Would Saudi Arabia come to the opening or only to multilateral talks where subjects of obvious mutual interest – environment, water, economic co-operation in the area – were slated for discussion? And so on and so forth. All this, against a background of some dissension within the Likud and more especially in the parties to our right, who charged the Government with making 'concessions' to the

Administration and gleefully anticipated the total failure of Baker's efforts.

That same April, I squeezed in a quick, useful trip to Europe. Ostensibly I went for the formal inauguration of BERD (the European Bank for Reconstruction and Development, a financial institution established to rebuild the economies of Eastern Europe), of which Israel was a founding member. But in fact I went to see and to be seen, to renew contacts, to shore up Anglo–Israeli relations and to meet various European leaders, among the thirty-odd heads of state from East and West gathered in London for the ceremony. It is not often that Israelis have a chance to mingle in this way, to show our faces in an atmosphere, unlike that at the UN, which is not politically and negatively charged. One of the disadvantages of being a small, unaffiliated country like Israel is that you don't fit in neatly anywhere; you are not attached to any bloc. Most countries belong somewhere: to the EEC, to NATO, to Benelux, to the Arab League, to the Third World. We belong everywhere and nowhere. So a gathering like BERD seemed worth the effort involved, even though a Baker visit awaited me upon my return as well as the physically and emotionally arduous schedules of Israel's Memorial Days followed by the celebration of our independence. Nor did my instincts mislead me. The praise, the compliments, the warmth that flowed in my direction were extraordinary. Everyone wanted to talk to me, including heads of states I had never met before: the President of Cyprus, the Prime Ministers of Norway and Portugal, and the President of Switzerland. Everyone who could shook hands, saying how much they hoped and believed peace was on its way; everyone stressed the 'wisdom and courage' of our policy during the Gulf War. It was as if from being a frog I had suddenly turned into a prince.

There were also old acquaintances: Ilon Iliescu, the fluent, rather mannered President of Romania; Czechoslovakia's brilliant, always friendly Vaclav Havel; and President François Mitterrand.

Mitterrand was as sceptical, as clear-headed, as sure of himself as ever, his bearing so strikingly reminiscent of de Gaulle that it was almost mimicry. And he had all of de Gaulle's impatience with lesser beings. Cameramen crowded around us, asking that we shake hands for their benefit. Mitterrand waved them off. 'This isn't a circus,' he said. He was very polite, protested his friendship for Jews, his knowledge of our history, his sympathy, but he wouldn't be told, he said to me coldly, to whom he could speak (meaning Yasser Arafat) or how he should think. My meeting with Prime Minister John Major was more to my liking. I was again struck by his directness and his lack of arrogance. He made no bones, I remember, about not being especially impressed by our peace proposal, but was unstinting in his appreciation of our restraint during the war and said he 'quite understood' that we could well have arrived at other conclusions. In 1992, when the Likud lost the elections, he took the trouble to write me a short charming farewell note to much the same effect.

Even warmer was my meeting with the Dutch Prime Minister, Ruud Lubbers. The relationship between Holland and Israel, between the Dutch people and the Jews, is unique in our experience, I think, dating back much further than the incomparable decency with which the Government and most of the people of Holland, to the extent of their ability, treated the Jews in the terrible days of World War II, all the way back to the sixteenth and seventeenth centuries. There were many mixed emotions in Israel during the weeks of the Gulf War, but now and again something would happen that broke, like the sun through clouds, through the loneliness, the isolation and the fear. Sometimes it was a personal gesture: Zubin Mehta's immediate decision to be with us and 'his' Israel Philharmonic Orchestra in those difficult days. Sometimes it was a more formal act, the equally quick decision of the Dutch to send us – without our asking for it – a Patriot battery and the experts to man it. In London, when I thanked Holland's Prime Minister for this, all he said was: 'It was the least we could do.' We talked for a while also about the thousands of immigrants from the USSR pouring into Israel and the huge economic burden we had accordingly undertaken. Mr Lubbers at once suggested that the European Community might be prepared to help in this endeavour, the only person I ever met to make such a suggestion. Not that anything was to come of it, as I could have told him, but didn't. I thought of him and the Dutch again when I drove back to Jerusalem next day past the masses of tulips which the Dutch send us each year for the adornment of the city.

I also had a session with Prime Minister Valentin Pavlov in one of the tremendous rooms of the Soviet Embassy in London, with good vodka and Lenin, his portrait hanging on the wall in splendid solitude, looking at me sternly as the Soviet Minister spoke of 'this historic meeting'. International politics being what they are, I wasn't taken aback by the Soviet hope that we might be able to help Russia in its great economic distress by using our connection with rich Jews abroad, with many of whose names, again not really surprisingly, the Minister was entirely familiar. We spoke also of the peace process and USSR–US participation. 'It makes things hard for the Soviet Union not only in Arab countries,' he said, 'but in Soviet republics with large or predominantly Moslem populations.' 'If it makes trouble for you,' I volunteered, 'forget it.' Soviet participation was not something we couldn't live without. 'No, no,' he was very quick to dismiss my solicitude.

In general, whenever I spoke, in those days, to European leaders, the question of European representation in the peace talks unfailing arose, with the Europeans demanding the right to attend in a status similar to that of the two co-sponsors, i.e. the US and the USSR. The Arabs, in the main, were inclined to back the idea. Why not? The European Community had always backed them. But we were in a different position: we couldn't and wouldn't agree to any arrangement that even in the slightest interfered with, or changed the character of, the direct negotiations on which, from the very beginning, we had insisted.

In September, there came a major explosion. The Bush Administration decided to delay for 120 days the granting of our request for the $10 billion loan guarantee on the astonishing grounds that to approve the guarantees before that period might harm the Peace Conference, even though the loan guarantees patently had nothing to do with the search for peace.

President Bush's decision came in response to the Arab demand that the United States refrain from taking a step perceived by the Arabs to be significantly supportive of Israel, in particular, and, most undesirably from their point of view, of Jewish immigration to the Jewish state. It should not be forgotten that, till this very day, the Arabs regard Jewish immigration to Israel as endangering the Arab world! Apart from this, the President was openly making the granting of guarantees conditional on Israel's committing itself not to engage in what was called 'settlement activity' beyond the cease-fire line of 1949–67. This was, as I have already stated and now wish to emphasize, the first time that the US Government decided to make humanitarian aid to Israel conditional on Israel's acceptance of a policy under dispute between the two countries. Not that this was the first dispute ever to arise between Israel and the United States. Not at all – but it set a precedent for the use of political pressure under such circumstances, something that no other President had done. Little wonder that American Jewry so strongly opposed this development and made such an effort to get Congress to take action against it.

Beyond the gravity of the President's decision (which was considerable), it also caused an extraordinary commotion. Mr Bush and Mr Baker themselves embarked forthwith on a telephone crusade to members of Congress asking for support while the American Jewish leadership rose to the challenge, protesting the Administration's linkage between the loan guarantees for immigrant absorption and the various deadlocks, inevitable in those complicated circumstances, punctuating and thus delaying Baker's operations in the Middle East – though the 'punishment' for these was meted out only to Israel. Various delegations of Jews from communities throughout the United States arrived on Capitol Hill to talk to their senators about instant approval of the guarantees. This enraged the President, who at a televised press conference saw fit to call upon the American people to back him against what he termed 'powerful political forces'.

'I heard today', he said angrily, 'that a thousand lobbyists on the Hill are working the other side of the question. We've only got one lonely little guy here.' In full view of millions, the President lost his temper, attacking the pro-Israel lobby with extraordinary harshness, and stressing that Israel's insistence on the guarantees was not only a threat to the Middle East Peace Conference but to world peace. He informed America:

It is my best judgment that a rancorous debate now is literally minuscule in importance compared to the objective of peace ... who is going to get hurt? What possibly could work against that reasonable request from an administration that's brought this thing from square one right up to a peak that nobody really believed we could achieve; getting these countries together and the work that's gone into it?

Then, banging on the podium, he referred to his own future, to the US elections of 1992, saying, 'I don't care if I get only one vote. ... I believe the American people will be with me ... on this question of principle,' and found it necessary, in his rage, to declare that 'just months ago, American men and women in uniform risked their lives to defend Israelis in the face of Iraqi Scud missiles, and indeed Desert Storm, while winning a war against aggression, also achieved the defeat of Israel's most dangerous adversary'.

In Paris, where I had addressed a meeting of the European Democratic Union's conservative leaders, I saw to it that my response should be cool, aimed at lowering rather than raising the temperature in Washington. I am positive that Bush did not realize what his words revealed about his true feelings, his most basic attitudes, towards the Jews and the Jewish state and also that, if challenged, he would in all sincerity, in horror even, deny the evidence. But I was determined not to be drawn into a direct confrontation with the Administration – even if this was what he wanted. I thought my thoughts about his behaviour, what he had said, the associations he had invited America to share with him, but for public consumption and to the media I said only that the issue seemed to me to be not between the United States and Israel, but between the United States and Congress. Not that I didn't understand all too well the implication for American Jewry of what the President had said to them, which amounted to 'Vote for me or for Israel', or that he had now proved to the Arabs once more that he meant business, that he was a man of his word. He had said he would go to war against Iraq and had done so. Now he was demonstrating that same iron will in dealing with us, whether the US Congress and US Jewry liked it or not. The pill he administered to Israel, suddenly stripped of its sugar-coating, not only had to be swallowed by us but had to be seen by the Arabs as swallowed.

I didn't even permit myself to be more than mildly annoyed by the gratuitous public statement made a few days later by the President's guest, visiting German Chancellor Kohl, who announced that he 'knew of no American who had done as much for the State of Israel as President George Bush'. We had to go on with the negotiations and there was no other broker in sight. So I comforted myself with the knowledge that we couldn't be made to accept the unacceptable or to agree to our own destruction. But I still couldn't shake the growing feeling that some specific arrangement with the Arabs was being worked out behind our backs and, considering that we were about to enter peace talks, I found the US attempt to face us with preconditions troubling. But mounting protests and making dramatic speeches wouldn't help. All that could be done was to weigh everything very carefully, examine options under a microscope, draw on whatever resources or patience we had and, above all, remember that nothing is static for ever, and that given time, frequently our most precious ally, the situation might change.

In the meantime, Presidents Bush and Gorbachev set an October deadline for the Conference, though the Palestinians had still not finally decided whether to attend or not in the face of PLO demands for assurances, among other things, that there would be a Palestine co-chairman of the joint delegation with Jordan. But Baker was not going to wait any longer: 'The bus is not going to come by again,' he told the Palestinians.

In the middle of October, joint invitations went out over the two Presidents' names to the Conference participants giving them only ten days' notice. Sent to Israel, Syria, Jordan, Lebanon and the Palestinians, the invitation was actually a statement of intent:

The US and the Soviet Union are prepared to assist the parties to achieve a just, lasting and comprehensive peace settlement through direct negotiations along two tracks ... direct bilateral negotiations will begin four days after the opening ... those who wish to attend multilateral negotiations will convene two weeks after the opening ... to organize them.

A joint, and therefore 'symbolic', press conference was held in Jerusalem on 20 October at which the Soviet Foreign Minister, Boris Pankin, said a few words, in notably minor key, about the restoration of full diplomatic relations with Israel and 'the opportunity history was holding out' to the entire Middle East, and Secretary Baker spoke of 'old suspicions' not disappearing quickly and his hope that the Government of Israel would continue 'on its present course'. The Palestinians had turned in a final list of seven delegates and their alternatives with Dr Haider Abdul-Shafi, a doctor from Gaza, as probable Palestinian chairman – which he became; Madrid had already been chosen as the surprise but not unsuitable venue for the Conference; and a special session of the Cabinet was scheduled to take place two days later upon my return from Strasbourg, where I was to address the European Parliament. I had accepted the Parliament's invitation because I felt that we should use every chance we had of participating in European events – even though most of the Parliament's members were opposed to our policy and some, on the extreme left, were actively hostile to it and to me.

It was in Strasbourg, answering dozens of questions and asking a few myself, that I began to think that I ought to go to Madrid, that it was my responsibility to be there. The drama of this first historic confrontation between Israel and its neighbours, the presence of the Presidents of the United States and of the USSR, to say nothing of some 2,000 media representatives, in fact everything about the meeting in Madrid in the autumn of 1991 formed an unparalleled background for the retelling of our story to a worldwide audience. My expectations of the Conference were not high nor my state of mind euphoric, but as I tried to envisage that opening, the firmer became my decision to be present at it, even though it occurred to me that President Bush would probably be less than delighted to see me there and that I would be the only Prime Minister to participate. It wasn't, it seemed, as important for the heads of Arab states to attend as it was for me. But then, nor was peace itself. When I told him that I was going to attend the Conference, Foreign Minister David Levy said that if so, he would not come, so I took along Deputy Foreign Minister Binyamin Netanyahu, who did an outstanding job as our chief spokesman. The rest of the delegation was made up, for the most part, of people who had, by now, worked with me for years: Eli Rubinstein; Yossi Ben-Aharon; Eliahu Ben Elissar, formerly our Ambassador to Egypt; Uzi Landau and Sarah Doron, ranking Likud Members of the Knesset; Assad Assad, my adviser on Druze affairs; and Israel's Ambassador to Spain, Shlomo Ben Ami – all people whom I trusted, without reservation.

As soon as I arrived in Madrid, I met with President Bush and Secretary Baker. We had been misled about the much-haggled-over and publicized Jordanian–Palestinian delegation; it was only in Spain that we learned that each of the two components had been allotted equal time to address the Conference and that the Palestinians were being treated as an entity unto themselves. I said what I had to say on the subject; and the President and the Secretary assured me that they were glad I had come and told me again that I need not worry: the United States was an honest broker. I hadn't seen the President for a long time but we skated over the very thin ice together, he clearly making an effort not to antagonize me, even telling me that he would not mention the words 'territory for peace'. Nor did he.

In the magnificent hall, with its tapestry-hung walls, crystal chandeliers and ceilings full of cherubs – an odd setting, I thought, for the coming-together of Middle Eastern peoples – the President spoke of 'Peace, real peace. ... Treaties. Security. Diplomatic relations. Trade. Investment. Cultural exchange. Even tourism.' It was a list I could have made myself, relating to real life, to the network of standard connections between nations, the everyday ties which the Arabs had denied us ever since the state was born. He spoke of territorial compromise, but made no demands for cessation of Jewish settlement and said nothing about a second Palestinian state. As he spoke, I kept my eyes on him or on my notes, only rarely looking around and then sometimes catching a Syrian or Jordanian delegate peering curiously at me. I thought I could read their thoughts: was this really Yitzhak Shamir? What would this Conference lead to?

Later, I heard reactions to the President's balanced, appropriate speech. He had greatly disappointed the Arabs. Words like 'territorial compromise' are not much used in their Arab states; the Palestinians particularly, with their rich imaginations, were disappointed. They had hoped that they were already there, already independent, triumphant; now their excitement and anticipation lessened. After the speeches, the Israelis had hoped for some thawing, perhaps even a handshake or two, but there was nothing; no gesture of friendship. The Arabs demonstratively stayed apart, hostile. On the other hand, they were there; and so were we; at a conference based ultimately on Israel's peace initiative, on the Likud policy with its insistence on direct talks. There would yet be many ups and downs, but perhaps the conflict that had taken up lifetimes would, one day, be over and perhaps the Madrid meeting would have played a role in the healing process.

In the meantime, another shorter lesson in the mysterious workings of history awaited me at the Soviet Embassy, where I met with President Gorbachev. It was jolting for me, sad even, to see him make an effort to hide his own recognition of his and the Soviet Union's profoundly altered status, both so clearly delineated in the glow of Madrid. The Embassy itself, its great chandeliers and marble columns, like those of the Royal Palace, expressed imperial pomp and power though these were now gone from the Soviet Union. There was a feeling (or had I brought it with me?) of a twilight of the gods. Mr Gorbachev was hospitable, rather anxious to talk. 'You're not as tough as described,' he said at one point. Nor, I thought to myself, are you, any more. He knew a great deal about Israel and spoke frankly about the immigration of Soviet Jewry. 'I hope our situation improves,' he said, 'so there will be fewer emigrants.' His presence at the Conference had attracted relatively little attention, his speech, which had been mostly about the Soviet Union, even less; and he didn't talk to me at all about the peace process or the Middle East. He had other problems to worry about.

My address was the first of the three delivered on Thursday, 31 October. I had hardly changed the first draft, written in Jerusalem two days before, though I had gone over it again and again. Almost everything was there: past, present, future, crammed into forty-five minutes. I began with the heart of the conflict, with the Land and the relationship between it and us:

We are the only people who have lived in the Land of Israel without interruption for nearly 4,000 years. We are the only people, except for a short crusader kingdom, who have had an independent sovereignty in this land. We are the only people for whom Jerusalem has been a capital. We are the only people whose sacred places are only in the Land of Israel. No nation has expressed its bond with its land with as much intensity and consistency as we have. For millennia our people repeated ... the cry of the psalmist: 'If I forget thee, O Jerusalem, may my right hand lose its cunning!' For millennia we have encouraged each other with the greeting, 'Next year in Jerusalem!' For millennia our prayers, literature and folklore have expressed powerful longing to return to our land. Only Eretz Israel, the Land of Israel, is our true homeland. Any other country, no matter how hospitable, is still a diaspora, a temporary station on the way home.

I took my listeners, those in the Hall of Columns and those all over the world but invisible to me, quickly through the history of the Zionist claim to the Land of Israel, of the international recognition that claim had won, of the armed Arab rejection of it and deadly assaults upon the state that came into being, and of

Arab hostility to Israel which has also brought tragic human suffering to the Arab people. Tens of thousands have been killed and wounded. Hundreds of thousands of Arabs who lived in Mandatory Palestine were encouraged by their own leaders to flee from their homes. Their suffering is a blot on humanity. No decent person, least of all a Jew of this era, can be oblivious to this suffering.

Turning to the present, I said:

I stand before you today in yet another quest for peace, not only on behalf of the State of Israel, but in the name of the entire Jewish people. ... We have always believed that only direct, bilateral talks can bring peace. We have agreed to precede such talks with this ceremonial conference, but hope that Arab consent to direct, bilateral talks indicates understanding that there is no other way to peace. In the Middle East, this has special meaning because such talks imply mutual acceptance; and the root cause of the conflict is Arab refusal to recognize the legitimacy of the State of Israel. The multilateral talks ... are a vital component in the process. ... There cannot be genuine peace in our region unless these regional issues are addressed and resolved. We believe the goal of the bilateral negotiations is to sign peace treaties between Israel and its neighbours, and to reach an agreement on interim self-government arrangements with the Palestinian Arabs. But nothing can be achieved without goodwill.

I appeal to the Arab leaders, those who are here and those who have not yet joined the process: show us and the world that you accept Israel's existence. Demonstrate your readiness to accept Israel as a permanent entity in the region. Let the people in our region hear you speak in the language of reconciliation, coexistence and peace with Israel. In Israel there is almost total consensus for the need for peace. We differ only on the best ways to achieve it. In most Arab countries the opposite seems to be true: the only differences are over ways to push Israel into a defenceless position and ... to destruction ...

As to the future, I continued:

We know our partners to the negotiations will make territorial demands on Israel. But as examination of the conflict's long history makes clear, its nature is not territorial. It raged well before Israel acquired Judea, Samaria, Gaza and Golan in a defensive war. There was no hint of recognition of Israel before that war in 1967 when the territories in question were not under Israeli control. We are a nation of four million. The Arab nations from the Atlantic to the Gulf number 170 million. We control only 28,000 square kilometres. The Arabs possess a land mass of 14 million square kilometres. The issue is not territory but our existence. It will be regrettable if the talks focus primarily and exclusively on territory. It will be the quickest way to an impasse. ... The issues are complex. ... The negotiations will be lengthy and difficult. We submit that the best venue for the talks is in our region, in close proximity to the decision-makers, not in a foreign land. We invite our partners to this process to come to Israel for the first round of talks. We, for our part, are ready to go to Jordan, to Lebanon and Syria for the same purpose. There is no better way to make peace than to talk in each other's home. Avoiding such talks is a denial of the purpose of the negotiations. I would welcome a positive answer from the representatives of these states, here and now.

I ended by saying:

I am sure that no Arab mother wants her son to die in battle – just as there is no Jewish mother who wants her son to die in war. ... For hundreds of years, wars, deep antagonism and terrible suffering cursed this continent on which we meet. The nations of Europe saw the rise of dictators and their defeat after lengthy, painful struggles. Now, they are together – former bitter enemies – in a united community. ... I envy them and I believe that, despite all differences between us, we should be able, gradually, to build a united regional community. Today it is a dream – but we have seen, in our lifetimes, fantastic dreams become reality. ...

We, who have had to fight seven wars and sacrifice many thousands of lives, glorify neither death nor war. We pray for peace. ... Let us resolve to leave this hall united in the determination that from now on any differences we may have will be solved only by negotiations, goodwill and mutual tolerance. Let us declare an end to war, to belligerency and to hostility. Let us march forward together, to reconciliation and peace.

The two other speakers that day were the head of the Palestinian delegation and the Syrian Foreign Minister, Farouk Al-Sharaa. The Palestinian's speech addressed us directly, predictably called for the division of the Land of Israel into two states, demanded an end to the settlements, spoke of the right to self-determination, of exile and of the 'blind and violent occupation'. Like, I suppose my own address, it contained nothing that was new to the other delegations or to Secretary Baker. Nor was anything new in the speech of Mr Al-Sharaa, who demanded Israel's withdrawal from 'the occupied Syrian Golan', Judea, Samaria, Jerusalem, the Gaza district and south Lebanon, termed the establishment of Jewish settlements as illegal actions and, describing Arab history as a long chronicle of peace, justice and tolerance, referred to the life of Jews living among Moslems as 'walking in grace and dignity, participating in all walks of life'.

The next morning was set aside for rebuttals and for the Secretary's closing statement. Since I was due to leave immediately after my response, so that I would be back in Israel before the Sabbath began, I kept my rebuttals brief and delivered a message or two. To the Syrian representative, I merely said that his claim that Syria was a model of freedom and of the protection of human rights 'stretched incredulity to infinite proportions ... the ancient Jewish community of Syria has been exposed to cruel oppression, torture and discrimination of the worst kind'. To the Lebanese, suffering so acutely under the Syrian yoke even as I spoke, I sent Israel's sympathy and understanding and repeated the assurance that we had no designs on Lebanese territory. To Jordan, I conveyed a re-statement of our belief that a peace treaty between our countries was both necessary and 'achievable'. As for the Palestinian delegation, I corrected some of the grosser 'errors' in the chairman's address, 'because these are our closest neighbours, whose lives, in many respects, are intertwined with ours,' and called to his attention that

even to this very day, under conditions you describe as occupation, any Jew who strays into an Arab village risks his life, but tens of thousands of Palestinian Arabs walk freely in every town and village in Israel. ... We have presented the Palestinians a fair proposal, one that offers them a chance to improve their lot immensely. I appeal to them to accept our proposal and join us in negotiations.

I then left Madrid. The prelude was over; I had spoken on behalf of the nation, expressing a consensus, and knew that my address had been well received at home, its purpose understood and applauded; as was the fact that I had returned to Jerusalem for the Sabbath, something that moved and pleased Jews in the Diaspora, including those still living in Arab countries. In the plane, homeward bound, half-dozing, I thought fleetingly about the international conference, my battle to prevent it and how time had not betrayed us. The world had shifted; Madrid and Washington were surely safer, sounder, more promising than any international conference could have been.

And the unfinished business in Madrid? The PLO had not been present officially, but it had worked hard in the ranks of the 'advisers' to the 'joint' Jordanian-Palestinian team. More than that, they had been a central media attraction, never out of the limelight for long. I couldn't know how the bilaterals would go. Or what the Syrians would do since they had announced that they would not join the multilateral talks until 'progress' had been made in the bilaterals, but, still, they had not refused to attend the latter. After I had left Madrid, Farouk Al-Sharaa presented his rebuttal. Creating a small sensation, he held up a British police poster from the 1940s showing me as a 'wanted man'. 'Let me show you', he said, 'an old picture of Shamir when he was thirty-two.' He continued to talk about me for a few more minutes, I was told, and then sat down.

In the course of the months that followed, some of the salient facts about Madrid emerged with greater clarity. It was possible to establish where the Peace Conference had succeeded and where not: Israelis and Arabs (Syria included) had sat across one table from each other and talked. Procedure had led to substance, tacit recognition to exchange, however limited, however sporadic. The bilateral talks seemed safe enough, though in the first session held in Madrid right after the opening the cause of true peace suffered a public blow when the Arabs turned down our suggestion for alternate locations in the Middle East for the bilateral talks. In the end, we had failed to move the talks to the places they were about and Washington became the site, as it still is. None the less, on 4 November, one day after the bilaterals began, a day filled with bickering and bargaining, Israel's Eli Rubinstein, Palestinian Abdel Shafi and Jordanian Abdel Salem el Majli finally shook hands for the camera. Peace, however, was not in the picture and it is still not there as I write, while President Bush, President Gorbachev, Secretary Baker and I have all, in the meanwhile, left the stage.

12

SUMMING UP

THE LAST TIME I met with President Bush was at the end of November 1991. I had undertaken what was for me a relatively long trip to the States, ten days in which I hoped to cement ties further with the American Jewish community – still very shaken by the President's remarks, only a few weeks earlier, regarding 'the powerful lobby' and so forth – and also to look for potential investors who might join forces with us to meet the demands of immigrant absorption. If Israel's overall image abroad had improved as a result of Madrid, and I thought this was the case, I could discern no such change in the Administration's attitude towards us (though the President had tried not very successfully in the interim to mend fences with the Jewish community) and it seemed to me not at all impossible that, when the fateful 120 days were up, the loan guarantees might well be postponed again. At all events, my schedule was not planned to include a visit to the White House, nor had I received any prior indication that I would be invited there.

In the Oval Office, Ambassador Shoval and I were greeted also by Secretary Baker and General Scowcroft. The President seemed to be in fine spirits, even rather forthcoming. We began with an exchange of compliments. 'I much appreciate your leadership in the matter of the peace process,' the President said. 'I don't know when you decided to come to Madrid, but it was good that you did and that you were there.' He went on to say that, 'as I told the Jewish leaders', the Administration neither would nor could impose anything on Israel, and stressed that its concern for Israel's security remained a priority. 'Perhaps you would like to say something about ways in which the various parties could be brought closer to each other?' It was, I understood, an invitation to candour. So I was candid. But first I, too, proferred a verbal bouquet, congratulating the President, and especially the Secretary, for what I saw as an impressive American success.

Then I told the President how much I regretted the decision that had been arrived at, so suddenly, to hold the bilateral talks in Washington, where they would, of necessity, be influenced by the proximity and accessibility of the Administration and that I could foresee the Arabs 'coming to talk to you, Mr President, instead of to us, which they will always think is the sounder of the two alternatives, and not good for Israel'. 'I, on the other hand,' the President replied, 'hear that the Arabs are unhappy about Washington, where they think you have the upper hand.' I reminded the President and the Secretary of State that Israel had been faced by a fait accompli, that the invitation to the bilaterals had been sent to Jerusalem in my absence (which could hardly have been accidental) and without my knowledge, and that, making matters worse, it had been accompanied by what amounted to a prepared 'agenda' for the talks. I didn't use phrases like 'breach of faith' (though that would have been accurate) or charge that the invitations, as they now stood, turned the talks into the very antithesis of what they were intended, at least by us, to be, or ask why this kind of 'surprise' had been sprung on us so discourteously although all the steps of the process, without exception, were to have been taken in consultation with Jerusalem.

What I did tell the President, however, was that I was most unhappy about the actions taken, that I strongly opposed the Administration's decision regarding Washington and that, after due consultations with the Cabinet, I would indeed recommend that Israel should not accept this proposal. 'Well, what's wrong with Cyprus?' the President asked. 'The Jordanians don't want it,' said Baker. I tried to explain that it wasn't geography that caused the problem. It was that the Arabs didn't want to talk to Israel, only to the sponsors – i.e. to the United States, which, they thought, had shifted its position and now supported them. 'I think you're mistaken. But if that's what they think,' said the President, 'they have made a mistake and will have a rude awakening.' 'We accepted all the Israeli positions regarding the peace process,' Baker added. 'Maybe that's what the Arabs think, but we won't deliver Israel.'

As I recall that conversation, I also recall how, from the very start, Baker had made clear to me when we talked informally that, insofar as the question of the territories was concerned, the sole policy-maker was President Bush, who was deeply convinced that the Arab claim was justified and that Israel must withdraw from Judea, Samaria and the Gaza district to the 1967 lines. As for his own responsibility, explained the Secretary, it was 'only' that of the man who had to get the job done. He was the producer, the expediter, but in no way the architect, of the President's policy for the Middle East. It was hard for me to reconcile these protestations with some of Baker's less friendly statements, but, at one stage, he suggested that it might be a good idea if I had a 'real' talk with the President about our radically differing points of view. 'Perhaps it will help,' the Secretary had said. I, too, had thought it might be a good idea, provided that we concentrated on the central theme and didn't get sidetracked into discussion of ongoing disputes. But, apparently, the President hadn't been interested. I regret this, though I probably wouldn't have changed his mind, but at least we would both have known that we had done our very best to try to communicate and come to some understanding.

We went on talking about the venue. The Secretary's solution: two meetings in Washington, then let's see. He kept pushing for places outside the Middle East. Lausanne ('if I can persuade the Arabs') was better than Washington, he said, and I agreed. 'I'm sorry', said the President before we parted, 'that there are these little differences of approach. I don't want this meeting to appear to have been negative. We've had enough of those in the past. Let's give it a positive look.' He was talking, I suppose, about what I'd say to the press later on. I didn't see the President again so that was his final message to me. Or, almost final. A year later, he replied to a letter I wrote to him right after the Israeli elections of 1992. I had not been Israel's Prime Minister when Jonathan Pollard, a US Naval Intelligence analyst, was arrested in Washington DC in November 1985 and charged with espionage on Israel's behalf, thus creating considerable tension between the Government of Israel and the Reagan Administration. But before and during his trial, in 1987, both Governments had consulted frequently. The United States, I thought, had not been generous; sentencing Pollard to life imprisonment seemed to me, in the light of the relationship between the two countries, to be unduly harsh, and in a last communication with the President (it was, in fact, to be one of the last letters I wrote as Prime Minister), I asked for Presidential commutation of Pollard's sentence. In his brief answer Bush explained that since the case was under Supreme Court review, my request could not be considered until that process was complete. 'I would also like to take this opportunity to note the achievements that marked your long tenure as Israel's Prime Minister,' the President added. 'Your decision to attend the Madrid Peace Conference ... was historic as was our collaboration to open the doors for Jewish

immigration from the former Soviet Union and Ethiopia. A strong
Israel at peace with its neighbours must remain our common goal.'
There was nothing more for us to say to each other.

But that was later. For the moment, in the heat (or, more precisely,
the chill) of the discussions about venue, no time remained to talk
about the guarantees (which, also perhaps, was not accidental). As
soon as I left, the United States made public its 'take it or leave it'
policy. The Secretary's spokeswoman announced that US diplomats
had been instructed not to haggle over any conditions, just to convey
the message to the parties involved: 'There's the proposal. Washington
DC. December 4. Let us know.' The venue issue had been the
Administration's first test post-Madrid as an 'honest broker' and it
had failed to pass it. Israel and Jordan had promised to decide on the
venue together but the broker had intervened. I got the impression
afterwards that our openly expressed dissatisfaction with the enforced
choice of Washington DC for the bilateral talks had influenced the
Administration's behaviour when the talks actually began and the
United States scrupulously limited itself to the organizational aspects,
making no attempt at all to interfere on any level, for which I was
grateful and said so, though the Arabs, of course, felt that they had
been let down.

I had come to Washington following the warmest possible reception
by Jewish communities throughout the Boston area (showing not a
glimpse of that famous New England reserve of which I was warned).
The excitement with which I had been greeted during my three-day
stay there, the singing, cheering thousands who had turned out to
welcome me also in Baltimore, and the interest and encouragement
voiced by US business leaders who met, publicly and privately, with
me and with the fifteen top Israeli industrialists accompanying me
on this 'job-hunting' expedition reaffirmed the relationship that had
been quietly created over the years between myself and the Jews of
the United States. Wherever I went I spoke about ending the state of
war and starting on the road to peace, about our refusal to partition
the Land of Israel again or to compromise its security, and about the
guarantees: 'One thing is certain, we shall not ask a single Jew in
the Soviet Union, Ethiopia or elsewhere to wait 120 days, or 90 days,
or 200 days until such technicalities can be arranged. Their departure
... in some cases a life-saving operation ... should not be linked to
political matters or disagreements.' And everywhere I spoke too of
Israel's economy, urging my listeners to 'shake off outdated
impressions and sterectypes' and to make a 'fresh analytical evaluation of the prospects of doing business in Israel'.

In Baltimore, speaking at the General Assembly of the Jewish Federations of North America and before one of the largest crowds I have ever addressed (though mass meetings had, by then, become standard in my US itineraries), I spoke of Jewish history, and of the 'miraculous transformation' in the status and fortune of the Jews:

Not long ago [I said], a friend brought me a copy of the front page of the London *Times* of 9 November 1917. On it were two news items, one reporting a coup d'état in Petrograd, in which Lenin deposed Kerensky, in the October Revolution that paved the way to the Bolshevik regime; the other reporting the decision of the British Government to facilitate establishment of a national home for the Jewish people in Palestine. This was, of course, the Balfour Declaration, the first political success of the Zionist Organization, later endorsed by the US Congress and incorporated in the League of Nations Mandate awarding Palestine to the Jewish people. There they were, in 1917, two movements, two ideologies, two philosophies entering the international arena, more or less at the same time; for most of the subsequent years, two movements in sharp and bitter conflict. Communism was to become an active opponent of Zionism and of Jewish life: our religious practices forbidden, synagogues closed, the Hebrew language not taught and many thousands imprisoned for their Zionist belief.

And now ... we have seen the collapse of Communism in the Soviet Union and the failure of that doctrine throughout Eastern Europe. While the Jews endured to survive three generations of oppression and persecution. Today Hebrew is taught in the Soviet Union; Israeli songs resound in its towns and villages; the blue-white flag waves over Israel's Embassy building in Moscow; and the Zionist dream is realized before our eyes. With joy, optimism, and infinite faith, we can proclaim that Israel lives, that Zionism succeeded.

I also took the opportunity to warn against 'entrenched distortions of Middle Eastern history. They are not unlike the fabrications which, for decades, typified the treatment of Communism in the West. Then, as now,' I said, 'some of the most brilliant intellectuals and journalists became the servants of the totalitarian version of history.'

Here and there, as when Boston University's President, Dr John Silber, presented me with an honorary law degree (he had placed a similar mantle on the shoulders of George Bush two years earlier), Arab demonstrators tried to disrupt the proceedings – calling for a halt to the settlements, shouting 'Death to Israel' and waving Palestinian flags – but didn't succeed in doing so. The University ceremony had been attended, among others, by my old friend Nobel Laureate Elie Wiesel, who had spoken of peace – '... not as God's offering to man but as human beings' gift to one another'; by Rhode Island

Governor Bruce Sunlin, at the time the only Jewish governor in the United States, who told the assembly that 'Israel has given the Jews in America greater strength, dignity and approval'; and by Massachusetts Governor William Weld, who was to lead a trade mission to Israel in the summer.

I, too, in my turn, spoke of peace or, rather, of the difficulty of attaining it. Thanking the University 'for granting me today with no special effort on my part, the degree for which I should have worked when I left my studies in Warsaw in 1935 to fight for a Jewish state', I talked of 'totalitarian, dictatorial, militaristic regimes that go to peace conferences to lull their potential victims, treat peace agreements as temporary conveniences not as binding contracts, and talk peace while they plan the next war'. I named no regime, but there was hardly a single account of my words in the many press stories that appeared which did not venture the possibility that it was to Syria that I referred.

In Los Angeles, apart from the pleasure of meeting George Shultz again (as I've described), I had accelerated the already hectic pace, compressing into hours newspaper and TV interviews, sessions with the community's Jewish leaders and a full-fledged address before the influential Los Angeles Economic Forum, where I talked of 'new realities that require new thinking' and, in some detail, of the Government's commitment to nurturing a climate attractive to private investment. I liked Los Angeles, its informality and climate (so like our own), and I had long ago accepted the fact that Los Angeles county alone had double the population of the State of Israel though, as I told the Forum, not half as much attention! On the whole it was what one might describe as a 'triumphant' tour of duty, the triumph being Israel's. I met a great many people in business and academic circles, some of whom had made clear to me that they would involve themselves in our future using their money or know-how or talent. And I had witnessed the depth of the belief of thousands of American Jews, stung though they had been by the President's hurtful words, that it was possible, even perhaps necessary, to be a good American and at the same time a Jew proud and supportive of the Jewish state.

In the weeks that followed my return to Jerusalem, there was, I felt, a resurgence of Administration hostility to us which found its expression in a series of 'misunderstandings' and unsubstantiated claims. Not all these charges against the Government of Israel were new: a recycled allegation (popular also in Alignment ranks) was that whenever Baker had visited Israel, a new Jewish settlement had been defiantly established somewhere or other in Samaria, Judea or the Gaza district, even though during all that time exactly one new settlement had, in fact, been created. Then a story regarding the supposed transfer by Israel of Patriot technology to China, though patently absurd, surprisingly found a prominent place for itself in the eminently respectable *New York Times* and the *Washington Post*. There was also an outburst of apparent US support for the Arab 'right of return' (a phrase devoid of real meaning but not of sinister overtones), first floated, then hastily explained away, by the Secretary of State's spokeswoman as 'a misunderstanding'. What made the disinformation and leaks more astonishing to me was that while critically important events were occurring almost everywhere in the world then – including the agonizing metamorphosis of the USSR into separate republics, the Serbian–Croatian war, Saddam Hussein's continuing control over Iraq and the famine in Somalia, to name just a few – so much of the US Administration's attention remained focused on Israel and the loan guarantees that were still being withheld. Significantly enough, they were finally granted only at the end of 1992 when the Likud was no longer in power.

In February, testifying before a Congressional sub-committee, Secretary Baker, repeating that 'we have an absolute, total, unwavering commitment to Israel's security', called for 'a halt or an end to new construction' in the territories, carefully defining both the word 'new' ('as of 1 January 1992') and 'construction' ('road, sewage, water and other infrastructure work'), and also explained that when the guarantees were granted, it would be in a manner that would enable the Administration to cut them off at will. Asked by a pro-Israel member of the committee, Representative Larry Smith of Florida, why he had made 'no such demands on the Arab dictatorships', Baker answered, 'Nobody else asks for $10 billion in addition to the $3–4 billion we give each year.' 'True,' said Smith, who went on to accuse the Secretary of misleading the American people by suggesting that Israel was asking for more money rather than for guarantees. To that, Baker made no reply.

However, not only the Bush Administration was out to unseat the Likud. The small parties to the right of the Likud – Tehiyya, Tsomet and Moledet – blinded by their extremism, though knowing that the Government was committed to uphold the right of Jews to settle everywhere in the Land of Israel – and that I myself was as fervent an advocate of this policy as any of their members – began to distrust and defy me. To this day, I cannot grasp why this should have been so. There were issues on which these parties disagreed with the Likud: they opposed Israel's commitment to the Camp David Accords;

they were in favour of more drastic punishment for captured terrorists; they regarded Israeli participation in the peace talks with disapproval, most especially the question of autonomy. But these differences of opinion, like their incessant squabbling among themselves, hardly formed a reasonable basis for their frequent, hostile and often hysterical attacks against the Likud and against me, for our 'moderation', the slowness with which we were proceeding with Jewish settlement in Judea, Samaria and the Gaza district, and our lack of 'toughness' in putting down the *intifada*. Anyone who has read this far in these memoirs knows, and the leaders and members of these parties surely knew, that those charges were all ridiculous. None the less, they persisted in placing pressure on the Government, in fact in weakening it, often leaving us with a majority of one vote, sometimes not even that. Between them, Tehiyya, Tsomet and Moledet had only seven seats, but that was sufficient to lend weight (apart from nuisance value) to their constant threats that, if not yielded to, they would bolt the coalition. All this, of course, was a bonus for the Alignment and for the media, but not for the public image of the Likud, which was being projected as leading a weak government, unable even to rely on its own partners. The most active of the three parties in this regard was Tehiyya (with three Knesset seats); its flag-bearer, Geulah Cohen, increasingly devoting her energy to bringing down the Government, though the only alternative to it was the left wing she had fought with the same vehemence all her life. Moledet, headed by Rehavam Zeevi, a tiny party which, as I have mentioned, advocated the physical removal of the Arab minority from the Land of Israel, had nothing else to say and neither is, nor was, worth discussing. In between was Rafael Eitan's Tsomet, which went its own capricious way, sometimes bitterly castigating the Government, sometimes not, but never to be seriously counted upon and, like the others, for ever in the headlines.

It was as though these parties were bent on self-destruction, incapable of understanding that if they wounded the Likud badly enough, the Alignment (backed by some of the Arab parties that always supported Labour) would be returned to power, bringing with it a return to the 1967 borders. I have no explanation for their behaviour, which I view as irrational, other than that all three had persuaded themselves that, regardless of what they said or did, the Likud would not be dislodged. How wrong they were, as they themselves were to learn; how short-sighted, how costly their fanaticism turned out to be, as fanaticism always is. But they had paid no attention to my warnings (of which there were many), or to

Parliamentary realities, and the resultant damage they did to Israel was severe. Later I asked myself whether I could have acted differently and repudiated the Camp David Accords, their validity and relevance, so that a Likud-led government might survive. Should I have 'bought' right-wing unity for the cause in which I believe? When I posed those and other questions to myself, the answer always remained the same: that I had no alternative other than to remain loyal to the guidelines of the Likud and my own conscience.

In January 1992, the Tehiyya and Moledet ministers finally resigned from the Cabinet (Tsomet having done so earlier), leaving the Government with fifty-nine out of 120 Members of the Knesset on its side. Not many choices faced me now. I could keep the Government alive (even if barely so) until November, when general elections were due, but that seemed pointless to me: it would have made a drama out of every Knesset vote and, in the end, I might have had to resign as the result of a Parliamentary defeat which would not have helped the Likud at the polls – though it would have gratified the Opposition. Or I could resign, leaving behind me a transitional government, a minority coalition, powerless to fend off whatever attacks might be made on it, from within or without. But there was a third possibility and that was the one I chose: to call for early elections. If elected, I decided I would not serve till the following elections but rather, at some appropriate time, help to pick my successor so that there would still be another Likud Prime Minister, someone younger than myself, for which the time had come. On 19 January, I announced my decision and, together with the coalition and opposition parties, set the date for new elections to be held on 23 June, only five months earlier than originally scheduled.

Despite the problems, I was confident of a Likud victory. We had abundant achievements to our credit, a better record (item by item) to set before the electorate than any other Israeli party had ever had – and I make this statement advisedly.

In the all-important area of security, we were in very good shape, all things considered. The state was no longer in danger from any external source; Israel's armed strength and deterrent power had lost none of their ability to impress. Internally, though the *intifada* was not over, it had been contained and was waning; Arab terror and the terrorist movements had not been eliminated but the resourcefulness, courage and sophistication of the IDF and Israel's security forces had proved themselves in the capture of many terrorists (while many others despairingly gave themselves up) and in what then was the ever-improving situation on the roads of Judea, Samaria and the Gaza district.

However difficult its initial stages had been, the peace process was well and truly under way. The Syrian–Israel, Lebanon–Israel, Jordanian and Palestinian–Israel talks had taken place at the agreed-upon times and discussions had begun in earnest. The people we had chosen to head the Israeli delegations, Yosef Ben-Aharon, Eli Rubinstein, Uri Lubrani and Yosef Hadas, had brought with them to Washington not only their expertise and deep understanding of the Middle East in all its intricacy, but also close identification with their historic mission. We had secured the best possible conditions for these talks by the positions we had taken and which had been agreed upon by the US and Arab representatives prior to the opening of the Madrid Conference. All preceding Israeli Governments had worked hard to arrive at direct, face-to-face negotiations with our neighbours and failed, but we had succeeded. We sat opposite them and talked, free of the intervention of mediators, not even the co-sponsors or their representatives in attendance. We had permitted no preconditions though the Arabs always demanded these and we had seen to it also that the UN would not participate, despite the pressure applied to us by the United States and, chiefly, by the Arabs. It was only our unwavering, if much maligned, determination that had made Madrid possible and, after Madrid, Washington.

Our international standing had improved markedly, due mostly to policies we had pursued during the Gulf War and regarding Madrid; Israel's prestige had risen notably throughout the world; nations that had formerly distanced themselves from us now sought renewed ties with us. The state's long isolation had ended. Over the past two years alone, no fewer than thirty-five countries, among them the USSR (and various members of the Soviet bloc including Poland, Hungary, and Czechoslovakia), China, India and Nigeria had entered into diplomatic relations with us, dramatically expanding our once shrunken diplomatic map – and at the UN, we had won the protracted battle to reverse the monstrous anti-Israeli Resolution of 1975 which dared to equate Zionism with racism. All this, it must be stressed, took place at a time when at home the Likud was ceaselessly accused by the Opposition of having devastated Israel's good name abroad.

And, of course, there was the greatest of our achievements: the mass immigration that reached our shores between 1989 and 1992 and which continues – the homecoming of over 400,000 Jews from the Soviet Union and more than 30,000 from Ethiopia. Of this unique historic development, for which the Likud was fully entitled to take credit, I have already written, but I shall come back to it in another context.

As for settlement, its forward surge reached unmatched heights under the Likud's auspices, most especially in the populating of territories under Israel's control in the wake of the Six Day War as well as elsewhere. In the past decade and a half, Jewish settlement throughout the Land of Israel has literally flowered: building is everywhere, in the Galilee, the Negev, Jerusalem and its environs, on the Golan Heights, in Judea, Samaria and the Gaza district. From the time the Likud assumed power, 272 new settlements have been established in the whole of the Land of Israel and some 300,000 Israelis are living across the 1967 borders.

The same pattern holds true for the national economy. Under the Likud, Israel's overall economic situation improved appreciably, certainly relative to pre-Likud years. True, we had not reached all our goals; there was no reason yet for wild celebration, but we had done well. For the two years prior to the 1992 elections, the rate of inflation had dropped from twenty per cent to ten per cent, still high but clearly heading in the right direction; the rate of economic growth had risen by five–six per cent per annum, which, if one took a look at the global situation, was an achievement in itself. Tourism was up; there was a great deal to be seen and done and ample and good accommodation for everyone. The national debt had dropped and the standard of living of the average 'old-timer' had soared. Not that there weren't clouds in the sky, the most serious of which, though anticipated, was unemployment. Due largely to the ten per cent increase in Israel's population as a result of the mass immigration, it was less than we had feared it might be, but that didn't make it either acceptable or tolerable. Nor was I much consoled by knowing that this immigration, with its unusual level of professional com-petence, would itself eventually contribute to a considerably more prosperous future for the entire nation. If achievement meant any-thing, I could foresee no likelihood of our not being empowered to go on with the job, though I was prepared for the contest to be a close one.

It turned out to be a very tough campaign. The Alignment wanted blood and few, if any, holds were barred, especially where I myself was concerned. The Opposition had waited fifteen years to stage a comeback and neither delicacy nor concern for truth was going to distract it now. As for us, we campaigned on our record, sure of the continuing loyalty of the Likud's traditional supporters – the masses in the big cities and small towns who had brought it to power – and sure also, as I still think was legitimate, that the new immigrants, to a man (and woman), would exercise their unfamiliar right to participate in democratic elections by casting their vote for the Likud Government that brought them here.

On election day, Shulamit and I cast our votes in Tel Aviv, still our official place of residence. In the evening, Israel Television's early forecasts, based on exit polls, were to begin and I settled myself in an armchair to await the first results. Then came the anchorman's announcement: an 'upheaval', he reported, in favour of the Alignment. It seemed impossible and yet, as soon as I heard the words, I knew it had happened, though there were still hours to go before the votes were all in and the count even nearing conclusion. I sat on, feeling as though I were being battered in a storm. We had been mistaken. The Likud had lost the elections. Not that the Alignment had won a landslide victory. In all, the 65–55 division which had kept the Likud in power swung to a 61–59 balance: a right-wing-plus-Orthodox coalition made way for a left-wing-plus-Arab bloc. But it wasn't the numbers that stunned me, nor the sense of rejection that one cannot escape in political defeat, nor that in the course of a few hours my 'political career' had essentially come to its end. My commitment to Zionism was not a 'career'. It had been part of my life for as long as I could remember and neither political victory nor failure could change it. No, it was something else I felt: a rush of fear for the fate of the Land of Israel, for I knew that now crucial positions over which the Likud and I had stood vigil might be yielded and Jewish settlement frozen in Judea, Samaria, the Gaza district and the Golan Heights. Yitzhak Rabin would become Prime Minister (and Minister of Defence) and Shimon Peres would be his Foreign Minister; their beliefs, attitudes and judgments about this were only too familiar to me and I knew that the apprehension which had flooded me was not groundless.

Next day, the inevitable, grim post-mortems commenced. How had it happened? Why did so many voters turn their backs on the Likud, despite that glittering list of accomplishments? Had the man-in-the-street taken it all for granted, forgetting how hard we had fought for every inch of the way? Or had part of the public denied us its votes because some of our ministers had been seen as addicted to power games, and the Likud as a party for ever torn by inner strife? Could the bickering, ineffective and harmless in itself, have really weighed more heavily, meant more, to erstwhile Likud supporters than our successful international negotiations, more than the peace talks, more than the longed-for immigration or dynamic settlement programme?

Was this conceivable? In retrospect, I suppose it was, though one will never know. I had never referred publicly to the Likud in-fighting, though I had intensely disliked it, thought it time-consuming and wished it had not been made available so readily (or at all) to the media. But it hadn't ever impinged in the least, in my view, on my ministers' considerable ability to carry out properly the responsibilities they undertook at my request. What really counted for me was whether they possessed the dedication and talent required for Israel's greatest good. And it is no mere formality or parting gesture when I write that the senior Likud members of my Cabinet, without exception, were men with whom any prime minister would have been pleased to work, and to whom the State of Israel owes much.

What did hurt and bitterly disappointed me, and I have known disappointment before in life, had little to do with either political defeat or politicians. It was that so many of the new immigrants denied the Likud their votes. For days after the elections the rebuff haunted me, above all else. They had meant so much to me that they had become a part of me. For years, barely a day went by that I didn't think about the Jews of the Soviet Union, work to release them from their misery, suffer their deprivations in my heart and mind, plan and re-plan ways and means of bringing them to Israel. I cannot recall a single conversation I held either as Foreign Minister or as Prime Minister, with any head of state, who, even in the remotest fashion, might be useful, in which I did not introduce the subject of the urgent need to assist Soviet Jewry to come to us. And when they finally started to arrive, there was no end to my relief and joy. I knew life here was not easy for them, and I worried constantly about that, though I also knew as certainly that their conditions would improve and yearned to give each one that reassurance myself. It has taken me time to get over the heartache; it is one thing to understand, another to accept. But I am reconciled by now to the fact that someone had to be blamed for the anxiety, the confusion, the often overwhelming hardships that the immigrants encountered in this land whose customs and language they had to learn and where life is lived so differently from anything they had known before. Who had time, vigour or the desire to think about Israel's future when their own futures seemed so unclear? They needed to punish someone and they had only one address: the Government. So in their anger, turmoil and frustration, they cast their votes against us. Ungrateful? Yes, but it was their only weapon against the trauma of their absorption and I am the last to refuse forgiveness though my sense of having been betrayed took months to fade. And it still moves me in a special way when, as I go on my daily walk, Russian immigrants come up to me, as they so often do, just to say 'Thank you for having brought us here. Thank you for what you did.'

In the meantime, there were things to do: to rest from the campaign; to deal with the chairmanship of the Likud, until I could legally submit my resignation; and to take my seat in the thirteenth Knesset, whose oldest member I am delighted to be.

There was also a personal matter to which I wanted to attend: a visit to Rujenoy, which I had left in the early 1930s and for which I had never experienced the slightest nostalgia – perhaps because I knew that, for me, all that was left of the town would be desolation, death and bereavement. But in September 1992, I decided that I wanted to return to the scene of my childhood, and with the assistance of the Belorus Government that is what I did. Two military helicopters, placed at our disposal (one carrying a physician, 'just in case'), flew Shulamit, myself and a small escorting party from Minsk to Rujenoy, where a crowd informed by Minsk TV of the time of our arrival had gathered. Incongruously enough, it was a little like a village celebration: a fine crisp day, men and women in their best clothes, children holding flowers for us, speeches of welcome, even a banquet. But first there was the Jewish cemetery. Very little was left of the large graveyard I could recall, only a few graves dated from before 1900, their names now illegible. Where had the massive tombstones gone? I suppose into buildings, pavements, the walls of houses.

The Rujenoy of my growing-up had shrunk; the two churches in the centre of town were where they had always been but of the six or seven synagogues, only one still stood, in ruins. The crowd moved everywhere with us, as though impelled by some force to follow us. Some of the people were very old and could still remember the way Rujenoy used to be. I looked for the houses in which we had once lived – my mother and father, my sisters and I – but no houses remained. Nor any Jews. The last Jew in Rujenoy – a man I had known – died in 1987. In the crowd, there were people who wanted to explain: the guilt was not theirs; the Nazis, the Fascists were to blame; not they; none of them. Someone showed me where an entire family called Kaplinsky – a son had gone to school with me – had taken poison rather than fall into German hands when the Nazis came to the area. There was nothing in Rujenoy any more for me. I was glad I had gone there, glad that I had seen the nothingness for myself, but, above all, glad that I was returning to the land to which I belong and which belongs to me.

Everything that has happened to me since I left Rujenoy for the first time so long ago has been a privilege. I have been able to take part in momentous events of which the greatest, without question, has been the coming-into-being of a Jewish state in the Land of Israel. I have borne arms and worked with the bravest and the finest of men and women who shared perilous missions and arduous responsibilities with me; I have lived for half a century with Shulamit, who has been not only my companion in life but also my closest comrade; my children – Yair and Gilada – and my grandchildren – Shai, Michal, Dror, Tali and Elad – have all been unfailing sources of pleasure, pride and love. If history remembers me at all, in any way, I hope it will be as a man who loved the Land of Israel and watched over it in every way he could, all his life.

EPILOGUE

IN THE LATE SUMMER and early autumn of 1993 a series of events took place which may change the course of Israeli history, face the State of Israel with dangers greater than any it has known since it came into being half a century ago, and drastically affect its immediate future. I refer, of course, to the negotiations so hurriedly and recklessly entered into with the PLO by Israel's Labour Government as soon as it took office in the summer of 1992 and which resulted, by the summer of 1993, in the signing of accords between Israel and that murderous organization. By the time this had happened, I had already finished making final corrections in the proofs of this book and regarded it as completed. In the normal course of events, nothing would have persuaded me to return to it in order to comment on current affairs. I had resigned from the Chairmanship of the Likud Central Committee, played no role in its decisions and restricted my political activities to my membership in the Knesset and to writing articles, now and then speaking in public both at home and abroad. But the implications of what has occurred are so grave, in my unhappy view, that I feel I cannot end my memoirs without entering into them – for those who have read them thus far and those who may read them in years to come – my most unhappy and considered opinion that these developments bear within them the seeds of disaster for the Jewish state.

Historians will perhaps wonder what lay behind the almost indecent haste, not to speak of the total secrecy, with which the Rabin Government moved towards the sealing of its formerly unthinkable partnership with Yasser Arafat, considering the dimensions of the risks involved to Israel's most vital national interests. After all, there could be no objective doubt that at Madrid and even long after it in the draining, frustrating but essential discussions that followed, Israel stood on the very threshold of peace, refusing to cross it until it was beyond dispute that what would be attained would be peace in the broadest, not the shallowest, sense of that much-abused word. What we sought was not peace in name only; not 'peace in our time' and on Arab terms; not the kind of peace that would diminish Israel, but a peace that guaranteed (to whatever extent might be possible) the state's strength and security. And while I was Prime Minister, there was one additional basic requirement: not peace that would override or set aside the Zionist ideals which have, up until now, been the guiding light and raison d'être of the Jewish state. So we knew that it would take time, maybe years, and that along the way there would be stones and tears and certainly no applause.

But we also knew, and were right about this, that gradually the Arabs, especially the Palestinians, would learn to accept that if they wanted peace and self-government, they would have to talk to us; prove their goodwill and intentions, and end the Arab terror, the *intifada* and the boycott. It wasn't Israel that had ever been the aggressor nor Israel that had ever lost the wars the Arabs forced us to fight if we wanted the state to survive – and we too had conditions they would have had to meet. If we had only been able to persist, I am sure Israel would have arrived at peace, security and the chance to realize the Zionist dream to its fullest. So we concentrated on the nature of the peace we sought rather than the speed and drama with which the world could be informed of our accomplishment.

The truth is that, in the final analysis, the search for peace has always been a matter of who would tire of the struggle first, and blink. Would it be the Arabs, finally accepting, as they had started to do, Israel's conditions for a genuine and lasting peace? Or, one day, might an Israeli government – as indeed happened – believing in the doctrine of 'land for peace', giving way to impatience and political ambition, capitulate to Arab demands at the possible cost of Israel's future? The answer came almost the instant the Likud lost the elections. Someone blinked, but it wasn't the Arabs who got tired of waiting. It was the leaders of Israel's new government who had, at last, taken over and were determined, however hazardous their course might be, that it would be they who would be able to claim the presenting of the longed-for peace to Israel. Ignoring the lessons of history, losing faith both in the ability of the people of Israel to hold out against the stresses and griefs of Arab aggression and in the Zionist vision itself, they surrendered to the many temptations of peace now.

In the middle of September, two agreements – a 'Declaration of Principles' for Palestinian self-rule in the territories, 'beginning with

Gaza and Jericho', and an agreement of 'mutual recognition' between the PLO and Israel – were signed with much fanfare on the White House lawn: Prime Minister Rabin and Foreign Minister Peres representing the Government of the sovereign State of Israel; Yasser Arafat, sovereign over nothing, representing a disintegrating organization still, as I write, committed to Israel's destruction and with whose members, only weeks before, Israelis were forbidden by law to meet. For me that ceremony, presided over by a beaming President Clinton and attended by three former US Presidents, symbolized the euphoria that, within days, had enveloped most of the personalities involved – with the one exception, I imagine, of Arafat himself. For him, participation in the ceremony made it the occasion of his public absolution and undreamt-of elevation, officially sealed by the Rabin handshake that so delighted the global media. Bankrupt, increasingly discredited in the Arab world – his *intifada*, though hard for Israel to bear, solved nothing and was harder yet for the Palestinians, with no prospect of success on any front and not even the USSR to help him – Arafat was literally saved by Rabin and Peres. I am sure that he knows as well as I do that if Israel had only been a little more patient, as I had urged for so long, the PLO would have very soon collapsed in any case – and, a bitter foe gone, we would have moved on, along a safer, infinitely better road to new relationships in the Arab world. As it was, Arafat left Washington DC rehabilitated: a new man; his past seemingly forgotten, his state-to-be assured, huge funds about to descend upon him from major international sources. And what better guarantors could he have conceivably found than Rabin and Peres?

It was as though the excitement generated by the PLO's willingness to acknowledge Israel's right to exist had suddenly blinded intelligent people everywhere, including in Israel itself, to the real significance of what had happened. For the first time ever, an Israeli government had consented to give away parts of the Land of Israel, thus helping to pave the way to the virtually inevitable establishment of a Palestinian state in Judea, Samaria and Gaza – though its leaders have repeatedly pledged that this grim possibility will never be realized. Yet here we are, I profoundly believe, well on the way to it. None the less, within Israel too, for a while, euphoria reigned, but it didn't last. There was too much confusion, sometimes even a sense of panic, too little information from a government that sent emissaries tearing around the world but didn't once, in the first few days, address itself seriously to an overwhelmed population to which, when it spoke, it was only in clichés about the bright new tomorrow that awaited

Israel in a changed world. There were also too many fiery statements and over-long speeches, pathetic because the die had been cast and no one who could or would do anything was listening.

Rabin informed Knesset members comprising the Labour-led coalition that the Government regarded the vote on the pact as a vote of confidence in it and the Party whips worked hard. But though the pact was approved, it was only by a very small majority. In the two-day debate that preceded the vote, and at which each member of Knesset was allotted ten minutes to register his views, I had my short say too. 'It is very rare', I said, 'in the history of nations for a government to make so many mistakes in such a short time. The maximum number of mistakes have been made by this Government in the minimum amount of time. ... This chapter in Israel's history will go down as a perfect example of how one can lose the war after winning so many battles.' But I knew that no one who could or would do anything about it was listening to me either. The Prime Minister had been quite candid about his lack of interest in what people were saying or thinking.

Departing from democratic tradition, he declared coldly that he had no use for, and couldn't be bothered with, anyone who opposed him. No use and no time even for the leaders of the Opposition or the 130,000 settlers who had made their homes in Judea, Samaria and Gaza with the full approval and encouragement of their Government. No ranking member of his Government saw fit, or had been told, to extend a hand to them in their grief and anger or to explain the situation to them as the Government actually perceived it. Though it was their lives, in the first instance, that were to be placed at risk by the new policy, despite Rabin's boast that 'this time' (as opposed to Israel's withdrawal from Sinai) no settlement would be uprooted and no settler forced to leave. According to the agreement, they could stay where they were, but apart from the promise that their physical protection would remain in Israeli hands – however that could be done in territory soon de facto to be under full PLO control – in all other respects they would have to fend for themselves. I know these brave and hard-working men and women and I know also the depth of their conviction that the Land of Israel must remain intact and that it is they themselves who must help to determine its borders. I shall be very surprised indeed if they voluntarily abandon the settlements they have created. What is certain but unfortunately does not surprise me, is that in the minds of Israel's policy-makers not only the territories but also those who settled them are expendable.

Nor is it reasonable to assume that Arab demands will be limited to control over Judea, Samaria and Gaza. Arafat himself articulated his unaltered goals after the Washington agreements were signed and, in this context, what he said counts: 'The agreement fulfils only a small part of our rights ...', he told a meeting of Arab foreign ministers a few days after the signing ceremony. 'Our first goal is the liberation of all occupied territories and the return of all refugees, self-determination for the Palestinians and the establishment of a Palestinian state whose capital is Jerusalem.' And who can blame him? Having done so well with Judea, Samaria and Gaza which he received without effort or sacrifice, why not try for the rest? Why not demand the 'return' to Israel of the descendants of Arabs who left Israeli-controlled territory in 1948? Should it be 400,000 or 800,000 or what? And what other parts of the Land will be asked for – and given? If Judea, Samaria and Gaza are the model, then how will the Government hold out, if it tries to, when the new Arab state demands rights in East Jerusalem, though ceding East Jerusalem is to annul the unification of the city that is Israel's eternal capital and chief pride and joy. And the rest will surely follow because that is the set pattern of appeasement, as every blackmailer knows. Military experts throughout the world have pronounced the Golan Heights vital to Israel's security but will that suffice to preclude their restoration, partial or total, to Syrian control whenever Syria's dictator also decides that 'land for peace' makes sound sense?

And then what? Perhaps the semblance of peace of a sort for a time; Israel pushed all the way back, hemmed in by the intolerable borders of 1967 before the Six Day War; the surge of settlement over and done with; the settlements themselves surviving as if under siege; immigration reduced by Israel to a trickle though the Ingathering was once our central purpose; a nation led by men who made peace paramount, like a golden calf, to be worshipped at the expense of the values and aspirations that made Israel unique and placed it at the heart of world Jewry. I can only hope that the people of Israel, in whose judgment and endurance I have such trust, will look for, and find, alternative paths – even if they are rockier and steeper – to lead them to a viable peace that has not been bought with their security, their land or their rights.

INDEX